The Myth of
FREE TRADE

The Pooring of America

DR. RAVI BATRA

A TOUCHSTONE BOOK
Published by Simon & Schuster

TOUCHSTONE
Rockefeller Center
1230 Avenue of the Americas
New York, NY 10020

First Touchstone Edition 1996
First Collier Books Edition 1994

TOUCHSTONE and colophon are registered trademarks
of Simon & Schuster Inc.

Manufactured in the United States of America

10 9 8 7 6 5 4 3 2 1

Library of Congress Cataloging-in-Publication Data

Batra, Raveendra N.
    [Myth of free trade]
    The pooring of America: competition and the myth of free trade / Ravi Batra.
        p.   cm.
    Originally published: The myth of free trade. New York: C. Scribner's Sons, © 1993.
    1. Free trade—United States.   2. United States—Foreign economic relations.   I. Title.
HF1455.B328   1994
382'.71'0973—dc20   93-35764   CIP

ISBN 0-684-83355-7

Previously published as *The Pooring of America*.

TO SUNITA

Where there is a will, there is a way.
Where there is no will, there are excuses.

CONTENTS

ACKNOWLEDGMENTS

Every work has its credits. In this case, I owe a huge debt of gratitude to my friends Clive Stephens, Thor Thorgeirsson, and Sanjay Unni for valuable research assistance. Robert Stewart, my editor at Scribners, gave me guidance at every step and helped me simplify my arguments. I am also indebted to C. T. Cruze and Joanne Madesen of Financial Mathematica, Inc., for their superb graphical techniques. The charts they have drawn for me are clear-cut and elegant; they helped me present complex matter in a simple and intelligible way.

Finally, I am grateful to my wife, Sunita, for carefully going through the manuscript and for constantly inspiring me to finish this work on time.

THE MYTH OF FREE TRADE

Introduction: America at a Crossroads

Ever since the Second World War, economists and the American government have trumpeted the benefits of free trade. Various administrations, Democratic as well as Republican, have championed laissez-faire in foreign commerce. Slowly but steadily, most trade barriers have been eliminated, and today America's dependence on international commerce, particularly its addiction to imports, is the highest ever in its history.

By now the idea of free trade has acquired a myth of its own. To be for laissez-faire is to be for progress, prosperity, and peace; to be against it is to invite the wrath of economists, Wall Street, political pundits, and much of the press. Baby boomers of the 1950s grew up with the gospel of free trade; in fact, the idea is now embraced as economic theology around the world.

In an increasingly global economy interlinked by satellites and multinational corporations, international trade undoubtedly deserves the attention it gets. It touches all of our lives. Americans today enjoy Sonys, Toyotas, BMWs, and Armanis, amid countless quality brands coming from abroad. Similarly, foreigners travel around in Boeings and Cadillacs, among products exported by the United States. Time and again, famines and global starvation have been averted because of bountiful American agriculture. International commerce thus plays a monumental role in the U.S. and global economy today, thanks to the postwar American policy of free trade.

The widely publicized North American Free Trade Agreement (NAFTA), signed by Canada, Mexico, and the United States in August 1992, is just the latest manifestation of laissez-faire. NAFTA seeks to eliminate trade and investment hurdles among signatories. It is yet to be ratified by legislatures in the three countries, but it has a tidal wave of political support behind it.

The opposite of free trade is protectionism, which means that domestic industries should be shielded from foreign competition through a variety of barriers such as tariffs and quotas. For a long time economists have denounced protectionism as a bankrupt idea devoid of logic and common sense. Protectionists have been proclaimed champions of a few vested interests who jeopardize the broader interest of the nation. Some even castigate protectionism as isolationist and immoral, suggesting it promotes monopolies and lazy unionized workers.

This book challenges the gospel of free trade. As in two of my other works, *The Downfall of Capitalism and Communism* and *The Great Depression of 1990*, I am once again throwing down a gauntlet to economic orthodoxy. In *Downfall*, published in 1978, I predicted the collapse of both capitalism and Communism by the year 2000. In *Great Depression*, published in 1985, I prophesied a global economic crisis beginning as a recession in 1990.

Two of my seemingly farfetched forecasts have unfolded before your very eyes: to the utter surprise of my vociferous critics, Soviet Communism has ended, and the United States is now in the midst of the longest recession since the cataclysmic 1930s. When I wrote these books, I knew my career was on the line, but I had no choice. It is a tremendous burden and responsibility to have information and foresight that you know could shape the destiny of nations. How can you then remain silent? Once I discovered that we could face cataclysmic events in our lifetime, I had to share my knowledge with you. For me, then, there was no turning back.

In hindsight, if my words in *Downfall* had not been ignored, America need not have squandered countless billions on defense buildup to bring about the collapse of Communism: the Soviet empire, plagued by internal contradictions, was headed toward extinction anyway. The current work, which opposes the view cherished by conventional economists over the last two centuries, is offered to you in the same spirit as my previous volumes. Once again I am privy to knowledge and information crucial to the economic survival of our nation as well as our planet. This time I find fault with the orthodox view of free trade.

Economists generally sing the melodies of laissez-faire but slight its costs in terms of layoffs, lost wages, and environmental destruction. In the pages that follow I will show you that *every country except America has benefited from the American policy of free trade.* Laissez-faire has wrecked U.S. industry and shattered the American dream.

There is a bit of irony in this, because I have been a free trader all my life. In fact, in the early 1970s, I wrote two volumes promoting the idea of trade liberalization. But my recent analysis of the American economy has shaken my belief. I now find that trade liberalization in the United States has produced a sharp drop in inflation-adjusted wages for as much as 80 percent of the population.

When a person changes his long-held beliefs, there must be overwhelming evidence to justify the change. Briefly, my thesis is as follows:

The experience of most countries shows that prosperity lies in the expansion of manufacturing rather than agriculture and services. This is because manufacturing has much higher worker productivity than other sectors, so that its salaries tend to be 150 to 200 percent of those in other areas. When freer trade promotes manufacturing, it raises overall productivity as well as the general standard of living; but when it fosters services at the expense of manufacturing, productivity growth as well as real earnings decline.

Manufacturing, not trade, is the main source of prosperity. And history, recent and past, confirms this resoundingly. It is no secret that ever since the 1970s, services have far outpaced manufacturing in the United States. As a result, the entire economic landscape has been transformed. Trade liberalization turns out to be the main cause of this transformation, which is unprecedented in the American chronicle.

Today only 17 percent of the labor force is employed in the industrial sector, the rest being in services and agriculture. Therefore, it is not surprising that inflation-adjusted wages have declined by 19 percent since 1972, while the volume of trade has doubled and tariffs have plummeted to 5 percent. In retailing, real after-tax earnings now match those of the Great Depression.

Since the 1970s, cheap imports produced by foreign workers, sometimes laboring on pennies per day, have destroyed and even exterminated industry after industry in the United States, while the administrators, both Democrats and Republicans, have stood idly by. It's an open secret that local firms producing steel, cameras, TVs, VCRs, textiles, and shoes, among many others, have fallen prey to imports from Japan, Taiwan, Korea, Singapore, China, and Hong Kong. And despite the anguish of the American poor and unemployed, the flood of imports continues at an alarming pace.

If this trend persists, then by the end of this decade, the American auto industry would be all but extinct; and computers, machine tools, and pharmaceuticals could suffer the same fate. The reason is that when foreign labor is so cheap, no matter how superior American technology is, U.S. industries just can't compete with foreign products. Free trade has done to the United States what Hitler and Imperial Japan could not do during the war.

Despite such clear-cut evidence, why is free trade so popular and protectionism in disrepute? The United States is now in the midst of the longest recession since the war. Yet protectionist forces, which normally thrive in bad times, have found little political or academic support. In spite of so much industrial devastation, why have protectionists so little to show in terms of legislation that would impede the torrent of imports? It's because protectionists have not offered a coherent case. They have always favored what may be called "monopolistic protectionism," which means protecting domestic industries without altering their monopolistic structure. They have also failed to document the destructive impact of surging imports on the U.S. economy, while free traders have had a great propaganda lobby supported by the multinational firms and American elites.

This book is perhaps the first to produce a systematic and cogent case for protectionism. Not only do I demonstrate the irreversible damage done by trade liberalization, I also devise a proper protectionist policy to guard against the latter's potential ill effects. I have utilized figures supplied by the president's own economic report to show that the fruit of rising U.S. productivity has been reaped by foreign labor and the multinationals. If your wages sharply fall while you work harder and become more efficient, something is very wrong with the system. That is what free trade has done to America, and this book exposes the devastation wrought by this policy.

When trade hurts a country, protectionism alone cannot help. It has to be accompanied by increased domestic competition among firms and industries. Otherwise, local companies will simply raise prices, produce shoddy products, and pay their executives enormous bonuses. This is exactly what monopolistic protectionism does. However, this book calls for competitive protectionism, which means breaking up import-competing monopolies into smaller firms while at the same time vigorously protecting them from predatory foreign competition.

The benefits of protectionism today are not limited to the living standard. Few people realize that *international trade is the worst polluter among all economic activities;* in fact, trade uses more than twice the amount of energy utilized by equivalent local production. Foreign trade ravages the environment far more than manufacturing, agriculture, and services.

If America were to adopt competitive protectionism—that is, shield domestic monopolies from foreign competition while breaking them up into smaller units—it would be able to cure virtually all its economic ills in a short time. Productivity, wages, and real incomes would soar, while the budget deficit and energy prices would plummet. Similarly, the foreign trade deficit would vanish, and, above all, global pollution would come under control. All this from the simple step of raising the tariff rate from the current average of 5 percent to about 40 percent.

You are skeptical, to say the least. However, I am sure my argument and the supporting evidence will make a believer out of you.

This work appears at a time when the country is debating the free trade accord with Mexico and Canada. Let me state it bluntly: NAFTA would deal another crippling blow to America's shrinking living standard. In *Great Depression,* I warned the government against its policy of financial deregulation and enrichment of the rich. My warning was unheeded, and now the nation is saddled with huge losses in the banking and thrift industries, an unprecedented social tumor of wealth concentration, and mass unemployment.

Time and again, the establishment has disregarded my critique of its policies. I can only hope that my current warnings about NAFTA are not greeted by deaf ears.

America today stands at a crossroads. The passionate debate stirred up by NAFTA suggests that the proposed accord could make or break the system. With our myriad socioeconomic ills, I feel strongly that the free trade agreement could be the straw that breaks America's back.

1

In Search of a Culprit

Nineteen ninety-one was a year of ultimate irony for the United States. It began with a stunning American victory in the Gulf War and ended with the collapse of the Soviet Union, leaving the United States not only victorious in the long, bitter cold war but also the sole superpower in the world. Yet Americans were smitten with gloom. Instead of celebrating their victories, one unexpectedly swift and the other unexpected, they were moaning and groaning about the future. The general mood revealed at best apprehension and anxiety, at worst, a sense of impending doom.

What was wrong? Was it the recession that had begun in July 1990? Or was it some hidden cause, eluding experts and amateurs alike, that had its roots in distant years?

At the end of 1991, the pundits, normally locked in perpetual conflict, were in agreement on at least one point: the recession that had begun a year before was too shallow and mild to create the general American mood of gloom. It was, after all, not all that unexpected. Economists had looked for it throughout the 1980s. In fact, it had come after an eight-year-long expansion, unprecedented in U.S. history.

The street panic at the end of 1991 easily bested that of the deep recession of 1974–75; it even dwarfed the panic of 1981–82, when the United States suffered the worst slump since the Second World War. In no respect was the recession of 1990–91 as severe as the preceding downturn.

In a cover story, *Time* was moved to ask, "Well, why are Americans so gloomy, fearful and even panicked about the current economic slump? . . . Inflation is at the lowest level in five years, and home mortgages are available at interest rates not seen since 1974. . . . The official unemployment rate is nowhere as severe as it was at the depth of the 1981–82 recession, and the contraction in the gross national product (so far 1.4%) has been far less sharp."[1]

Between 1990 and 1991, 1.7 million jobs were lost, but during 1981–82, the loss approached 3 million. Moreover, the New York Stock Exchange broke six records in a row at the end of 1991, whereas in the previous recession the stock market had repeatedly hit lows for the period. Yet all these statistics, to paraphrase Mark Twain, were damn lies. "In one of history's most painful paradoxes," *Time* continued on the same page, "U.S. consumers suddenly seem disillusioned with the American dream of rising prosperity even as capitalism and democracy have consigned the Soviet Union to history's trash heap."[2]

The American gloom of 1991 was more deep seated than indicated by that year's mild and seemingly innocuous slump. A number of negative trends that had been nagging the public for years had now come to the surface. Debt among consumers, corporations, and the government had been rising; educational standards and achievements had been on the decline; productivity growth had been stagnant.

Inequality had begun a slow but steady rise, shrinking the middle class; soaring imports had decimated industry after industry in many parts of the United States; millions of Americans were without health insurance and medical care; the environment was suffering increasing abuse and pollution; urban roads and bridges were full of potholes; families were breaking apart; drugs and violence pervaded the schools and the streets. To top it all, the government was all but paralyzed, unable to lead the country out of the spreading morass.

All these festering wounds were hidden just beneath the skin as long as Americans had hopes about their legendary dream. Despite increasingly ominous signs, the official propaganda, reminiscent of the behavior of the former Soviet Union, quieted the simmering anxiety of the public during the 1980s.

The histrionics and communicative skills of President Reagan had kept American hopes alive. The gross national product, after all, was still growing; per capita GNP continued its upward trend; the U.S. economic machine regularly churned out millions of new jobs. Foreigners found America to be so attractive that they poured hundreds of billions of dollars into U.S. assets. What else could you ask for?

Never mind that the prosperity was bought by record debt, or that the foreign fondness for America was sudden and thus suspicious, or that billionaires and centimillionaires, along with the homeless, were mushrooming, or that banks and savings and loan associations were straining, or that the manufacturing hub was rapidly shrinking. Never mind all that.

As long as people had jobs, even at subsistence wages, nothing else—debt, deficits, productivity slack, family breakdown, political corruption—mattered. America was still a great country in the mind of its public. The winners of the Super Bowl still called themselves world champions, even though American-style football is limited to North America; the victors of the World Series were still the world conquerors.

Politicians continued to brag about America's superiority throughout the 1980s, and the public was seduced by all the rhetoric. But the slump of 1990 shattered the fake cocoon of job security.

Around Christmas 1991 General Motors announced it would lay off 75,000 workers over the next four years; International Business Machines put its new layoffs at 20,000, in addition to the same number it had laid off before. These firings seemed to be endless and created the feeling that few had a secure job. That's when the American anxiety, heretofore drowned by shrill official trumpets, erupted in a floodtide. The endless optimism of the roaring 1980s gave way to the endless pessimism of the 1990s, despite, as mentioned earlier, the richly deserved American triumphs in the Gulf War and the cold war.

Today, few doubt that the United States has been in a long period of economic decline. Official statistics, numerous and self-contradictory, cannot mask what the general public feels. The gloom is too widespread to be silenced by barren averages such as GNP and per capita income, which confuse the prosperity of the few with the mediocre living of the masses. Even those who in their self-interest have to tout the government optimism now concede that the country has slid into a long economic malaise. The productivity slump, after all, is not a sudden development.

Some believe that the U.S. economic erosion began in 1973. *Time* quoted Allen Sinai, chief economist of the Boston Company, as saying that "the 1973 period marked the beginning of the decline of the American standard of living."[3] This statement is a shock to all those who have been led to believe that the 1980s were a decade of unprecedented boom; yet it contains a germ of truth. Despite vast official propaganda to the contrary, the reality, as subsequently made clear, is that the so-called prosperity of the 1980s was a mirage, a façade, and a big lie. Thus, on the eve of the 1992 election, the country had suffered twenty years of steady economic erosion.[4] In a nation of free press and full freedom of speech, it is a great credit to the government's statistical machine that this ugly phenomenon took two decades to surface.

What is the cause of this long decline? Why is something happening in America that has never occurred in its history extending over three centuries? The question actually contains the seeds of the answer.

Never in its history has the United States faced declining prosperity over two decades. Even during the Great Depression, so cataclysmic in its sweep and effect, the country suffered for only one decade. Nothing like the Great Depression has afflicted the nation again; but the steady erosion of the living standard since 1973 has moved some economists such as Wallace Peterson to call it the "silent depression."[5] Silent or not, it is clear that something occurred in the recent past that sparked a long period of economic decline, beginning in 1973. Moreover, this "something" must have never happened before, because it is the first time in history that Americans have suffered such a long slide with no end in sight.

So here's the puzzle. What is this "something" that is a totally new phenomenon in American annals? Since the two-decade decline is unique in history, its cause must also be unique. The theories offered by economists and pundits to explain the erosion must pass this test of uniqueness; otherwise, these explanations are self-serving, misleading, or incomplete.

Traditional Explanations

Let us briefly examine the reasons often cited for the declining living standard. You may rest assured that in the next chapter I will offer you decisive proof of this decline. Let's take for granted for the moment that at least half, and as much as 80 percent, of the population today is worse off than in 1973.

It is now commonplace to compare the United States with Germany and Japan. Even those doubtful of U.S. decline acknowledge that these nations, which were in a shambles in the aftermath of the Second World War, have caught up with the United States and may even have surpassed it in some areas.

Germany and Japan have become highly competitive in world markets, and many are afraid that the United States has either lost its once formidable competitive edge or is about to lose it forever. Others like to use a military metaphor. "We may have won the Gulf War and the cold war," they say, "but we are badly losing the war of competitiveness."

This feeling is pervasive in America today. It spreads across the ideological spectrum. Americans of all persuasions—Democrats and Republicans, whites, African Americans, and ethnic minorities—are alarmed about the growing industrial might, especially of Japan, which over the last decade has had a huge surplus in its trade with the United States.

The reason America has lost its competitive edge is said to be the slow growth of productivity in its economy. Both Germany and Japan enjoyed astounding growth in national output per hour during the 1960s, 1970s, and 1980s, as displayed in Figure 1.1.

As Steven Greenhouse writes, "Overall, the United States still leads in productivity, but its rate of productivity growth continues to lag competitors'."[6] Using 1960 as the base year, Figure 1.1 shows that the gross domestic product (GDP) per employee rose from 100 to about 155 in the United States, whereas in Germany it rose to more than 240 and in Japan to over 460. In other words, in thirty years, productivity grew by 55 percent in America, 140 percent in Germany, and a staggering 360 percent in Japan. Other measures of productivity, such as the output per hour in the business sector, are somewhat more favorable to the United States. But even there productivity grew by no more than 70 percent.

Before reacting to these shocking numbers, you must remember that both Germany and Japan were devastated by the war and were starting from a very low base. They are also in a slump at this time. In spite of these caveats, both countries have undoubtedly enjoyed astonishing gains. Britain, France, and Italy, other parties to the war, have, like the United States, been laggards in the productivity race.

What are the reasons behind the U.S. productivity slide? Not only has the nation lagged behind Germany and Japan, its productivity growth during the 1980s was just a third of its own rate during the 1960s. And for some years in the 1970s, the growth was actually negative. Some of the reasons commonly cited for the productivity debacle are as follows:[7]

1. The rate of saving is abysmally low in the United States, at less than 5 percent of disposable income, as opposed to over 14 percent in both Germany and Japan.

2. Since savings are the backbone of investment, the rate of investment is also much lower in America than in other nations.

3. Since investment is the backbone of productivity, the productivity gain in the United States is much smaller than in Germany and Japan.

FIGURE 1.1
Real Gross Domestic Product per Employee

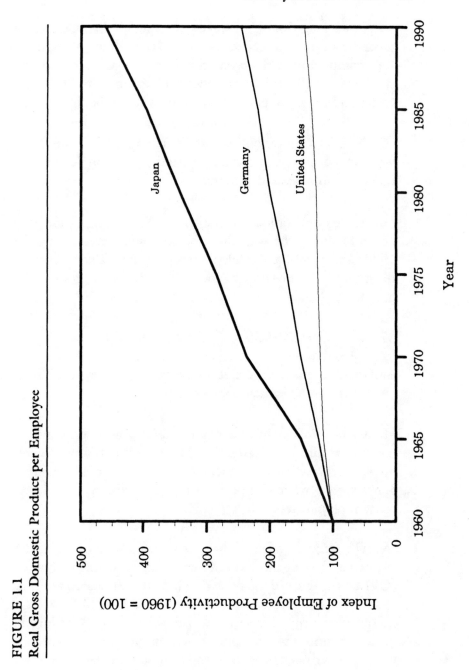

4. For a long time U.S. wages were higher than German or Japanese wages. This gave an additional cost advantage to America's competitors. (However, this is no longer true. German wages were $20 per hour in 1992, whereas in both the United States and Japan, wages approximated $15 per hour).

5. American education has suffered a long-term decline; U.S. workers are not being trained to handle increasingly sophisticated technologies and equipment.

6. Some have argued that the United States had a great baby boom following the war; those babies came of age during the 1970s and 1980s, and while the economy was able to provide them jobs, their lower skills and education caused productivity growth to slacken.

7. Huge federal deficits and debt kept the interest rates higher in the United States than in Germany and Japan. As a result, American companies were at a disadvantage in borrowing for investment vis-à-vis their competitors.

8. In the 1980s, while Germany and Japan were busy investing in their future, American companies were frantically buying up other companies; consequently, corporate debt in the United States soared, while corporate spending on research and development plummeted.

9. The standard of living has been declining since 1973, the year when the Organization of Petroleum Exporting Countries (OPEC) quadrupled the price of oil. This price soared again in 1979 after the revolution in Iran. In order to pay for high energy costs, firms all over the world had to cut back on investment; but since the low-taxed American oil was much cheaper than in other nations, U.S. companies suffered far more than their competitors, which were already used to the higher energy burden.

10. Finally, the deindustrialization of America, in the face of cheap imports from abroad, has caused a sharp drop in productivity growth as more and more Americans have had to seek jobs in service industries, which have much lower productivity than manufacturing.[8]

Incomplete Answers

The ten reasons presented above are commonly cited to explain the American productivity slide of the 1970s and 1980s. Do they explain the longest decline in U.S. prosperity? Do they pass the uniqueness test that I proposed above. The answer is no. At best, they offer incomplete explanations; at worst, they are incorrect and misleading. However, they are not self-serving explanations such as American taxes are too high or capital gains are overly taxed. U.S. tax rates are much lower than those in competing nations.

At the risk of repetition, let me state this again: the slide in the living standard since 1973 has been the longest in three centuries of U.S. history. It is therefore a unique phenomenon that calls for a unique explanation.

Among the ten reasons offered above, there are only two that stand the test of uniqueness. Our giant peacetime federal deficit is one, the deindustrialization of America the other. Yet they are both partial answers. First, the federal debt and deficit began to soar only after 1980, whereas the slide in prosperity began in 1973. The deindustrialization process began even before 1970, as the proportion of the labor force employed in manufacturing began a long-term decline. But the authors of the deindustrialization hypothesis failed to look at its root cause.

Deindustrialization is indeed new in the U.S. chronicle, but what is its true cause? Volumes have been written on this hypothesis, but hardly anyone has discovered the culprit.

Before I name the culprit, let me examine the rest of the conventional explanations for the productivity slide. The low savings rate in the United States is as much an effect as a cause. When a person faces downward mobility, as most Americans did after 1973, savings fall faster than incomes. Once acclimated to a high standard of living, people try to maintain their lifestyle even with an income slide either by borrowing or by consuming their past savings.

Second, the U.S. rate of investment, as measured by the investment/GNP ratio, has been steady since the 1950s. It even crept upward during the 1980s. Why, then, didn't the productivity slide begin in the 1950s? Why did it wait until the 1970s?

Third, American wages have been higher than wages in other nations for much of U.S. history. Why have they become a significant factor now?

About U.S. education; it is well known that the United States is a nation of immigrants. Time and again the country has been hit by waves of immigrants who were often illiterate and unskilled. But the nation was able to train them and convert them into skilled workers. The educational problem is not a new factor.

About the baby boom; the United States has experienced far greater baby booms before in its history. Again, nothing new.

About the 1980s merger mania: such manias have afflicted the United States many times before. There was a great merger wave in the 1870s, another in the 1920s, and yet another in the 1950s. There were, of course, harmful consequences from these waves, but none generated a two-decade-long slide.[9]

About the price of oil; this is nothing new either. Energy prices rose sharply during the 1910s as well as the 1940s but failed to make a big dent in the economy. They also rose periodically in the nineteenth century without creating extraordinarily ill effects. Furthermore, the price of oil fell sharply during the second half of the 1980s without reversing the U.S. economic decline. At the end of 1991, the inflation-adjusted price of oil was back about where it had been in 1973, the year of the first oil price shock.

Thus the only valid explanations left are the gargantuan federal deficit and the deindustrialization of America. As suggested earlier, the federal deficit is only a partial answer to the puzzle of the productivity slide, whereas the deindustrialization hypothesis has failed to finger the true culprit.

The deindustrialization of America is justly blamed on competition from Germany and Japan; but the presence of foreign competitors is also nothing new to the U.S. economy. During the nineteenth century, U.S. products faced stiff competition from Britain, France, and Germany, whereas during the years leading up to the Second World War, competition came from these countries as well as—yes—Japan. Thus, the fact that today the United States faces strong competitors abroad is also not new. What is new is the game plan—the ease with which foreigners have been allowed to compete on U.S. turf since the 1950s. What is new is America's commerical policy. The culprit, dear reader, is free trade.

However, before describing the villain in detail, I must turn to the question of the long slide in the U.S. living standard. Despite frequent reports of rising poverty, hunger, and homelessness, some still believe that at least the 1980s saw an unprecedented boom and affluence. Back then the government and the conservative media constantly reminded us of the eight-year-long economic expansion, supposed to be the longest in history.[10] Is prosperity truly a legacy of the Reagan-Bush years? So it appears at the superficial level, but an in-depth analysis exposes the lie.

2

The Shattered Dream

What is the legendary dream that has been the folklore of U.S. society for two centuries? The great American dream is a cliché that is too often used or abused by people of all stripes. The media speak about it, scholars write about it, politicians gripe about it.

Those in office commonly say their actions brought the American dream within reach; those out of office, on the contrary, say the American dream is increasingly inaccessible. To an outsider this would be an exercise in futility; for why worry about a dream?

The American dream has been the subject of endless debates in U.S. history, and the present is no exception. But what is the dream? Michael Wolff et al. explain it better than I can. The American dream, in modern terms, means "a home of your own, money in the bank, a big car, appliances galore, all provided by a single wage earner."[1]

This is not just an American dream; it's a global dream. But it is associated with the United States, because for as long as I can remember, the country has been called a land of opportunity. America is a nation of immigrants. A pauper from abroad could come here and, with education, hard work, and some luck, even become a millionaire. This rarely happened in any other nation, and even today it rarely happens in other nations.

The dream meant upward mobility not only for the generations born in the United States, but also for swarms of immigrants. So productive was the country's economy that it provided rising incomes not only to natives but also to the millions coming from abroad. As a result the poor could join first the middle class, then the upper middle class, and finally the realm of the rich.

Compared to other peoples, the American poor were filthy rich. While elsewhere poverty meant hunger, illiteracy, and homelessness, for some in America it meant not owning a new car or a home. While the poor in other nations could not imagine having a telephone, a refrigerator, a heated house, hot running water, an electric oven, even a flush toilet, those in the United States took these amenities for granted. The American poor griped mostly about inadequate health care, insufficient educational opportunities, lack of air-conditioned cars; to the foreign poor such gripes were laughable—if comprehensible.

Every new generation in the United States, including the one that lived through the Great Depression, was better off than its predecessor. The nation indeed had its moments of poverty during numerous recessions and occasional depressions. But no episode of deprivation lasted beyond a decade; most recessions ended within two years and depressions within seven years.

Incomes kept growing, sometimes at breakneck speed, sometimes at a crawl. Every recession and depression was followed by a stronger boom. Individuals at times suffered from shrinking incomes, but a whole generation never did. And prosperity meant upward mobility for a vast majority of the population, not just for the privileged few. Such is the legend of the American dream.

Alas, the dream no longer exists. The amenities that Americans enjoyed during the 1950s and 1960s gradually slipped away from the grasp of the baby boomers. Initially the slippage was imperceptible—in fact, invisible. More and more women joined the labor force, so that the single-earner family gave way to the two-earner family. At first family income grew sharply, and even though family expenses also grew, income outpaced costs. Thus, in spite of the productivity slide, the American dream remained alive during the 1970s.

Social friction, of course, began to rise as families committed to their dreams had to spend an increasing number of hours to maintain their living standard. Less time was left for children, personal intimacy, elderly parents, and leisure. Families crumbled and the divorce rate soared. Yet the dream, though more difficult to achieve, endured.

However, productivity growth continued to fall, and when the 1980s came, everyone—consumers, corporations, and the government—sought to fulfill the dream through borrowing. Debt soared like never before, and even though the productivity slide was arrested, the erosion of the living standard was not reversed.

Today, the American dream stands shattered. The people and politicians are all perplexed; they are groping for answers. However, the politicians are not ready to admit the mistakes of their past policies. The facts are there, but often facts don't kill theories; only a new theory can eradicate old ideas.

Has the Living Standard Really Declined?

In spite of overwhelming anecdotal evidence, few economists believe that the living standard in the United States has been declining since 1973. It's not that they are unaware of the soaring homelessness, growing urban decay, crumbling roads and bridges, declining home ownership, and shriveling middle class, it is just that they pin their faith on a statistic called the gross national product (or gross domestic product) to measure the nation's well-being. Those who concede that GNP has its flaws then look to per capita income as a gauge of the living standard.

According to these two measures, the U.S. living standard has continued to rise in spite of the productivity debacle. Table 2.1 and its counterpart, Figure 2.1, reveal an upward trend in real or inflation-adjusted GNP as well as per capita income. Real GNP grew from $1,204 billion in 1950 to $4,156 billion in 1990, or

TABLE 2.1
Real GNP and Per Capita Income, 1950–1990*

Year	GNP (Billions of Dollars)	GNP Growth (%)	Per Capita Income†	Per Capita Income Growth (%)
1950	1,203.7		5,220	
1960	1,665.3	38	6,036	15.6
1970	2,416.2	45	8,134	34.8
1980	3,187.1	32	9,722	19.5
1990	4,155.8	30	11,508	18.0

SOURCE: Council of Economic Advisers, *Economic Report of the President* (Washington, D.C.: U.S. Government Printing Office, 1991).

* In 1982 dollars.
† Personal disposable income divided by the population.

roughly 3½ times. Its growth between 1950 and 1960 was 38 percent, which was close to its growth rates of 32 percent between 1970 and 1980 and 30 percent during the 1980s. According to this measure, growth did slow down but not by much, because the performance of the 1960s, when GNP grew by a huge 45 percent, was an aberration that the economy could not be expected to duplicate decade after decade.

Per capita income, defined as after-tax income per person, also rose sharply between 1950 and 1990, although here too growth slowed somewhat during the 1970s and the 1980s. Clearly, according to both these measures, the standard of living continued to rise despite the productivity slide. This is the view adopted by various administrations as well as mainstream economists. In this view, while the income statistics are disturbing, there is no cause for alarm.

Economists concede that GNP and per capita income are not ideal measures of national prosperity. The president's economic report for 1992, for instance, makes this statement: "Growth in real GNP or GDP does not ensure an increase in the standard of living. If real GDP grew less rapidly than the population, for example, real GDP per person would fall. But even real GDP per person is not a

FIGURE 2.1
Growth Rates of Real GNP and Per Capita Income per Decade,
1950–1990

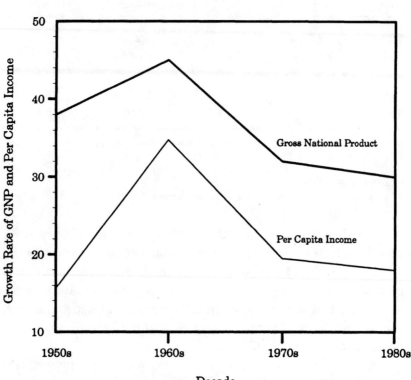

perfect measure of economic well-being because some transactions
are not recorded in GDP."[2]

Despite this caveat, mainstream economists have not abandoned
GNP or GDP as a measure of prosperity. If such statistics are to be
believed, the United States in 1990 enjoyed the highest living standard in its history. Anyone taking an objective look at the state of
the country would simply laugh at this claim. Both GNP and per
capita GNP were at an all-time high in 1992. Can you believe that
a nation with the highest-ever debt per person is actually at the peak
of its prosperity? American households are the world's biggest bor-
rowers. Yet the GNP figure would have us believe that historically

they are now at the zenith of affluence. How myopic can you be? What about the homeless millions, urban blight, crumbling roads and bridges, declining test scores, unaffordable homes, desolate factory towns and parking lots? None of that matters to the GNP figures.

Thus, real GNP (or GDP) and per capita GNP or income measures can be extremely misleading, especially in an economy with growing inequality. In times of declining inequality, GNP and per capita income may accurately measure a country's well-being, but certainly not when inequality rises.

What is the difference between GNP and GDP? Not much, especially in the formulation of policy with which this work is concerned. GNP, or gross national product, is the yearly value of goods and services produced by all Americans here and abroad, whereas GDP, or gross domestic product, is the annual value of goods and services produced inside U.S. borders. For instance, if you worked anywhere outside America last year, your income would be included in GNP but not in GDP. Both GNP and GDP are normally within 1 percent of each other and are standard measures of economic activity.

Most countries use the GDP accounting system, whereas the United States used the GNP framework until 1991. But for all practical purposes, the two frameworks are identical.

Study after study shows that income disparity has grown steadily since 1970. Under these circumstances, aggregate measures such as GNP and per capita income can be highly misleading, because they lump the rising prosperity of a few rich families with other people's incomes, which may or may not have risen. Thus the aggregate average can rise when the incomes of a large majority actually decline.

The aggregate income measures also become suspect when higher numbers of people join the labor force or employees have to work longer hours. For instance, suppose your income stays constant but you need to work only half as many hours as before. You are now easily better off. You are in a position to enjoy the good life. But suppose your income rises by 5 percent while your working hours rise by 20 percent. You will not be amiss in thinking you are worse off than before even though your income has grown.

During the 1970s and 1980s, women in increasing numbers left their household work behind and began to work in a variety of occupations.[3] A per capita income rise under these conditions does not necessarily reflect rising prosperity, because the value of household work is not included in GNP figures, whereas a woman's wages from outside work are. For all these reasons, a country's average wage adjusted for inflation is a far better gauge of well-being than either GNP or per capita income. Even though the average wage is also an aggregate measure and may still distort perceptions in times of rising inequality, it is free from the aggregate bias resulting from declining leisure time or growing family participation in the labor force.

There is an official statistic called "average weekly earnings" that applies to production or nonsupervisory workers, who, according to the Bureau of Labor Statistics, constitute some 80 percent of all employees. These statistics exclude executives, managers, and professionals such as doctors and lawyers but include the vast majority of the labor force. For this reason the behavior of real (inflation-adjusted) average weekly earnings, which are not completely aggregated as they exclude supervisory workers, is the best available measure for the standard of living.

Let's now examine Table 2.2 and Figure 2.2, which graphs real average weekly earnings from 1950 to 1991. Table 2.2 presents these data for every fifth year plus 1991, which is the latest year for which figures are available, and for 1973, the year that marks a turning point in U.S. history. Real earnings peaked at 315 that year, after rising from 213 in 1950, amounting to a growth of 48 percent. Since 1973 they have been on the decline. This is what moved economist Wallace Peterson to call 1973 a watershed year that marked the beginning of the "silent depression." As he puts it: "It is silent because the deterioration is slow and insidious like a cancer, hardly noticed by either the press or policy-makers. It is depression because it has continued for so long."[4]

When a mainstream economist is confronted with these data, his first response is one of staunch denial: "It just can't be." His second response is to question your patriotism. When that doesn't work, he questions the veracity of your data. But the figures in

TABLE 2.2
Real Wages in the United States, 1950–1991*

Year	Real Wage†	Real Wage Growth (%)
1950	213	
1955	244	15
1960	262	7
1965	292	12
1970	298	2
1973	315	6
1975	293	− 7
1980	275	− 6
1985	271	− 1
1990	260	− 3
1991	256	− 2

SOURCE: Council of Economic Advisers, *Economic Report of the President* (Washington, D.C.: U.S. Government Printing Office, 1991 and 1992).

* In 1982 dollars.
† Average weekly earnings of production or nonsupervisory workers.

Table 2.2 came out of the president's own economic report. They are as reliable as all those the government constantly used to trumpet the eight-year-long, debt-driven expansion of the 1980s.

In the third column of the table, the earnings figures have been converted into percentages to measure the rate of growth or decline in real wages. Between 1950 and 1955, wages grew by 15 percent, by another 7 percent over the next five years, followed by a 12 percent growth between 1960 and 1965. That is when wage growth slackened, because it plummeted to 2 percent over the following five years. There was then a brief spurt, causing wages to peak in 1973. Since then earnings have been dropping.

At first the fall was sharp, 7 percent between 1973 and 1975 and then another 6 percent over the subsequent five years. The so-called roaring eighties only slowed the decline, and by the eve of the 1992 election, wages had plummeted by a whopping 19 percent from their peak.

FIGURE 2.2
Average Weekly Earnings in 1982 Dollars, 1950–1991

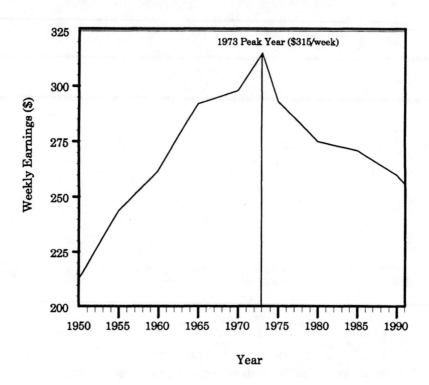

Average weekly earnings data, as mentioned earlier, apply to 80 percent of America's work force. Thus, for over three fourths of the nation, the living standard has declined by 19 percent, with no end in sight.

But this is not all. The decline mentioned above is before taxes. If rising Social Security taxes and sales taxes are taken into account, the earnings fall is even greater.

More shocking figures are displayed in Table 2.3 and Figure 2.3. Table 2.3 is a disaggregated version of aggregated average weekly earnings. In Table 2.3, real earnings figures are presented for three important sectors—manufacturing, construction, and retail trade. Construction was and is the highest-wage industry among the three. In all three, earnings rose consistently between 1950 and

TABLE 2.3
Real Average Weekly Earnings in Selected Sectors, 1950–1991*

Year	Manufacturing	Construction	Retail Trade†
1950	$233	$279	$165
1955	271	327	182
1960	291	366	195
1965	329	423	212
1970	332	486	212
1973	361	512	219
1975	342	477	202
1980	337	430	178
1985	350	421	162
1990	338	400	149
1991	328	390	146

SOURCE: Council of Economic Advisers, *Economic Report of the President* (Washington, D.C.: U.S. Government Printing Office, 1991 and 1992); Bureau of Labor Statistics, *Employment Hours and Earnings, 1909–90* (Washington, D.C.: U.S. Government Printing Office, 1991).

* In 1982 dollars.
† Obtained by dividing current dollar figures by the consumer price index.

1965, then slowed in their advance and finally peaked in the pivotal year of 1973. But by 1991, manufacturing wages, at $328 per week, had dropped below their 1965 level, whereas construction earnings had fallen close to their 1960 level. To top it all, real earnings in retail trade had plummeted even beyond their 1950 lows. In real terms, retail employees in 1991 earned nearly 12 percent less than what they had more than forty years ago.

In 1991, the state sales tax rate averaged 7 percent, while the federal Social Security tax was 7.65 percent. In 1950 each of these taxes averaged about 2 percent. When such sharp tax rises are taken into account, the living standard of retail employees by the 1992 election had dropped more than 20 percent below the 1950 low. In fact, it is now approaching the 1939 level, when the country, with an unemployment rate of 15 percent, was still reeling under the Depression.

FIGURE 2.3
Average Weekly Earnings in 1982 Dollars in Construction,
Manufacturing, and Retail Trade, 1950–1991

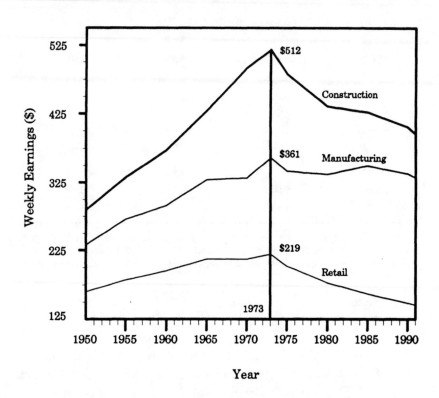

How many retail employees are there, anyway? Nineteen million, at last count. No wonder there is so much gloom in the
country today. For millions of Americans, the current silent depression is as painful as the still-roaring Depression in 1939.

Rising Inequality

Those reared in the cradle of GNP or per capita income figures may
still be unconvinced by all the evidence I have presented above. But
there are other measures to corroborate that the American dream
stands shattered with no cure in sight.

Just examine the data about the family distribution of income presented in Table 2.4. This distribution can be described by estimating the share of income received by families at different levels of income. Family income includes all income received from private channels as well as that received from the government.

Table 2.4 displays the income share received by families grouped by level of income. For instance, the second column shows the income share received by the poorest 20 percent of families from 1950 to 1989, whereas the last column reveals the income share enjoyed by the richest 5 percent.

The table confirms the earlier evidence of the declining trend in real earnings of 80 percent of Americans. Since real wages rose from 1950 to 1973, we should expect a fall in income disparity over these years. Then wages began to fall, which means that the disparity should have been rising since the mid-1970s. This is exactly what a close look at Table 2.4 reveals.

In fact, the rise in disparity closely matches the fall in real earn-

TABLE 2.4
Distribution of Family Income in Selected Years, 1950–1989*

Year	Lowest Fifth	Fourth Fifth	Third Fifth	Second Fifth	Highest Fifth	Top 5%
1950	4.5	12.0	17.4	23.4	42.7	17.3
1955	4.8	12.3	17.8	23.7	41.3	16.4
1960	4.8	12.2	17.8	24.0	41.3	15.9
1965	5.2	12.2	17.8	23.9	40.9	15.5
1970	5.4	12.2	17.6	23.8	41.0	15.6
1973	5.5	11.9	17.5	24.0	41.1	15.5
1975	5.4	11.8	17.6	24.1	41.1	15.5
1980	5.1	11.6	17.5	24.3	41.6	15.3
1985	4.6	10.9	16.9	24.2	43.5	16.7
1989	4.6	10.7	16.7	23.7	44.0	17.9

SOURCE: Bureau of the Census, Current Population Reports p.60, No. 168, *Trends in Income by Selected Characteristics: 1947–1989* (Washington, D.C.: U.S. Government Printing Office, 1991).

* In percent.

ings. Between 1975 and 1989, the inequality rate rose by 15 percent, as the share of the top 5 percent rose from 15.5 percent to 17.9; whereas from Table 2.2, real wages between 1973 and 1990 fell by 17 percent.

With rising GNP and per capita income, the earnings decline should cause a breathtaking jump in the prosperity of the wealthy. Another study, conducted by the Congressional Budget Office and presented in Table 2.5, confirms this in a resounding way.

Displayed in Table 2.5 is the family income distribution by deciles (tenths) in two years—1977 and 1988. The extent of real income loss revealed by these figures is even more startling than the conclusion I reached before. From Table 2.2, I had concluded that 80 percent of Americans had suffered an income decline since the early 1970s; the congressional study also concludes that as many as

TABLE 2.5
Average Family Income in Constant Dollars by Deciles, 1977 and 1988

Decile	1977	1988	Change Dollars	%
Tenth	4,113	3,504	−609	−14.8
Ninth	8,334	7,669	−665	−8.0
Eighth	13,104	12,327	−777	−5.9
Seventh	18,436	17,220	−1,216	−6.6
Sixth	23,896	22,389	−1,057	−4.4
Fifth	29,824	28,205	−1,619	−5.4
Fourth	36,405	34,828	−1,577	−4.3
Third	44,305	43,507	−798	−1.8
Second	55,487	56,064	577	1.0
First	102,722	119,635	16,913	16.5
Top 5%	134,543	166,016	32,473	23.4
Top 1%	270,053	404,566	134,513	49.8

SOURCE: Congressional Budget Office, *The Changing Distribution of Federal Taxes: 1975–1988* (Washington, D.C.: U.S. Government Printing Office, 1991), p. 39.

80 percent became worse off between 1977 and 1988. Every group from the tenth to the third deciles suffered a real income loss, but those in the top 20 percent gained. Of the losers, the poorest were the biggest percentage losers, and of the gainers, the richest, or top 1 percent, were the biggest gainers.

When 80 percent lose and 20 percent gain, I say the general living standard has suffered a free-fall. According to the latest figures, the top 1 percent of Americans have more wealth than the bottom 90 percent.[5]

Family Poverty

Further confirmation of the shattered dream comes from figures on family poverty.[6] The official poverty measure is based on a definition of minimum needs. If a person's income is below the level needed to buy a nutritious diet, he/she is defined to be poor. Poverty income varies with family size, age and sex of the head of the household, number of children, and, of course, inflation. In 1990, the poverty line for a family of four was drawn at an income level of $13,300 before taxes.

Table 2.6 examines the trends in American poverty from 1960 to 1990 over selected years. Analytically, there are two concepts of poverty—absolute and relative. With the first, you look at the absolute number of poor families, whereas with the second, you examine the percentage of poor families in any year. Both the absolute and relative poverty rates declined from 1960 to 1973 but then began to rise. This once again confirms that 1973 was a momentous year that marked the beginning of a two-decade long economic decline. Poverty figures are not available for the years before 1959. If they were, I am sure they would show that poverty, at least in absolute terms, is as bad today as in 1950.

1973: The Watershed Year

Nineteen seventy-three marked a turning point in U.S. history, because the legendary American living standard, which had begun its

TABLE 2.6
Families in Poverty in Selected Years, 1960–1990

Year	Number in Poverty (Millions)	Rate of Poverty (%)
1960	8.2	18.1
1965	6.7	13.9
1970	5.3	10.1
1973	4.8	8.8
1975	5.5	9.7
1980	6.2	10.3
1985	7.2	11.4
1990	7.1	10.7

SOURCE: Council of Economic Advisers, *Economic Report of the President* (Washington, D.C.: U.S. Government Printing Office, 1983 and 1992).

Watershed Year–1973

long upward march after the revolution of 1776, peaked that year. Ever since then, average real earnings of as much as 80 percent of the work force have been on the decline. Such a protracted fall is unique not only in the postwar period but in the entire history of the nation. That is why 1973 is a watershed year;[7] it initiated something the United States had never faced before.

Figure 2.4 dramatizes the monumental significance of 1973 in American annals by bringing together the individual charts for three variables in the postwar period. It shows that all these variables either peaked or bottomed around the watershed year. Thus real wages reached their all-time high, while poverty bottomed out. Similarly, the income share of the poorest 20 percent of the population peaked around 1973, whereas that of the top 5 percent (not included in the figure) hit a low.

Long held beliefs, especially pleasant ones, die hard. Expectations of upward mobility and rising real incomes are ingrained in the American psyche. As a result, in spite of the overwhelming evidence of the steady economic erosion, mainstream economists and various administrations ignored reality and continued to trumpet the illusion of rising prosperity. They should take a cue

FIGURE 2.4
Real Wages, Family Poverty, and Inequality, 1950–1991

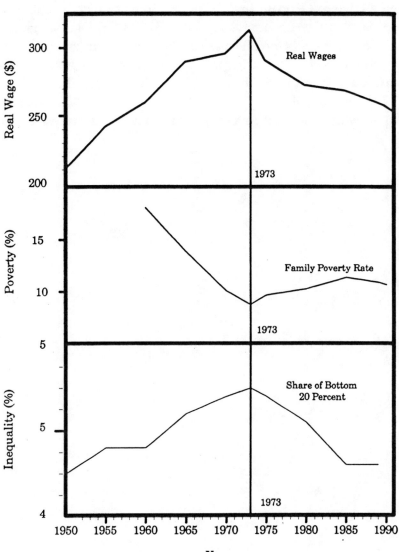

from the bloody Los Angeles riots of April 1992, which undoubt-edly reflected the rage of the poor subsisting amidst opulence.

Many people are aware that the United States has lost its tech-nical edge to Germany and Japan; yet some of them continue to believe that the American living standard is still rising, though at a lower rate than before. Typical of them are Michael Wolff et al. when they write, "It is truer to say that the world is getting richer than that America is getting poorer."[8] However, in the spring of 1993, with the silent depression in its twenty-first year, it is evident to many that the great American dream is now just that—a dream.

3

Free Trade: The Real Culprit

The facts are clear, the evidence overwhelming: the great American dream of increased prosperity for each generation lies shattered. In fact, there is even talk of the country sinking into a Third World–type hole, and a vicious circle of poverty. With the media, politicians, and pundits all in confusion, there is a frantic search for diagnosis and cure. The irony of it all is that as the debate on NAFTA grows, few realize that the real cause of America's unprecedented economic debacle is the policy of free trade. We are about to sink deeper into what is already the quicksand of American industry and earnings.

The twenty-year slide in the real wage of the U.S. production worker between 1973 and 1992 is a new phenomenon, unseen even during the decade-long Great Depression. A new event calls for a unique explanation, and the only thing new in the American chronicle is free trade.

In the aftermath of the Second World War various U.S. administrations went after trade liberalization with gusto. In 1947, after many rounds of talks, the United States helped forge a global agreement called GATT, or the General Agreement on Tariffs and Trade, whose purpose was to reduce or eliminate barriers that countries had erected against the free international flow of goods and services.

A tariff is a tax imposed on foreign products at the port of entry. The tax raises the prices of foreign goods, discouraging their consumption and import. As a result of GATT large cuts in U.S. tariffs were made in 1947 and 1948, and the average duty fell from 27 percent to 15 percent. New cuts were made following another global agreement called the Kennedy Round, in which tariffs on manufactures were lowered by one third. Another cut occurred after the so-called Tokyo Round of trade negotiations, completed in 1979. Today the average American tariff rate stands at 5 percent.

Such a low tariff rate is unprecedented in U.S. history.[1] Over the past two centuries, tariffs were rarely below 30 percent. This is the only phenomenon that is new. There are indeed other explanations for the real-wage decline since 1973, but they are either partial or misleading. I examined them briefly in Chapter 1; here I shall analyze them in detail. But first let me show you why and how free trade or the low tariff rate is responsible for crippling the American dream.

Free Trade in the United States

As far as trade is concerned, there are two generic types of economies—open and closed. Economists define a closed economy as one functioning without any imports or exports. This is a self-sufficient nation that invests and consumes all it produces. Foreign products are totally absent from its markets. A closed economy has no headaches about exchange rates, balance of payments, foreign debt, or investment.[2]

An open economy, by contrast, is one where a country trades with other nations. It imports certain products and exports others in exchange. Its currency is convertible into a foreign currency at a rate called the rate of exchange. An open economy is concerned with questions of the balance of trade or balance of payments, international debt and investment, capital and technology transfer, and so on. Needless to say, a free trade country is an open economy dependent on foreign commerce.[3]

No country today is a closed economy, nor has there been one in centuries. But some countries rely so little on foreign trade that for all practical purposes, they are closed to international commerce. The Soviet Union was more or less a closed economy; so are Russia and Ukraine today. On the other hand, Britain, Germany, Japan, Canada, and Australia, among many others, are clearly open economies because a large proportion of their economic activity depends on foreign trade. It is worth noting here that Japan is an open economy but not a free trade country because of its high barriers to imports.

What about the United States? Throughout its history, at least until 1970, America was practically a closed economy.[4] An economy's degree of openness may be measured by its dependence on exports, imports, or both. In an expanding economy, demand rises for most goods, including foreign products: when the rest of the world grows, it demands more of our products. Thus both exports and imports tend to increase with rising GNP at home and abroad. For this reason, the degree of openness can be measured not by absolute levels of exports or imports but by their ratio to GNP. It may also be partly indicated by the growth rates of exports, imports, or total trade.[5]

From our discussion so far we may conclude that a free trade country is an open economy with a zero or low level of tariffs. It has a high volume of exports, imports, and total commerce as a percentage of GNP.

Postwar data reveal that the United States became a free trade economy in 1973, when it experienced a sudden surge in the trade/GNP ratio. While tariff rates had been falling ever since the first GATT accord in 1947, the trade ratio had been more or less constant. In fact, as the third column in Table 3.1 reveals, the trade ratio of 1970 was almost the same as that of 1947. In 1973, for the first time, the ratio not only took off but also surged in subsequent years, never to fall below 20 percent.

Similarly, the exports/GNP ratio soared in 1973 and subsequently never fell below the previous high of 8.5 percent achieved

TABLE 3.1
Relationship of Exports, Imports, and Total Trade to GNP in
Selected Years, 1947–1990

Year	Exports (% of GNP)	Imports (% of GNP)	Total Trade (% of GNP)
1947	8.5	3.5	12.0
1950	5.1	4.3	9.4
1955	5.2	4.4	9.6
1960	5.8	4.7	10.5
1965	6.1	4.7	10.8
1970	6.8	6.0	12.8
1972	6.7	6.4	13.1
1973	8.4	7.2	15.6
1975	10.1	8.2	18.3
1980	12.9	11.7	24.6
1985	9.2	11.2	20.4
1990	12.3	13.0	25.3

SOURCE: Council of Economic Advisers, *Economic Report of the President* (Washington, D.C.: U.S. Government Printing Office, 1991), pp. 286–7.

in 1947. The imports/GNP ratio behaved in the same way. It jumped in 1973 and reached an all-time high in 1990.

In 1973, the average U.S. tariff was 7 percent, compared to 27 percent in 1947. This low rate along with the sudden surge in the volume of trade suggests that 1973 was the first postwar year when the United States became an open economy with free trade. This is not only because the average tariff was then paltry, but also because foreign commerce became large enough to transform the nation into a trade-dependent economy.

What about other years? Here we should examine the volume of trade before 1947.

An economy is impacted both by exports and imports. For instance, exports create jobs, whereas imports tend to destroy employment opportunities, although they do hold inflation in check. Thus both exports and imports exert a strong influence on an open economy. That is why the best measure of an economy's openness is the volume of trade, which is defined as the ratio of the sum of exports and imports to GNP.

A small trade/GNP ratio implies that the country is practically self-reliant, whereas a higher ratio signifies trade dependence. But what is small or large in this connection? This is determined by a country's history. Large economies are less dependent on trade than small ones, which find it difficult to meet all their needs from local production. A country's own history, not international comparisons, determines whether or not an economy is self-sufficient.

For the United States, reliable trade/GNP ratios are available from 1890 to 1990.[6] The average value of these figures turns out to be 13.7 percent, which provides us a benchmark to determine whether or not the U.S. economy is closed. In other words, the U.S. economy may be said to be practically self-reliant as long as trade is no more than 13.7 percent of GNP. Normally, exports match imports over time. Hence, a 13.7 percent trade volume implies that export dependence and import dependence are each worth 6.85 percent. Surely, when exports are below 7 percent of total economic activity, the economy may be reasonably called closed.

Historically, before 1973, the U.S. volume of trade rarely exceeded this benchmark, except during the two world wars, which were exceptional times. From the analysis in Table 3.1, we see that a sharp, sustained surge in both exports and imports qualified 1973 as the first postwar year as an open economy. Now we find that the historical benchmark of 13.7 percent reinforces this conclusion. From 1947 to 1972, the trade/GNP ratio was below the benchmark, but since then it has been consistently higher. This, along with low tariffs, suggests that America has been a free trade country since 1973. Such a shift is bound to have profound consequences.

Moreover, it turns out that 1973 was the first year in its entire history when the United States became an open economy with free trade. A close look at Figure 3.1, which graphs the yearly behavior of the trade/GNP ratio between 1890 and 1990, reveals this. There are four periods during which the trade/GNP ratio is above the average line—1890–1900, 1915–20, 1943–44, and after 1973. Of

FIGURE 3.1
Trade/GNP Ratio, 1890–1990

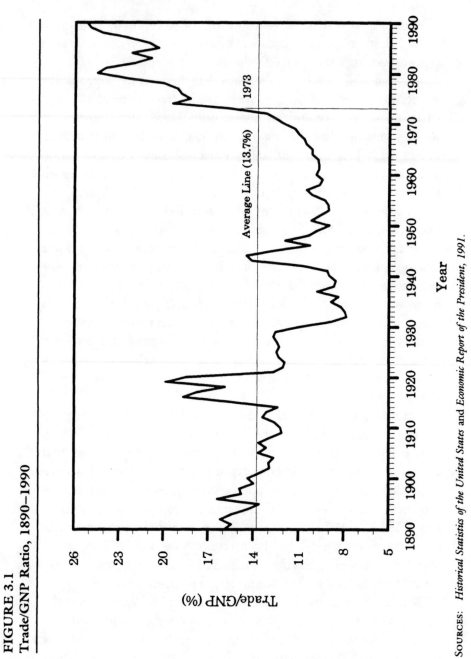

SOURCES: *Historical Statistics of the United States* and *Economic Report of the President, 1991.*

these, the first occurred toward the end of the nineteenth century and the next two during the world wars.

The first period was temporary and barely above the average line, indicating that the economy was minimally open. After 1900 the economy became increasingly closed to foreign commerce.

What about the years before 1890? Unfortunately, reliable GNP figures are unavailable for those years, although we do have good data on trade. Therefore, it is not possible to obtain dependable figures regarding the trade/GNP ratio, which is the best gauge of an economy's degree of openness. Yet we do know about average tariffs, and in the nineteenth century they were as high as 59 percent.

During the two world wars the trade/GNP ratio was above the closed economy mark of 13.7 percent. However, even the war years did not alter the fundamentally closed stance of the economy. Wartimes are not normal. Forced by a struggle to survive, individuals and nations do what they wouldn't do in other circumstances. Wartime openness is also temporary, and transient episodes leave the economy essentially unscathed. Throughout history, after each war the United States returned to its usual closed stance.[7] But not after 1973. This time, the U.S. dependence on trade continued to grow and except for a minor blip has been growing ever since. Furthermore, average tariffs during the wars were as high as 30 percent.

From all this we conclude that *in 1973, for the first time ever in its three-century history, the United States became a free trade economy, and has remained so ever since.* Thus 1973 was also a watershed year as far as America's foreign commerce is concerned. It is a mere coincidence that oil prices also soared at the time, masking the true significance of that year. Energy prices had surged many times before, but never before had America been a laissez-faire economy.[8] Until 1973 either tariffs were exorbitant or trade was too small to be relevant to the U.S. economy.

Thus, what makes 1973 so unique in the American chronicle is the fundamental shift from a closed stance to an open, free trade state, which forever altered the nature of the economy. Such a shift is monumental, comparable to an earthquake of 8.0 on the Richter scale. It cannot but cause loud reverberations, with echoes in every nook and cranny of society.

What caused this monumental transformation? In the aftermath of the Second World War, the United States emerged as the predominant economy in the world. While England, France, Italy, Germany, and Japan lay in a shambles, American manufacturing was at its zenith. Confident that the United States could outcompete all others, the federal government vigorously pursued laissez-faire around the globe. It also offered the Marshall Plan to rebuild Western Europe and assisted Japan through liberal exports of technology. By every possible measure, America's economic might was unchallenged for two decades after 1945.

However, by the late 1960s, it was evident that the United States had been overly successful in its zeal to rebuild the economies of its trading partners. Both Europe and Japan had emerged to challenge America's dominance in manufacturing. The once formidable U.S. industrial pillars were beginning to crumble. The foreign onslaught was first felt in low-tech industries such as footwear and textiles; then came the turn of radios, televisions, automobiles, motorcycles, refrigerators, air conditioners, generators, turbines, cameras, and numerous other manufactured products in which the Americans had held a near monopoly for two decades.

In the early 1960s, America's retreat was slow, barely perceptible. American workers and businessmen remained smug, complacent, and blind to the emerging challenge that would nearly rout them in the next decade. While the Europeans and Japanese were studying, saving, and investing their way out of the ruins, Americans were becoming lethargic, litigious, and extravagant. The world conserved and harnessed its energy, while America wasted it with abandon.

Europe and Japan, through grit and perseverance, increasingly exported manufactures to the United States. Sony, Honda, Mercedes-Benz, and Chanel became household names, perhaps more so than RCA, Zenith, General Motors—the American industrial giants that now seem as endangered as pandas. Apparently, the import surge in 1973 was so great that it catapulted the United States into an open economy. As tariffs had already tumbled, the country thus became an open economy with free trade. Since 1973, America's trade dependence, particularly its import addiction, has continued to rise with no end in sight. At present, the average tariff rate is 5 percent, not too far below the 7 percent rate of 1973, and the trade ratio, at 25 percent, is at its all-time high.

Free Trade and Real Earnings

I have argued before that the best available measure of living standard is the average real wage of production or nonsupervisory workers. This is because, according to the Bureau of Labor Statistics, these workers constitute some 80 percent of the work force of the United States, and it is their prosperity or poverty that should be the primary determinant of the U.S. living standard, not the GNP figures commonly used for this purpose by the administrations or mainstream economists.

Of course, to be consistent other countries should also be judged by the same measure. A rising living standard must mean rising incomes for at least a majority of a country's people, not just a small minority. With sharply rising inequality, GNP figures can grow while real employee wages consistently fall.

What has free trade done to real wages in the United States? The answer will surprise most orthodox economists: free trade has decimated the real earnings of a vast majority of Americans, a conclusion that emerges shockingly from a study of Figure 3.2.

Figure 3.2 puts together the official figures on trade and real earnings in postwar America. It is divided into two parts, with the lower part displaying the behavior of the trade/GNP ratio and the upper part displaying the real weekly earnings of all nonsupervisory workers as well as those in retail trade and manufacturing.

All the earnings lines reveal an upward trend until 1973 and after that a downward trend. Between 1950 and 1970, the trade ratio was more or less constant, as it rose from 9.4 percent in 1950 to 12.8 percent in 1970. For all these years the trade/GNP ratio was below the closed economy line of 13.7 percent. After 1972, however, the trade/GNP ratio moved up steeply, and within a year earnings peaked in many sectors and for all production workers.

As long as the United States was a closed economy, real earn-

FIGURE 3.2
Trade/GNP Ratio and Real Wages, 1950–1991

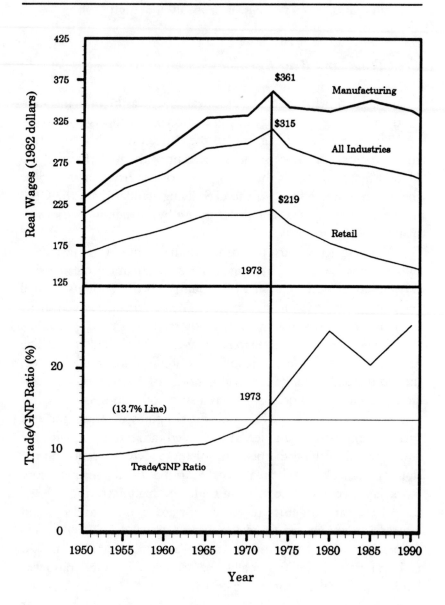

ings grew each year. But when America became a fair trade economy in 1973, real wages peaked and began a long decline. The basic message of Figure 3.2 is that once the U.S. economy shifted to free trade, as the trade/GNP ratio rose, workers' real earnings fell. In other words, after the economy switched from near self-reliance to trade dependence, real wages declined as U.S. trade dependence continued to increase.

Why free trade has reduced real earnings will be explained later. For now you should note that there is a negative association between U.S. trade dependence and your real income. It is clear that free trade has crippled the American living standard by reducing the real earnings of as much as 80 percent of the work force. Indeed, the government's policy of trade liberalization amounts to shooting oneself in the foot.

Productivity and Real Earnings

Another factor that impacts earnings is overall productivity in the economy. As the 1992 *Economic Report of the President* puts it: "Workers' earnings are closely related to their productivity: In a competitive market economy, a worker will tend to be paid an amount equal to the contribution he or she makes to the value of the employer's output."[9]

This statement clearly explains what determines real wages in a market economy. Economic theory suggests that a worker is paid what he or she is worth to an employer. A business looks at the productivity of a new worker and the price at which the worker's output can be sold in the marketplace. Productivity, however, depends on technology and capital equipment. Someone working with a word processor is far more productive than another person using a typewriter. The computer operator is thus paid more than the typist. Therefore, the higher the productivity, the higher the wage rate.

In monopolistic industries, however, in which one or two firms dominate, rising productivity does not always ensure rising salaries for employees. Or wages may rise by only a small fraction of the growth in productivity. This is because firms with growing monopoly power have strong control over wages. But if the entire economy is expanding, so that the demand for labor in many sectors grows, wages must rise in some proportion to the gain in labor productivity.[10]

On the other side of the spectrum, labor unions may force an employer to pay salaries that outpace productivity gains. For a while, some workers may earn more than their contribution to the firm warrants. However, this cannot persist for long, because soon the firm will become unprofitable and begin to lay off employees. The union will then have to relent and accept a lower wage.[11]

Unemployment also has an effect on employee earnings. With rising unemployment, competition for scarce jobs grows, and workers and their unions become willing to work for lower pay. Businesses then feel little pressure to offer higher salaries in order to attract skilled persons from other industries. Thus, in times of high unemployment, or recessions, salaries may not move with productivity gains.

In the long run, however, recessions and even depressions are followed by booms; labor markets become tight again, and employees' salaries can then catch up with their higher productivity.

The upshot of all this is that in the long run wage growth in a market economy is commensurate with productivity growth. Any discrepancy between salaries and productivity that may occur from time to time or in certain monopolistic industries is generally (though not always) a temporary, short-run phenomenon.

Note that economic theory does not say that wages generally rise only if productivity growth rises. All textbooks, whether at the freshman or graduate level, agree on this point and have done so since Adam Smith wrote his *Wealth of Nations* in 1776. For salaries to increase, only productivity has to rise, not necessarily productivity growth. Of course, wage growth accelerates if productivity growth does. This is an important point in understanding how a business normally behaves. The positive connection is between real wages and productivity, not between wages and productivity growth. As Alan Dillingham et al. write in their recent text: "As productivity increases, so does the level of real income earned by labor."[12]

What is the difference between productivity and productivity growth? To illustrate, let us explore the familiar concepts of prices and inflation.

Inflation is the percentage increase in prices per year. Stated otherwise, inflation is the same thing as annual price growth. But prices rise even if inflation falls. A drop in inflation or price growth means a decline in the rate at which prices rise from year to year. In the same way, a fall in productivity growth signifies a fall in the rate at which productivity rises from one year to the next. Thus, productivity rises even though productivity growth may decline, just as prices nowadays keep rising even though price growth, or inflation, has tumbled.

According to economic analysis, if productivity rises, wages also increase even though productivity growth may decrease. What is important is that in America worker productivity continues to rise even though productivity growth, that is, the annual rate of productivity increase, has dropped. In other words, U.S. productivity is continuing to go up, although more slowly than before. The productivity gains of the 1970s and the 1980s paled before those of the 1950s and the 1960s; yet they were gains.

Anyone who blames America's declining real wages on declining productivity growth, does not understand economics. Ford Motors today produces roughly the same number of cars and trucks as in 1975 with only about half the number of employees. This means that worker productivity there has practically doubled in eighteen years; yet Ford workers have lower real earnings (adjusted for inflation) than they did in 1975. Can we blame the drop in their living standard on their lower productivity? Of course not.

The productivity of the American worker has risen steadily even since 1973; the only thing that has declined is the annual rate of growth of productivity. But why should that by itself reduce your earning ability?

Something is amiss here. Those who blame your shrinking real wages on declining productivity growth would flunk even freshman economics, because productivity growth is irrelevant to the wage determination process—unless, of course, there is free trade. *Never in pre-1973 history did American wages fall while productivity rose.*

Wages and Productivity in the United States

Economic history generally confirms the positive relationship between the economy's overall productivity and real, inflation-adjusted earnings. Figure 3.3 presents the behavior of two variables between 1874 and 1950. Reliable productivity data go as far back

FIGURE 3.3
Productivity and Real Employee Earnings, 1874–1950

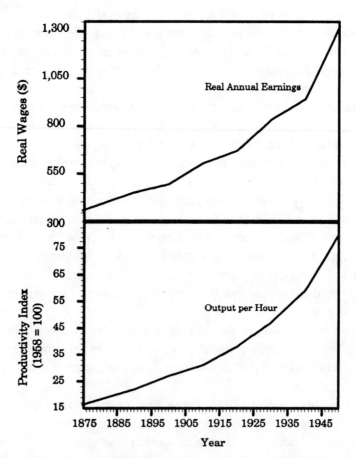

SOURCE: *Historical Statistics of the United States, Series D683, D726, and D737.*

as 1874, and earnings figures are available from 1860 on. However, for both variables Figure 3.3 begins with 1874 to see if any connection exists between them.

The lower part of the figure displays the index of overall productivity as measured by output per hour, with a base year of 1958 = 100; the upper part depicts the index of real annual earnings of nonfarm employees with the base year of 1914.[13] These lines are almost parallel, indicating a one-to-one connection between real earnings and productivity. In fact, the productivity index rose from 16 in 1874 to 27 in 1900, and to 80 in 1950, whereas annual earnings jumped from $403 to $483 and then to $1,358. Thus productivity and nonfarm wages kept pace with each other between 1874 and 1950.

It doesn't matter what base year or measure of productivity we use—output per hour, nonfarm output per hour, or manufacturing output per hour. They all indicate a high and steady rise in worker productivity in the United States. Similarly, it matters little what measure of real earnings we use—annual earnings of all employees, employee earnings in the nonfarm sector, or wages of production workers in manufacturing. They all reveal giant gains in real earnings commensurate with the giant gains in productivity.

In manufacturing, for instance, productivity tripled between 1909 and 1950, while real earnings more than doubled. Annual employee wages jumped from $656 to $1,379 in 1914 dollars, whereas weekly earnings of production workers rose from $11.00 to $26.00. In other words, the enormous productivity gain in manufacturing was not fully enjoyed by its employees. Some of this gain filtered into other sectors. This is not an anomaly but a normal behavior of the economy, something that I explain in the next chapter.

Let's now examine some selected years to see the influence of short-run factors on real earnings. Specifically, let us see how productivity and the real earnings of production workers in manufacturing behaved in the decade of the Great Depression.

Between 1930 and 1934, real earnings remained unchanged, even though manufacturing productivity grew by 5.7 percent. Salaries, of course, plummeted, but so did prices, so that the purchasing power, or real wages, of those with full-time jobs remained essentially unscathed. On the other hand, industrial output tumbled, but manufacturing employment fell even more, so that output per worker actually rose.

Thus, in the first five years of the Depression, high unemployment severed the link between wages and productivity, but as the economy began to expand after 1934, wages and productivity resumed their positive association, and by 1940, real earnings had climbed by 28 percent, while productivity had risen by 20 percent. However, even though the worst of the slump was over in 1933, the Depression lasted through the entire decade, because even in 1939 the unemployment rate exceeded 15 percent of the labor force. What is of interest here is that even as cataclysmic an event as the Great Depression could not break the normal positive link between wages and productivity for long.

Earnings and Productivity During Wars

The Great Depression could not sever the positive link between wages and productivity, at least in manufacturing. Let's see if the two world wars had any success in this matter.

In the case of World War I, real weekly earnings in manufacturing jumped by 17 percent between 1914 and 1919. Productivity rose in the midst of the hostilities, but then came down to its starting level by 1919 even though wages continued to grow. This shows that tightness of the labor market can impact salaries in the short run. Unemployment had disappeared even before the war, and the great need for armaments production caused a jump in the demand for labor. As a result, workers were able to command wages that outstripped their productivity.

The experience during the Second World War was more or less the same. This time both productivity and wages grew during the hostilities, but wages grew by 46 percent from 1939 to 1943, whereas productivity rose by only 12 percent. After 1943, both wages and productivity fell, but production wages in 1947 still exceeded their prewar low by 29 percent, while productivity was up by only 8 percent.[14]

Thus the war years show that in addition to productivity, a tight labor market, or a low rate of unemployment, also determines the level of real earnings. Of course, these wage gains in manufacturing must have come at the expense of employees in other sectors of the economy.

You may be wondering that when economists generally agree about a positive link between productivity and real earnings, why have I spent so many pages illustrating this relationship? Why have I analyzed so many periods to make just one simple point? The reason becomes clear when you look at Figure 3.4, which underlines what has troubled our economy since it became free and open.

Figure 3.4 displays three trend lines, representing output per hour in manufacturing, real average weekly earnings of all production workers, and weekly production earnings in manufacturing. From 1950 to 1973 all these trends moved in the same direction. Both real earnings and productivity moved upward; but then a curious development occurred after 1973: while productivity continued to grow, real earnings declined in manufacturing as well as for all production workers.

This is unprecedented. What happened in 1973? You already know by now: the United States became a free trade economy for the first time in history. Between 1950 and 1973, the trade/GNP ratio was more or less constant and below the closed economy benchmark of 13.7 percent; in these years earnings grew because of rising productivity. But after 1973, as the trade/GNP ratio climbed, earnings fell in spite of the still rising productivity.

Not until 1973 was America a free trade economy, and not until 1973 was the generally positive link between wages and productivity—expected and preached by economists for decades—severed. Even the Great Depression could not destroy this link. Nor could the two world wars do any more than weaken it. Never before did wages fall while productivity rose. Once the U.S. economy switched to free trade, productivity continued to grow, even though at a slower pace than before, but wages began to tumble. Such is the devastation

FIGURE 3.4
Manufacturing Productivity Index and Real Wages in 1982 Dollars, 1950–1991

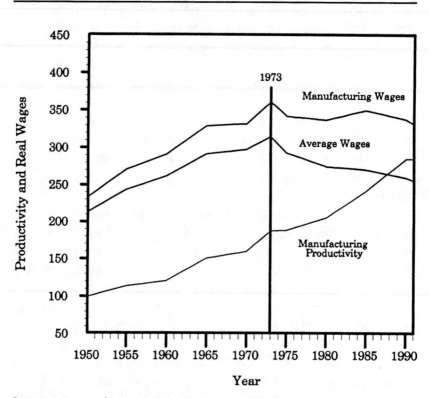

SOURCE: Bureau of Labor Statistics, *Employment and Earnings,* various years.

wrought by free trade; such is the earnings carnage of trade liberalization.

Specialists in international economics define free trade as a nation's switch from a closed to an open system, with zero or low rates of tariff. That is what the United States became in 1973, for the first time in history, and has been ever since. As long as the American economy remained closed, rising productivity induced an increase in real earnings; but once the country shifted to free trade, rising productivity was accompanied by declining earnings. Indeed, the nation has been paying a heavy price for the dogma of free trade.

There is a great outcry in America today about the declining growth of productivity. This is, of course, a matter of concern; but why should it induce a decline in earnings when the level of productivity is still rising? There has been no absolute decline in output per hour beyond one or two recession years. Productivity growth has decreased at times in the past, but that never produced a declining living standard. All it did was to generate a lower GNP growth, not lower wages. Remember the difference, as explained before, between productivity and productivity growth.

Between 1900 and 1910, labor productivity rose by 16 percent, or an average of 1.6 percent per year, but that was below the annual rate of 2.2 percent prevailing in the previous decade. That in turn fell far short of the annual rate of increase of 3.6 percent between 1874 and 1884. Yet earnings did not decline between 1874 and 1910. Yes, productivity growth fell, but not earnings.[15]

Free trade has done to America what even the Great Depression could not do. Even during the economic cataclysm of the 1930s, earnings rose with productivity because the United States was still a closed economy with high tariffs. But since 1973, earnings have declined while productivity has continued to rise. Eventually, free trade could be more devastating than even the Great Depression.

4

Roots of the Free Trade Fiasco

Three historically unprecedented phenomena have transpired in America since 1973. Real earnings have plummeted for over three fourths of Americans; the normally positive link between real wages and productivity has been severed; and the United States has become an open, free trade, import-addicted economy. Of these three, the third is a cause, the first two effects. Why? This is the question to which I now turn.

Association between any two events does not mean there is a causal link between them. When the National Football Conference wins the Super Bowl, the stock market usually jumps. Here there is an association, but no causal link. This association is simply a statistical quirk, a mere coincidence.

Could we say the same thing about the three phenomena mentioned above? No, we could not even if the cause-and-effect relationship was not apparent. This is because the three are part of the same discipline called international economics. Tradition has it that trade, productivity, and real earnings all move in the same direction. However, this tradition must now be abandoned.

The central question facing us is, why has free trade destroyed the American dream? In searching for the answer, let's go back to the analysis of the main factors affecting real earnings.

The 1992 *Economic Report of the President* explains in simple terms that in a competitive economy a worker receives a salary matching the contribution he or she makes to the value of an employer's production. No business will pay you more than the value of the output you produce for it. Your contribution depends on your productivity and the price your output fetches from the market. Thus, your earnings depend on the product price and your productivity.

Productivity is not the only determinant of earnings. Your salary also depends on how increased output affects the product price. Suppose a firm hires many new workers and thus raises its output substantially. If it has to reduce its price to attract new customers and sell the increased production, then it may have to lower the wage rate even if worker productivity is constant. In the summer of 1992, airlines slashed their ticket prices in half. While this was a boon to vacationers and business travelers, the airlines lost money despite heavy traffic. TWA and Continental employees, from pilots to flight attendants to ground personnel, had to work harder but accept lower salaries at the same time. Their productivity jumped as the same number of employees served more customers. Yet their earnings fell because ticket prices had been reduced so drastically. This shows that wages can fall in spite of higher employee productivity if product prices plummet. Once again, for emphasis, two, not one, factors determine your salary: your productivity is one, the market price is another.

Over the years, there has been an enormous increase, for instance, in labor productivity in agriculture. Today, only 2 percent of the American labor force produces enough farm products to feed not only the entire United States but also many other nations. Yet the rise in real wages in farming has been minuscule. Labor earnings in agriculture have risen by a tiny fraction of the enormous rise in productivity. Moreover, farm incomes and profits have actually declined.[1]

A farmhand in 1950 produced one bushel of wheat but now

produces seven; his productivity has thus jumped sevenfold. Yet his after-tax earnings, adjusted for inflation, have barely budged. The reason is that farm prices have lagged behind the prices of other products.[2] Agricultural goods have become extraordinarily cheap relative to other goods in the United States. The fraction of income that an average American spends on food today is close to its all-time low. Thus, productivity increase alone will not guarantee you a higher salary. The nature of the industry you work in is also important.

Why have farm prices tumbled relative to other prices? The reason is that for necessary goods, prices fall sharply in response to an increase in their supply.[3] Let us take food, a necessary good, as an example. We need food before we can have luxuries, and most Americans eat well—some say too well. Therefore, if the food supply goes up, people will not rush to grocery stores and stock up unless prices have been dramatically slashed. Whenever a grocery has a glut of potatoes, tomatoes, ice cream, coffee, or any other edible, it has to chop prices to clear its shelves. This explains why a rise in farm output causes a sharp fall in its price. Hence a rise in productivity is no guarantee of a rise in farm income.

With nonfarm goods, however, people's behavior is different. In the case of food, there are biological limits to consumption; but no such limits exist in manufacturing, services, or the quality of housing. In nonfarm industries, a rise in supply need not produce a sharp fall in prices.[4] For example, during the 1980s, house prices rose substantially even though new houses flooded the market. This is because while supply went up, demand for housing increased even more. Something like this could never happen in the market for wheat, soybeans, or even canned foods, because there are biological limits to the consumption of farm goods.

Product prices are determined by forces of supply and demand. An increase in supply alone normally generates a fall in the product price. But for nonfarm goods, the price fall is generally small, because the demand for such products rises sharply as their price drops. Suppose you go into a department store to buy a shirt. To your pleasant surprise, the price is 25 percent below what you had expected. Most likely you would want to stock up on shirts and buy two or more, instead of just the one that you originally intended to purchase. You end up spending more than you had planned. While the price was only 25 percent below your expectation, your demand jumped by 100 percent or more. Thus, for manufactured goods, especially high-ticket items such as cars, computers, and appliances, price exerts an enormous influence on demand. But the same is not true about farming.

An increase in your productivity will normally bring you a higher salary if you work in manufacturing, transportation, services, construction, or most other nonfarm industries, because increased output in such sectors generally results in only a slight price decline. Thus the key to understanding the impact of productivity growth is this: How steep is the price fall resulting from the productivity gain? If the price declines sharply, then your salary or profit may fall even if your productivity jumps. If you work for AT&T, hard work will normally bring you a large raise; but if you labor on a tobacco farm, your diligence is no guarantee of a higher salary. Thus, the nature of the industry in which you are employed also determines your living standard.[5]

When the price of a commodity falls, you expect to spend less on it. If you end up spending more, as in the example of the shirt above, such a commodity is said to have an elastic demand. But when price falls and you spend less, the product is said to have an inelastic demand.[6]

For instance, consider the case of salt. If its price falls by 25 percent or even 50 percent, you are not likely to consume more salt. On the other hand, if you are ambivalent between driving your old car or buying a new one, a 25 percent price decline will most likely make you go for the new automobile. You will end up spending a lot more than by just hanging on to your old car. Thus, goods whose price fall induces you to spend more have an elastic demand; if you end up spending less, then that demand is inelastic.

Necessary goods normally have inelastic demand, whereas manufactured and especially expensive products have elastic demand.[7] Elasticity of demand for your firm's product turns out to be a major determinant of your salary. It is at least as important as your productivity.

Analogy with Agriculture

Why am I harping on agriculture when the central question is the desirability of free trade? Many people easily understand the economics of farm earnings, because they have heard about the unique problems of agriculture and the special status farmers enjoy with politicians and administrations.[8] The media usually pay a great deal of attention to the recurring farm crisis, because thousands of farmers live in debt and have barely enough to make both ends meet. Unfortunately, the blight tormenting rural America for decades has now spread to the industrial heartland. *The horrors of farming have now become the horrors of U.S. industry.* If you follow this argument, you will easily see why free trade is crippling the American living standard.

From all measures, there has been a phenomenal productivity growth in U.S. agriculture, not just in recent years but ever since the birth of the nation. Rice, wheat, soybeans, milk, sugar, tobacco, beef, corn, and cotton now require less than 10 percent of the man-hours to produce the same output as in the 1920s.[9] Yet real farm incomes have not grown much, if at all. In fact, frequently rising productivity has been a major headache for the farmer, bringing misery instead of affluence.

In order to see why free trade has decimated the real earnings of most Americans, we need to understand how productivity gains affect farming.

Farmers operate in a highly competitive environment. They have little say in the determination of market prices, which are normally set by speculators in commodity markets, such as the Mercantile Exchange in Chicago. Each farmer therefore attempts to maximize his earnings through the use of new technology and other productivity improvement measures. No farmer by himself has a significant impact on price, but when many farmers use the new technology, there is an enormous increase in the supply of farm products.

Farm prices must then fall, as would the price of any product with an increased supply. But since farm products have inelastic demand, people spend less on these goods as prices fall. Thus, farmers end up with less money even though they have raised their productivity and output. In fact, productivity growth becomes a cause of their earnings decline.[10]

The reward of rising agricultural productivity goes to consumers. This is precisely why U.S. consumers pay some of the lowest farm prices in the world. It is hard to believe that the enormous growth in farm productivity has not produced prosperity for American farmers. In fact, the government has to constantly rescue them with generous subsidies. All this emerges clearly from a study of Figure 4.1, in which the upper part represents land productivity and net income in agriculture and the lower part, labor productivity and wages in 1982 dollars. Land productivity is crop production per acre, whereas farm income includes government subsidies.

Between 1950 and 1990, land productivity more than doubled, but real farm income fell from $57 billion to $36 billion, or by 37 percent. Indeed in 1929, farm income, at $42 billion, exceeded that of 1990. Are farmers then in a depression? Perhaps not.

While agricultural incomes have plummeted, the number of farmers has fallen even more. In 1950, there were 5.65 million farms but in 1990 only 2.16 million, or less than half that.[11] Therefore, real income per farm operator has risen somewhat. It is certainly higher than the 1929 level. In any case, the enormous productivity increase in farming has not produced commensurate profit for the farm sector.

The first year of America's switch to free trade, 1973, stands out again in the chart. This is the year in which postwar farm income peaked at $69 billion.[12] The best year ever for agriculture, however, was 1945, when farm income was at its all-time high of $78 billion.

Both 1945 and 1973 were years of inflation and a worldwide commodities boom. Both saw a big jump in international demand for U.S. farm products. In the first case, the cause was the war; in the second, it was a major crop failure in the Soviet Union. All this suggests that higher prices are perhaps more important to agricultural prosperity than technological improvements.

The story is the same for labor hired by farmers. There also big productivity gains have failed to produce commensurate gains in

FIGURE 4.1
Farm Productivity and Income in 1982 Dollars, 1950–1990

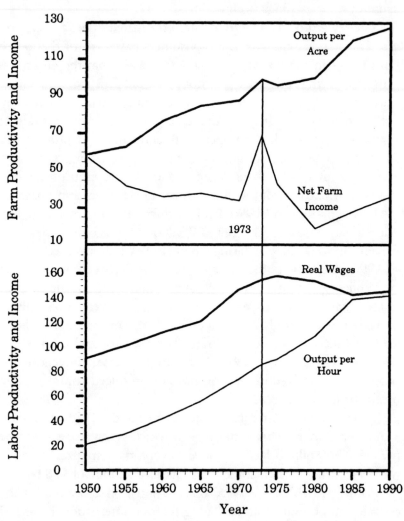

SOURCE: *Economic Report of the President,* 1991 and 1992.

real earnings. The lower part of Figure 4.1 reveals this even more poignantly than the upper part. The inflation-adjusted wage index is plotted against farm output per hour or labor productivity in agriculture. The index of labor earnings in 1982 dollars rose from 91 in 1950 to a peak of 158 in 1975, but then began to tumble, settling at 146 in 1990. The labor productivity index, however, rose from 22 in 1950 to 90 in 1975 and then to 142 in 1990. Thus, while labor earnings during the entire period rose by 62 percent, productivity soared by 545 percent. And after 1975, output per hour climbed by 58 percent, while real wages fell by 7 percent.

Such giant productivity gains give a new meaning to the dictum of poverty amid plenty. American agriculture is the most efficient and mechanized in the world; yet hundreds and thousands of destitute farmers have abandoned their farms. Technology is not an unmixed blessing, and U.S. agriculture proves it.

Inflation is a better friend of the farmer than scientific inventions. Agriculture has always prospered in times of rapidly rising prices and suffered when prices fall. Net farm income today is below that of 1929, the year the Great Depression began. However, farm prices are much higher now than at that time. Where, then, is the problem? What really matters to agriculture are farm prices relative to the prices of other goods.[13]

If agricultural prices rise faster than nonagricultural prices, farmers gain; otherwise, farmers lose. What really matters is the relative price, that is, the farm price relative to the nonfarm price. History shows that high relative farm prices are more important to agricultural prosperity than productivity. Farmers thrive during wars and periods of inflation, because the prices of goods they sell outpace the prices of goods they buy. Figure 4.2 demonstrates this clearly.

Figure 4.2 displays a causal relationship among relative farm prices, real wages, and farm income. This figure confirms what I have argued before, that real labor earnings are determined by two forces: labor productivity and relative prices. In 1950, the index of labor productivity was 22 and had risen to 90 by 1975, while real wages rose from an index of 91 to 158. Thus while productivity grew by 310 percent, earnings rose by only 74 percent. This is because the index of relative farm prices fell from 101 to 76, or by

FIGURE 4.2
Farm Real Wages, Relative Price, and Net Income, 1950–1990

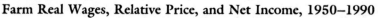

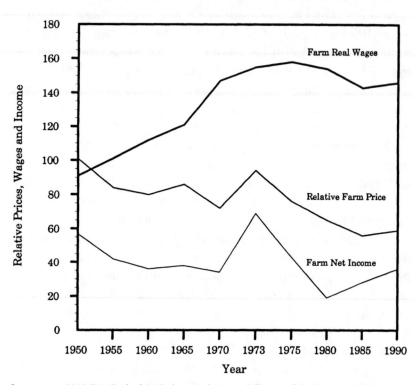

SOURCES: *1991 Fact Book of Agriculture* and *Economic Report of the President*, 1991.

some 24 percent. The analysis underscores the disproportionate influence of prices. Relative prices matter more to earnings than productivity.

Since 1975, productivity growth has slowed, as between 1975 and 1990 the index of output per hour grew from 90 to 142, or only 58 percent. The compound annual productivity growth between 1950 and 1975 was 5.8 percent; since 1975, it has been only 3 percent—indeed a sharp drop. But even though productivity growth tumbled, the absolute level of productivity continued to rise, and not at an unhealthy rate. Yet real earnings fell. The reason lies in the sharp drop in the index of relative farm prices, which fell from 76 in 1975 to 59 in 1990.

Between 1950 and 1975, when real earnings peaked, farm prices fell by 24 percent, or at a compound annual rate of 1.1 percent. But between 1975 and 1990, the corresponding fall was 22 percent, or an annual rate of 1.7 percent. Thus the farm price decline accelerated after 1975 and clearly overcame the positive effect of rising productivity on labor earnings. The story of net farm income is similar, as the two trend lines, represented by the relative farm price and farm net income, are almost parallel to each other. Whenever the relative farm price fell, net income tumbled.

Farm real earnings fell in spite of huge government subsidies to agriculture, amounting to $17 billion in 1992 alone.[14] This should demonstrate how strong the effect of declining relative prices can be on real wages and profits in an industry.

The "Agrification" of America

Most analysts—economists, historians, bankers, and columnists—are aware of the special problems of agriculture. *But few realize that, thanks to free trade, U.S. industry is now in the same boat as farming and has been there for the past two decades.* Farm troubles used to be considered so unique that the government statistical machine divided the economy into two areas: the farm sector and the nonfarm sector. Not anymore.

What has bedeviled U.S. agriculture over the past two centuries has now afflicted U.S. industry over the past two decades. The only difference is that farm troubles have stemmed from inelastic demand, whereas industry's headaches have come from free trade. Farm problems are natural; industrial problems are man-made.

Food demand is inelastic because of biological limits to consumption; but the manufacturing decline has been caused by a variety of contradictory economic policies of various administrations. Trade liberalization has been the quintessence of U.S. commercial policy since the war, and finally it has succeeded—to coin a word—in the "agrification" of U.S. industry, especially manufacturing.

I define the term "agrification" in this way: when an industry behaves or is made to behave like agriculture, we may say that it has been agrified. Agrification, then, means that various industries have the same troubles as the farm sector. The problems of agriculture are no longer unique; they afflict the entire economy. Since so many occupations, including as much as 80 percent of the labor force, have suffered a decline in real employee earnings, it is fair to say that there has been an agrification of America, not just its industry, in the past twenty years.

The agrification hypothesis becomes clear as you recall the analysis of manufacturing presented in the previous chapter. The special problem of agriculture was—and is—rising productivity and yet declining income and real wages. But isn't that also happening in American industry? Hasn't this characterized U.S. manufacturing over the past two decades? Today, workers at Kodak, Xerox, General Electric, Chrysler, Exxon, and RCA, among other pillars of American industry, are nearly twice as efficient as in the early 1970s. Yet their inflation-adjusted salaries are sharply down.[15]

It's true that industrial productivity growth is no match for that in U.S. agriculture. Yet the basic analysis of the two sectors is exactly the same. The nemesis of farming has been its declining relative price. The nemesis of recent U.S. industry turns out to be the same.

Analogous to farming, let us define industrial relative price as the ratio of the average price of products produced by industry to the price of goods and services produced elsewhere in the economy. Here the term "industry" means the sectors that produce nonfarm goods, as opposed to services and the government sector. The industrial sector mainly includes cars, furniture, computers, consumer electronics, appliances, machine tools, and so on, most of them the types of products for which the United States faces fierce competition from abroad.

These are also the nonfarm products that have much higher labor productivity than most other nonfarm sectors. Productivity growth was very strong in U.S. industry during the 1950s and 1960s; it tumbled in the 1970s, then rose again in the 1980s. Productivity growth was positive in all the postwar decades. No decade saw an absolute decline in productivity.

The industrial relative price can be computed in two ways. We can calculate it by dividing the consumer price index (CPI) of all commodities by the CPI of all items. Another way would be to divide the CPI of commodies or manufactured goods by the CPI of all services, which have been growing much faster than the rest of the economy.

Table 4.1 presents the second concept of the relative price, namely, the ratio of the CPI for manufactures to the CPI for services. These ratios are displayed in the fourth column, which reveals a relentless decline in the relative price of industrial goods, especially after 1975. From a peak of 1.72 in 1950, the price ratio dropped to 1.21 in 1975 and then to a low of 0.86 in 1991. In the first period, the drop was 30 percent over twenty-five years, or an annual rate of 1.4 percent; but after 1975 the drop is 29 percent over sixteen years, or a staggering annual rate of 2.2 percent. The decline in relative industrial prices is familiar to all of us. When you

TABLE 4.1
Industrial Price Ratio Between Manufactures and Services in Selected Years, 1950–1991

Year	CPIC*	CPIS	CPIC/CPIS
1950	29.0	16.9	1.72
1955	31.3	20.4	1.53
1960	33.6	24.1	1.39
1965	35.2	26.6	1.32
1970	41.7	35.0	1.19
1973	47.8	40.1	1.19
1975	58.2	48.0	1.21
1980	86.0	77.9	1.10
1985	105.4	109.9	0.96
1990	122.8	139.2	0.88
1991	126.6	146.3	0.86

Source: Council of Economic Advisers, *Economic Report of the President* (Washington, D.C.: U.S. Government Printing Office, 1991 and 1992).

* CPIC = consumer price index of all commodities; CPIS = consumer price index of all services.

purchase a camera, computer, fax, TV, or VCR, you don't see much increase in price from year to year. In fact, you may have even seen a sharp price fall for computers, faxes, and VCRs. But when you need the service of a doctor or a lawyer, you quickly get a sticker shock; or when you or your sons and daughters go to a university, the bill gives you a sinking feeling.

The soaring prices of health care, legal services, education, and so on are a great irritant to you, while you relish the price drop of manufactures. However, this phenomenon of tumbling relative industrial prices is more than an irritant, because, as explained shortly, it induces a relocation of productive resources from manufacturing into services and crimps living standards. Obviously, investment is attracted to those sectors where the price rise is high.

The industrial price slide is reminiscent of the declining farm relative price over the same years. Some of the reasons for this happening in industry are similar to those in agriculture: productivity growth in industry is larger than in services. Fast-growing sectors generally suffer a drop in relative price. This happened to agriculture as well as industry, because both enjoyed a faster productivity rise than the rest of the economy, which bulks large in services such as health care, entertainment, banking, restaurants, insurance, legal work, and so on. It is not, then, surprising that in both industry and agriculture real wages grew far more slowly than labor productivity. And since the mid-1970s, real incomes in both sectors have actually been falling.

But this is where the similarities end. In both industry and agriculture, real wages dropped because of the falling prices that accompanied the rise in productivity. But in agriculture the earnings drop resulted from inelastic demand, whereas in industry the culprit was free trade. As explained in the previous chapter, the United States has been a free trade economy ever since 1973, whereas before that it was more or less a closed economy. Now we see that the industrial relative price fell at a much faster rate after 1973 than before.

Between 1950 and 1973, as shown in Chapter 2, both productivity and industrial real wages soared; but after 1973, productivity continued to increase, while real wages tumbled. The culprit, obviously, was free trade, which caused such a sharp drop in industrial relative price that it overcame the positive effect of productivity gains on income. Before 1973, the U.S. economy was more or less closed and self-reliant, so that efficiency gains in industry generated only a modest price fall, and real earnings soared for all Americans.

In other words, free trade has brought about the agrification of America, because the phenomenon of rising productivity and falling earnings is precisely what has plagued U.S. agriculture over the past two centuries. What bedeviled farming in the past is now besetting U.S. industry, and for the same reason, namely, the excessive decline in the relative price. In a nutshell, the agrification syndrome, that is, the combination of rising productivity and declining wages, means that the American economy is now suffering from the same crisis as agriculture.

The syndrome is similar to what plagued the world during the early 1930s, when product prices fell sharply—by 24 percent in a matter of four years from 1929 to 1933. This price deflation in turn sent the U.S. unemployment rate soaring to 25 percent.[16]

Nothing so dramatic as the Great Depression has occurred since the free trade year of 1973, but industrial prices have relentlessly declined relative to the prices of services, which constitute the bulk of the economy. The relative price drop has had little effect on overall unemployment, but it has caused a sharp fall in the output and employment of the industrial sector. From New York in the east to Los Angeles in the west, from Chicago in the north to Dallas in the south, millions of manufacturing jobs have evaporated into thin air, thanks to the hefty and steady tumble in the industrial relative price.[17]

In city after city, industrial heartlands have turned into wastelands, only to be replaced by service businesses.[18] Those laid off by the likes of General Motors, IBM, Xerox, AT&T, Apple, and Westinghouse can now find jobs only in the likes of Burger King, McDonald's, Bloomingdale's, Macy's, K mart, Sears, and Wal-Mart, frequently at a fraction of their old salaries. Manufacturing jobs have been replaced by service jobs, and therein lies the tragedy of free trade.

Contrary to popular opinion, laissez-faire has not caused higher

[handwritten at top: Price in manufact ↓; Price in service ↑; thus investment moves away from manu. and $ more to service]

unemployment in the United States, only a pitiful drop in real earnings. This is because those displaced by foreign competition have generally been able to find jobs in the low-wage service sector.

In some ways, the lessons of the Great Depression and the policy of trade liberalization are the same, namely, that price upheaval can seriously disrupt and distort the economy. The assault of the Depression was swift and sharp, whereas that of free trade has been glacial and imperceptible.

The Great Depression sent all prices tumbling, and businesses, facing huge losses, had to lay off millions of workers. By contrast, free trade caused a sharp drop in manufacturing prices relative to those of services. Consequently, capital has been attracted to high-priced services, which have thrived at the expense of manufactures. The end result has been an erosion of the industrial base and real wages.

Thus, both the Great Depression and trade liberalization shattered the American dream by disrupting the price mechanism. The United States was able to overcome the calamity of the Depression, thanks to the Second World War, which restored the price level. The slow but steady calamity of laissez-faire can be overcome only by putting an end to free trade.

[handwritten: elastic demand]

Had the economy remained closed, the slide in productivity growth observed since 1973 would have slowed wage growth but earnings would still be rising. This is because industry has elastic demand, and, in an economy insulated from foreign competition, high elasticity is sufficient to generate rising earnings in an atmosphere of improving technology. With elastic demand, if the price of a product falls you end up spending more on it, so that the industry also earns more, raising business profits as well as workers' earnings.[19]

Earnings are determined not only by productivity but also by prices. In a closed economy, as productivity rises, product prices do fall, but in a smaller proportion, provided demand is elastic. This ensures a rise in profits and real wages.

However, in a free trade economy rising productivity may cause a larger fall in product prices, especially if foreign productivity is also rising. In fact, the greater the rise in foreign productivity in industrial goods, the larger the fall in the industrial relative price. This is because in a laissez-faire economy, there is only one market in which the producers of industrial goods compete—the global market. As technology in many countries improves, the rise in output and hence the price fall of manufactures are magnified. Countries with slower growth are then at a disadvantage, because the huge relative price drop has a much greater effect than their productivity rise. And since wages depend on both prices and productivity, the price fall overcomes the productivity gain, thereby generating the paradox of declining earnings amid increasing productivity in manufacturing.

There has been an enormous productivity growth in both Germany and Japan (see Chapter 1). The result has been a sharp worldwide fall in the industrial relative price. This, and only this, has caused American earnings to drop so steeply despite rising U.S. productivity. If America had not switched to free trade and had remained a nearly closed economy, as it had throughout its pre-1973 history, its markets would have been insulated from foreign production and technology. *U.S. earnings and living standards would have continued to grow even if Japanese productivity had grown a thousand times faster than U.S. productivity.* The slide in productivity growth is not the reason for America's economic decline; opening the nation's markets to foreign competition is the only cause.

In two centuries of developmental experience, productivity growth in the United States has fluctuated widely. At some times, the growth accelerated; at others, it slackened. But real wages never declined, except occasionally for two to four years during depressions.

However, thanks to four decades of foolhardy government policies, the country has now become a free trade economy, vulnerable to the depredations of high growth in other countries. Trade liberalization has proved to be a curse on the American dream.

What is puzzling is that the U.S. government was fully aware of this phenomenon and yet persisted with past policies. The 1988 *Economic Report of the President* had this to say about the pathetic wages in industry:

The increase in productivity growth in the business sector, and the increase in living standards since 1981, are explained largely by the dramatic strengthening of productivity growth in U.S. manufacturing. However, the benefits of stronger productivity growth in manufacturing have not been realized primarily in the real wages of manufacturing workers or in the profits of manufacturing enterprises. Instead, they have resulted in lower prices for manufactured products and greater purchasing power for consumers. This result reflects the normal operation of a competitive economy, supplemented by intense international competition in manufactured products.[20]

This statement deserves praise for its candor, as it admits the absence of wage gains in manufacturing owing to intense international competition despite an enormous rise in productivity in recent years. Yet the argument is deceptive and false. First, real wages actually fell, even in the 1980s; second, it assumes that consumers are different from workers, so that while workers suffer, at least consumers benefit. Real earnings actually dropped for 80 percent of workers and their families, all of whom are also consumers. Hence the living standard declined for four fifths of the consumers and population because of intense foreign competition.

Mixed Earnings in Services

It should now be clear that free trade, not a productivity slide, has been the real cause of falling wages in industry. But since relative prices for services have soared, why has there been a sharp drop in service wages as well? In fact, those employed in retail services are among the poorest workers. Their after-tax real incomes in 1991 were more than 20 percent below their 1950 lows and approached levels not seen since the Great Depression.

The fall in the industrial relative price implies an equivalent rise in the relative price of services, which reveals a mixed situation. Some service employees have definitely suffered, but a small minority has greatly prospered. Physicians, attorneys, investment bankers, scientists, computer engineers, and executives saw their earnings skyrocket during the 1980s, while many others employed in high-tech services enjoyed mediocre gains. In industry and agriculture, nearly all employees suffered, but in services, a minority, about a third of service workers, enjoyed such gigantic gains that they overcame the income sluggishness of the other two thirds of workers. This is precisely why, as discussed in Chapter 2, those in the top 5 percent income bracket of the population, according to the Congressional Budget Office, saw their real income rise by 23.4 percent between 1977 and 1988, while those in the top 1 percent bracket gained by nearly 50 percent.

In a brilliant analysis of wages in various sectors, Barry Bluestone[21] shows where and why earnings gains and losses occurred between 1963 and 1987. For expository purposes, I have divided his estimates into three tables. Table 4.2 presents real annual wages in industry and services. In both they grew smartly between 1963 and 1973; however, in percentage terms the gains in services were larger—23 percent versus 20 percent. This happened even though productivity growth of industry was much higher than that of services. The reason has already been explained: services enjoyed larger wage gains in spite of lower productivity growth because of a rise in their relative price.

Between 1973 and 1987, industrial wages fell by 2 percent but services enjoyed a 10 percent gain. The difference between the wage gains in the two sectors was thus 12 percent instead of the previous 3 percent. This can, of course, be explained by the much larger relative price shift in favor of services occurring after the economy switched to free trade in 1973.

TABLE 4.2
Real Annual Wages by Industry in Selected Years*

Year	Goods-Producing Industry	Change (%)	Services	Change (%)
1963	17,015		12,253	
1973	20,344	20	15,088	23
1987	19,864	−2	16,615	10

SOURCE: Barry Bluestone, "Comment," in *A Future of Lousy Jobs,* ed. Gary Burtless (Washington, D.C.: The Brookings Institution, 1990), p. 74.

* In 1987 dollars.

Table 4.3 reveals that once the U.S. economy became open and free, industrial workers at all levels of education lost income, although those with less than a high school education lost the most. The figures in parentheses measure the percentage gain or loss in different occupations requiring various degrees of education and skill. Thus low-skilled workers were the biggest losers from free trade.

Among services some lost, but overall there were gains. Table 4.4 shows that low-education workers took a great beating, suffering a wage loss of 18 percent. Most of these were retail trade employees. Those with high school diplomas also lost out, but those with some college education or more were big gainers.

The Hypothesis of Deindustrialization

The decline in the U.S. standard of living is not a new and abrupt phenomenon; it has been occurring since 1973, although the recession since 1990 and the election hoopla of 1992 have brought it into the media limelight. Despite benign neglect by the economics establishment, this unprecedented debacle has caught the attention of some respected economists. Among them are Bennett Harrison, a Carnegie-Mellon professor, and Barry Bluestone, a professor at

TABLE 4.3
Real Wages by Education in Industry in Selected Years*

Year	Less than High School	High School	Some College	College Degree or More
1963	14,563	17,621	19,567	30,791
1973	15,685	20,527	20,779	36,075
	(8%)	(16%)	(6%)	(17%)
1987	13,768	19,087	20,718	33,367
	(−12%)	(−7%)	(−0.3%)	(−8%)

SOURCE: Barry Bluestone, "Comment," in *A Future of Lousy Jobs,* ed. Gary Burtless (Washington, D.C.: The Brookings Institution, 1990), p. 74.

* In 1987 dollars.

TABLE 4.4
Real Wages by Education in Services in Selected Years*

Year	Less than High School	High School	Some College	College Degree or More
1963	9,163	12,649	12,356	20,157
1973	9,470	14,845	14,198	25,530
	(3%)	(17%)	(15%)	(27%)
1987	7,798	14,365	15,167	27,446
	(−18%)	(−3%)	(7%)	(8%)

SOURCE: Barry Bluestone, "Comment," in *A Future of Lousy Jobs*, ed. Gary Burtless (Washington, D.C.: The Brookings Institution, 1990), p. 74.

* In 1987 dollars.

the University of Massachusetts. Others are Katherine Newman at Columbia University, Gary Burtless, who is at the Brookings Institution, and Wallace Peterson, a distinguished professor of economics at the University of Nebraska.[22]

Bluestone and Harrison coined the term "deindustrialization of America" in a well-read book with the same title. They define deindustrialization as a steady erosion of the industrial base, especially in the northern part of the United States. Their main thesis is that this systematic decline since the 1970s has caused regional unemployment as well as lower earnings. Since their argument has both acolytes and critics, let's examine it at some length.

According to the deindustrialization hypothesis, following the Second World War, the United States emerged as the only advanced country with an unscathed industrial machine. American might was then unchallenged, both militarily and economically. Out of altruism or self-respect, the United States set out to help both Europe and Japan to reconstruct their economies; the assistance was in terms of money, technology, market access, and bearing the entire defense burden against the threat of Communism. All this enabled Western Europe and Asia to concentrate on their own industrial base and infrastructure.

At first, U.S. corporations, which had an incredible lead in technology and productivity, were able to outcompete their foreign counterparts with ease. As a result, wages, profits, and real incomes grew at an unprecedented pace. But by the early 1960s, Western Europe and Japan were ready to compete with American firms both in the United States and elsewhere. The rate of profit in the United States began to fall in the mid-1960s because of the growing power of unions as well as international competition, and the growth in income began to decline. Still, the absolute level of real incomes continued to rise.

U.S. corporations responded by shifting their plants out of high-wage areas both inside the country and abroad. Within the country, they shifted facilities from the North to the South, and outside the nation they moved their capital to Europe and Asia, where wages were but a small fraction of U.S. costs. As foreign competition intensified, plant closings became common, leading to an army of unemployed workers who either had to emigrate to the low-wage South or accept lower-paying jobs in their own localities.

During the 1970s competition from Japan and newly industrialized countries (NICs) such as South Korea, Hong Kong, Taiwan, and Singapore put a great squeeze on American profits, forcing companies to speed the relocation of their plants to Asia. This intensified the loss of jobs inside the United States, especially in occupations that could easily be performed by low-skilled workers abroad. Thus low-education American workers ended up competing with low-skilled foreign workers. Those without a high school diploma were the first to suffer wage losses; then came the turn of those with a high school diploma, followed by those with a college degree or more. Low-skilled workers in industry were the biggest losers. Workers displaced by foreign competition had to switch to service industries, especially restaurants, health care, and retailing. Hence, while manufacturing eroded, services grew apace.

In addition, in the 1980s the country went through a merger mania that created a huge debt burden on U.S. corporations, which responded with cost-cutting measures such as worker layoffs, postponement of research and development expenditures, cutbacks in investment, and a sacrifice of product quality. All this magnified the ugly consequences of the cutthroat global competition. Deindustrialization, in a nutshell, shattered the great American dream and caused a U-turn in the postwar climb in the U.S. living standard.

This, in brief, is the hypothesis of deindustrialization, which has evolved in the writings of various writers since 1982, when the term first appeared. William Greider, a *Washington Post* journalist, is among the latest to articulate this view. In his words, "The deleterious impact on American wages is likely to continue for at least another generation."[23]

The hypothesis has its critics, and you won't find more than a cursory discussion about it in textbooks, especially those of mainstream economists.[24] First, the critics question the erosion of the U.S. industrial base. Supporters point to figures such as those presented in Table 4.5, which shows that the share of output in GNP has systematically declined in both goods production and manufacturing. The share of labor employed by the two sectors has also met the same fate, falling to as low as 17 percent in manufacturing in 1990.

However, critics argue that the share of manufacturing production in GNP has stayed constant since 1950. Who is right? Obviously, both can't be correct. It turns out that the critics examine

TABLE 4.5
Output and Employment in Goods Production and Manufacturing in Selected Years*

Year	Goods Production† (% of GNP)	Manufacturing (% of GNP)	Goods Production's Share of Employment (%)†	Manufacturing Share of Employment (%)‡
1950	42	29	41	34
1970	32	25	33	27
1988	26	19	24	18
1990	NA	NA	23	17

SOURCE: Council of Economic Advisers, *Economic Report of the President* (Washington, D.C.: U.S. Government Printing Office, 1991),

* In current dollars.
† Includes mining, construction, and manufacturing.
‡ Percentage of total nonagricultural employment.

TABLE 4.6
Manufacturing Output and Its Share in GNP in Selected Years*

Year	Manufacturing (% of GNP)	Manufacturing Output (Billions of Dollars)
1950	21	258
1970	21	507
1988	23	928

SOURCE: Council of Economic Advisers, *Economic Report of the President* (Washington, D.C.: U.S. Government Printing Office, 1991),

* In 1982 dollars.

output figures presented in 1982 dollars, as shown in Table 4.6, whereas the supporters look at output in current dollars.

Using current-dollar figures, the production share of manufacturing tumbled from 29 percent in 1950 to 19 percent in 1988. Using 1982 dollar figures, however, the share actually grew slightly from 21 percent to 23 percent. There is a large discrepancy here. Normally, this kind of conflict does not arise, but, as we have seen before, there has been an enormous shift in the manufacturing relative price from 1950 to 1990. With the relative price falling steadily, the current-dollar figure will obviously reveal a much higher manufacturing share in the 1950s than in the 1980s.

Which view is correct? In computing shares and percentages, it is better to look at the current-dollar calculations than the constant-dollar ones, which may contain a measurement bias. Therefore, the view that the U.S. industrial base has eroded steadily is correct and the other view is false. The former is also supported by the vast evidence of massive job displacement and of plant closings by the hundreds and thousands.

The sharp drop in the manufacturing share of employment also points in the same direction. From 1950 to 1990, the employment share was cut by half, and in 1991, even the absolute level of manufacturing employment had declined to 18 million workers from its peak of 21 million in 1979.

No doubt the United States has suffered from deindustrialization on a vast scale. Yet the thesis does not explain the steady erosion of the American standard of living. Deindustrialization is not a cause of declining real earnings. It is a penetrating description of the process leading to the erosion, not of the causal factor. The cause is free trade. Deindustrialization has been caused by the agrification of America.

Why did the U.S. industrial base erode? The deindustrialization hypothesis blames it mainly on the multinational firms that relocated their facilities to the low-wage countries of Asia. This is a fact. Yet the multinational firms would not have rushed abroad, if they weren't free to import their goods back into the United States. It's the steady drop in American tariffs that encouraged them to invest heavily in Asia. In addition, U.S. corporations encountered faced intense international competition, forcing their emigration to low-wage countries.

If the United States had maintained its historical policy of being a nearly closed economy, there would have been no erosion of U.S. industry. America's laissez-faire policy enabled U.S. multinationals to relocate their factories abroad, produce their goods in low-wage nations, and then freely import those goods back into the United States. In August 1992, Smith-Corona announced the relocation of its typewriter-manufacturing plant to Tijuana, Mexico, and the layoff of 875 U.S. workers in the process.[25] Suppose the company were required to pay a hefty duty on typewriter imports; would it move its factory to Mexico? Of course not. The real cause of such plant relocation and the resulting decline in real wages is free trade, nothing else.

As a process explaining the steady erosion of the industrial base, the deindustrialization hypothesis is immaculate. I would, however, restate the thesis in this way. After the United States became a free trade economy in 1973, the rate of manufacturing profit fell to a new low because the industrial relative price began to fall at a higher rate. U.S. corporations responded by accelerating their emigration abroad and by cutting labor demand at the plants remaining at home. This in turn caused a massive loss of high-paying jobs, as many as 38 million by one estimate.[26] Most of the fired workers found employment in low-paying service industries, while a few entered the newly expanding high-tech services, where wages were soaring. To this add the restructuring of industry and the resulting job losses caused by the merger mania of the 1980s, and you have a complete explanation of the systematic decline in the American living standard.

The government neglect of merger mania reveals the total bankruptcy of official economic policy. Trade liberalization is supposed to generate competition between home and foreign producers; but mergers restrict domestic competition as one giant firm gobbles up others. In its wisdom, the government in the 1980s decided that foreign competition was preferable to domestic competition, that foreign predators were more trustworthy than local rivals.

What a bizarre idea! It should be the other way around. Competition is vital for efficiency. It is the cradle of giant productivity gains—but not when it comes from abroad. Given the choice, domestic competition is far better than foreign competition. Government policy was thus, at best, contradictory; at worst, self-destructive.

5

Productivity Growth: Is There Really a Serious Problem?

In recent years, economists and politicians have shed more crocodile tears over slackening productivity growth than on any other social ill. Almost every trouble is supposed to have arisen from the productivity slide that began in the early 1970s. If inflation rises somewhat, low productivity takes the blame; if unemployment jumps, low productivity is the culprit; if America cannot compete in global markets, low productivity takes a beating.

Low productivity is the whipping boy for most economic and social troubles in the United States: If only people were to strive harder and corporations were to invest more, economic ills would disappear, as productivity would surely climb.[1] Let's first see if the problem is as serious as everyone says it is, and then examine its true cause.

Productivity may be defined in a variety of ways. The most popular, and oft analyzed, measure, is output per hour in a company or a nation. This is an eminently plausible definition, because the amount of time we take to generate goods and services for our needs is a reasonable gauge of our contribution to society. For instance, in Japan an average worker puts in 16.8 hours to make a car, whereas a U.S. worker does the same job in 25.1 hours.[2] Clearly, Japanese auto workers are a third more productive than their U.S. counterparts. National output per hour is analogous to hourly industrial output.

Table 5.1 presents the historical record of national productivity. In 1890, the index of output per hour was only 14, and by 1990, 112. An enormous jump in national productivity has occurred over the last hundred years, during which output per hour has fluctuated widely. Between 1890 and 1900, productivity grew by 21 percent, or a 1.9 percent compound annual rate. The rate remained more or less stable until the 1930s, when it climbed to 2.5 percent per year. Surprisingly, the Great Depression was associated with a marked jump in productivity growth, suggesting that layoffs sharply ex-

TABLE 5.1
National Productivity in Selected Years, 1890–1990*

Year	Output per Hour†	Compound Annual Productivity Growth (%)
1890	14	
1900	17	1.9
1910	20	1.6
1920	24	1.8
1930	29	1.9
1940	37	2.5
1950	50	3.1
1960	66	2.8
1970	87	2.8
1980	99	1.3
1990	112	1.2

SOURCES: U.S. Department of Commerce, *Historical Statistics of the United States* (Washington, D.C.: U.S. Government Printing Office, 1975), vol. 1, p. 162; Council of Economic Advisers, *Economic Report of the President* (Washington, D.C.: U.S. Government Printing Office, 1991), p. 338.

* 1982 = 100.
† Figures from 1890 to 1940 were converted to the base year of 1982 by multiplying each of them by 0.625.

ceeded the fall in output. This kind of rise is, of course, unhealthy for the economy and society.

The largest jump occurred during the war decade when productivity soared at the rate of 3.1 percent per year. This rate was more or less duplicated over the next two decades. Since the 1970s, however, productivity growth has been less than half of that between 1940 and 1970.

There is no denying that a sharp slide has occurred in productivity growth since the 1970s, although productivity itself has continued to rise. (Note the difference between productivity and productivity growth, explained in Chapter 3.) But looking at the historical norm, the numbers of recent years don't fare as badly. Between 1890 to 1930, the rate of increase fluctuated between 1.6 and 1.9 percent; compared to these, the rates around 1.3 percent during the 1970s and the 1980s, even though lower, don't appear to be that far off.

In the historical context, productivity growth during the war decade and in its aftermath was an anomaly, unlikely to be matched again. Compared to other countries, America's current growth is stunningly low. But is that a cause for serious concern? The United States, after all, has many advantages that few other nations have. The country is well endowed with a vast expanse of productive land, a variety of minerals and raw materials, a labor force that is still among the most efficient in the world, a huge domestic market, unmatched military might, and so on.

Few nations have these assets. Japan, Germany, France, Britain, Taiwan, Sweden, South Korea—all lack the natural endowments of the United States. Other nations need higher labor productivity growth to enjoy higher living standards, but not the United States. Between 1900 and 1930, U.S. annual productivity growth hovered around 1.8 percent, far short of the growth recorded by Germany and Japan in recent years. Yet the real wage index in America then jumped from 496 to 834, or a staggering 68 percent. This was on top of the 10 percent rise recorded in the previous decade despite a depression.[3] All this happened in spite of a huge population growth that dwarfed the baby boom of the 1950s, as population soared from 62 million in 1890 to 122 million in 1930.

True, the recent slide in productivity growth is a cause for concern, but it is not nearly as serious as it is made out to be. It is not an unsurmountable hurdle, and can be easily fixed through proper action. Far more serious is the agrification of the country caused by misguided government policy. The sharp drop in the relative industrial price, as explained in the preceding chapter, is far more alarming than any other ill. In fact, by eliminating the industrial price crisis, we can even arrest the productivity slide.

Free Trade and Productivity Growth

More has been written on the productivity slide than any other economic ill in recent years. I gave you an inkling of that literature in the introduction, but few reasons mentioned by others survive closer scrutiny. The productivity slack has been blamed on inadequacy of savings, investment, spending on research and development, and education. It has also been blamed on booming spending on services and defense.

In most of these areas, the United States is inadequate because other countries are more than adequate. But we should not compare the country with other nations, because America has assets that others lack. We have to look at U.S. history to understand the true nature of the problem.

Compared to Germany's and Japan's, the U.S. saving and investment rates look awful. But compared to America's own historical norm, savings are still fairly high. True, individuals are saving less, but businesses save as much as ever before and individual savings have only been a third of total savings. Table 5.2 offers a true picture of the saving and investment rates in the economy. As you can see the saving rate actually peaked in 1980 at 18 percent of GNP, and even in 1990 it was not far below the rate in 1950. The same is true of the rate of investment, which peaked at 19 percent of GNP in 1950, but the 1990 rate of 15 percent compares favorably with the historical norm.

Some blame the recent productivity slide on heavy defense spending, which, however, has been decreasing as a proportion of

TABLE 5.2
Rate of Savings and Investment in Selected Years, 1929–1990

Year	Gross Savings (% of GNP)	Gross Investment (% of GNP)
1929	14	17
1940	14	13
1950	15	19
1960	16	15
1970	17	15
1980	18	16
1990	14	15

SOURCE: Council of Economic Advisers, *Economic Report of the President* (Washington, D.C.: U.S. Government Printing Office, 1991).

GNP since the 1950s. Thus, defense spending cannot be the true culprit either. Others fault research and development spending, but that as a percentage of GNP has also been constant. Some economists suggest that booming services have generated the productivity problem. But the services growth is an effect of something else. It is not a cause.

There are others who blame the baby boom for the productivity slide. All those babies born during the 1950s joined the labor force during the 1970s, stretching the economy to its limits. At the same time women came out in droves to work outside their homes. Investment failed to rise to match the sharp climb in the number of newcomers, thereby causing a productivity slowdown. However, this was not the first time that the U.S. labor force soared. As mentioned above, population doubled between 1890 and 1930 without any productivity slack and without a major rise in the rate of investment. Population did not hurt productivity in the past; why should it now?

The sharp rise in the price of oil during the 1970s is another culprit in the minds of many. As energy prices rose, so the argument goes, the firms had less money left for capital equipment that helps productivity grow. Hence the slide. However, oil prices fell sharply during the 1980s, but there was no relief from the productivity slack.

The only cause of the productivity slowdown is free trade. Take a look at Figure 5.1 Until 1970, both the trade/GNP ratio and the annual rate of productivity growth were nearly constant; but after 1973, when the country became a free trade economy, productivity growth plummeted with rising trade dependence as measured by the soaring trade ratio.

Until the economy switched to free trade, the yearly rate of productivity growth after the war was no less than 2.8 percent, and the rate of investment, being constant, was not a factor in the productivity slowdown. But after the early 1970s, as the trade/GNP ratio increased, productivity growth fell. There is only one conclu-

FIGURE 5.1
Trade/GNP Ratio and National Productivity Growth, 1950–1990

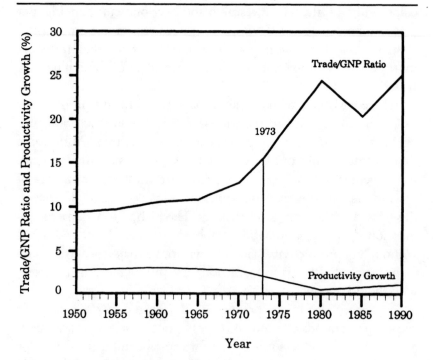

SOURCE: *Economic Report of the President, 1991.*

sion we can draw from this. Free trade caused the productivity growth slack and is continuing to do so.

How did free trade accomplish this? The process of the productivity slide is the same as that of the drop in real earnings. Manufacturing has much greater productivity than services do. As long as the economy was closed, the share of manufacturing in GNP was more or less constant, but after the nation's switch to laissez-faire, the manufacturing base began to fall in favor of services. When a slow-growth sector expands at the expense of a high-growth sector, overall national productivity is bound to decline. This is what happened during the 1970s and 1980s and continues without respite.

In fact, manufacturing is now slumping so fast that for the first time ever in history, government employees outnumber those in industry—by as much as half a million.[4] Thus free trade launched a double-barreled attack on real earnings in the United States. First, as explained in the previous chapter, it accelerated the decline in the relative price of industry, and secondly it led to a slowdown in national productivity growth. Even though productivity growth in manufacturing recovered somewhat during the 1980s, the relative price slide was so severe that real earnings continued to fall. In other words, even though the productivity problem is indeed a cause for concern, the bigger problem is the continuing drop in industrial prices relative to those in services.

Trade, however, has not always been bad for the United States. During the 1940s the American economy had also become open, though temporarily, and the nation enjoyed the highest rate of productivity growth in this century. The reason is that the United States was then an exporter of manufactures; therefore, increased trade stimulated industry, raising both employment and production in the high-productivity manufacturing sector. Trade is not always harmful to productivity growth; it hurts only when it crimps the industrial base.

6

Global Experience with Free Trade

Ever since the early 1950s, the world has witnessed a phenomenal growth in trade, which has expanded 1.5 times faster than global economic activity. Throughout history popular ideas have rationalized the status quo, and the phenomenon of soaring trade is no exception: it has the enthusiastic support of mainstream economists.

The acolytes of free trade claim that it increases productivity growth and living standards among all trading partners. To them trade is mostly a matter of exchange among individuals, and it cannot but be mutually beneficial. We have already seen that as far as the United States is concerned, this claim is totally false. Trade liberalization here has not only retarded productivity, it has also reduced real earnings by crippling the industrial base. Let's now see what freer trade has done for America's trading partners around the world.

Based on most criteria, all other nations have smaller economies than the United States. Conventional economics states that a small economy reaps higher gains from trade than a large economy. Let's see if the experience of smaller nations confirms this view.

Canada

Let us start with Canada, which in many ways is similar to the United States. America's northern neighbor is also well endowed with natural resources, has a highly productive agriculture, and was among the few economies unscathed by the war. Canada's labor force is educated and efficient, but it has a very small population in comparison with its neighbor. For this reason, Canada is a small economy relative to the United States; but the two are each other's largest trading partners, so that Canada's volume of trade as a percentage of its GNP has always been high. This makes the country a naturally open economy.

In many ways, Canada is a microcosm of its southern neighbor. It is a nation of immigrants, with a diverse population largely sharing a belief in Judeo-Christian ethics. As a measure of their cultural identity, Canada and America share the largest open border in the world. This may explain why the bulk of U.S. multinational investment has moved to the north. GM, GE, Ford, IBM, Exxon, McDonald's, and Kodak are as much a part of the business landscape in Canada as in the United States.

According to conventional analysis, trade stimulates productivity growth, which also depends on investment or the level of capital formation. The amount of money a country spends on machine tools, plant, and business equipment constitutes its investment, which is the same thing as an addition to its stock of capital. Table 6.1 presents figures for trade, investment, and productivity in selected years. Since the investment/GNP ratio, which is a common measure of capital formation, was more or less constant at around 22 percent between 1950 and 1990, it cannot explain the variations in productivity growth, which has fluctuated widely over the years.

The fifth column displays figures for annual productivity growth. The figure facing 1960, for example, is the annual productivity increase during the 1950s. This rate was then 3.9 percent and rose slightly to 4.1 percent during the next ten years. During these decades the trade/GNP ratio was nearly constant, and so was capital formation. Both of them were high relative to their values in the

TABLE 6.1
Trade, Investment, and Productivity in Canada in Selected Years,
1950–1990

Year	Trade (% of GNP)	Investment (% of GNP)	Manufacturing Productivity*	Productivity Growth (%)
1950	44	22	68	
1960	37	22	100	3.9
1970	43	22	149	4.1
1973	46	23	178	6.1
1980	56	24	194	1.2
1986	55	21	236	3.3
1990	51	22	260	2.5

SOURCES: Bureau of Labor Statistics, U.S. Department of Labor, *Productivity and the Economy: A Chart Book,* 1985 and 1988 (Washington, D.C.: U.S. Government Printing Office, 1986 and 1990); Bureau of Labor Statistics, U.S. Department of Labor, *International Comparisons of Manufacturing Productivity* (Washington, D.C.: U.S. Government Printing Office, 1991); *International Financial Statistics* (Washington, D.C.: International Monetary Fund, 1991).

* 1960 = 100.

United States, but there was not much variation. Not surprisingly, productivity growth was also nearly constant.

Between 1970 and 1973, the productivity rate jumped to 6.1 percent annually, then tumbled to 1.2 percent over the next seven years, only to pick up again during the following six years. Throughout this time, capital formation stayed high but trade fluctuated widely. The trade/GNP ratio jumped from 46 to 56 between 1973 and 1980, while productivity growth plummeted. Did the increased openness caused by worldwide reductions in tariffs hurt Canada's productivity? The evidence is inconclusive, especially because oil prices also soared during that period, and this could have caused a surge in trade, especially in Canadian oil exports, without affecting worker productivity. In fact, as oil prices plummeted after 1986, the trade/GNP ratio also fell, approaching the 46 percent figure of 1973. From 1973 to 1980, productivity growth fell as trade rose; after 1986 it fell again, but trade also declined. Thus the link between trade and productivity is, at best, inconclusive.

We may conclude the discussion of Table 6.1 saying that trade has by and large been very beneficial to America's northern neighbor. This is because the high overall rate of productivity growth in Canada was achieved in an environment of an open and relatively free trade economy. The petroleum price climb of the 1970s should have benefited the country, which is an exporter of oil. But it did not do so because Canada lives in the shadow of a giant; since the oil price shock caused first a deep recession and then stagnation in the United States, it also ended up hurting the Canadian economy, especially its productivity growth.

Table 6.1 shows that variations in Canadian trade occurred mostly after 1973, when oil prices shot up, and then again after 1986, when they tumbled. When oil became expensive, productivity growth plummeted, because the U.S. economy slowed down considerably. Thus, even though trade grew, productivity slackened. In other words, Canada's extreme dependence on the United States hurt its economy during the 1970s, even though almost all other exporters of oil prospered.

However, while productivity slackened, real earnings did not suffer as much. This is shown in Table 6.2. The index of real earnings in 1985 dollars is presented in the fourth column, which shows that, unlike its neighbor, Canada saw its real wages climb continuously between 1950 and 1986, as productivity kept rising. It is only after 1986 that there was a slight fall in real earnings, presumably because of the fall in the price of oil. Note that after 1973, as productivity growth fell, wage growth also fell substantially. Yet real wages continued to rise. A similar drop in U.S. productivity growth started the American earnings slide, which has yet to be arrested. This is because Canada, which has been an open economy throughout this century, did not face the same kind of traumatic switch from a closed system to laissez-faire. The country did not suffer the wrenching adjustment that the U.S. economy had to undergo after 1973 and is still undergoing.

Without trade with the United States, Canada's economic engine would nearly grind to a halt. But further openness would fail to produce any positive results. The free trade agreement between America and Canada that became effective in 1989 has not had

TABLE 6.2

Trade, Productivity, and Real Earnings in Canada in Selected Years, 1950–1990

Year	Trade (% of GNP)	Productivity Growth	Index of Real Earnings*	Wage Growth (%)
1950	44		46	
1960	37	3.9	60	2.7
1970	43	4.1	78	2.7
1973	46	6.1	86	3.3
1980	56	1.2	97	1.7
1986	55	3.3	100	0.5
1990	51	2.5	99	0.0

SOURCES: Bureau of Labor Statistics, U.S. Department of Labor, *Productivity and the Economy: A Chart Book,* 1985 and 1988 (Washington, D.C.: U.S. Government Printing Office, 1986 and 1990); Bureau of Labor Statistics, U.S. Department of Labor, *International Comparisons of Manufacturing Productivity* (Washington, D.C.: U.S. Government Printing Office, 1991); *International Financial Statistics* (Washington, D.C.: International Monetary Fund, 1991).

* 1985 = 100.

much impact on the Canadian economy. While productivity growth picked up during the 1980s, wage growth slackened; in fact, wages have been stagnant since 1986, while productivity has continued to rise. Is Canada now suffering from its own kind of agrification, which I defined in Chapter 4 as the association of rising productivity and stagnant or declining earnings? Is the trade agreement responsible for this?

It is too early to tell. All in all, Canada cannot prosper without its U.S. trade, but there is some evidence that this trade is now generating diminishing returns. Further openness in the economy should be halted until more evidence becomes available.

NAFTA would hurt Canada just as much as the United States. Both Canadian and U.S. multinationals would move some of their plants out of Canada into Mexico. Consequently, real wages would drop even more.

The 1988 *Economic Report of the President* describes the composition of U.S.-Canadian merchandise trade in 1986. While the two are each other's largest trading partners, America's trade with Canada constitutes only 18.9 percent of the U.S. total, whereas the U.S. share of Canada's foreign commerce is over 71 percent. Both countries trade with Japan, but the Japanese share of Canadian trade is only 5.6 percent. This does not mean that the agrification syndrome cannot afflict Canada.

You have earlier seen how huge productivity rises in manufacturing in Japan and other nations have combined with the openness of the U.S. economy since 1973 to generate a sharp fall in the industrial relative price in the United States. But Canada does not have much trade with Japan. Does that mean that Canada is immune to the effects of agrification? No.

The U.S. and Canadian economies are now interlinked through free trade and multinational investment. There is growing evidence that Canada may be in the early stage of agrification as well. The wage data reported by the International Monetary Fund and presented in Table 6.2 are about earnings in manufacturing. If we look at disaggregated figures in individual industries, we discover that real wages in 1991 had dropped about 2.5 percent below their 1984 levels in mining, construction, and services.[1] While this is a small drop over seven years, it does indicate the onset of the agrification process, as national productivity continued to rise during this period. Apparently Canada is beginning to catch the virus that has afflicted its southern neighbor since 1973.

Mexico

Mexico is America's neighbor to the south. It has a markedly different economy from that of the United States. Mexico is rich in oil, agriculture, and other minerals but has a very small industrial base. Much of its labor force is relatively low skilled, and for a long time the country followed protectionist policies while its giant neighbor to the north was busy opening its borders to foreign commerce.

Mexico's key statistics are presented in Table 6.3 for selected years from 1961 to 1988. What catches your eye immediately is the

TABLE 6.3
Key Statistics in Mexico in Selected Years, 1961–1988

Year	Index of Real Earnings*	CPI	Exports†	Imports†	GNP†	Investment†
1961	NA	1.6	18	19	164	24
1968	2.3	1.9	29	34	336	66
1970	2.4	2.0	37	43	484	88
1973	3.1	2.5	58	65	681	133
1975	4.5	3.6	76	106	1,082	236
1977	7.4	5.3	191	189	1,806	363
1980	12.2	9.3	537	578	4,159	1,033
1981	16.2	11.9	702	798	5,674	1,509
1985	100.0	100.0	7,306	4,897	43,337	9,048
1986	175.0	186.0	13,655	10,026	74,983	15,415
1987	412.0	432.0	38,076	24,226	183,636	36,485
1988	873.0	925.0	NA	NA	NA	NA

SOURCE: *International Financial Statistics* (Washington, D.C.: International Monetary Fund, 1991).

* 1985 = 100.
† Billions of pesos.

behavior of the consumer price index (CPI) over the years. From a low of 1.6 in 1961, the CPI soared to 925 in 1988, or at an annual rate of 26.6 percent over twenty-seven years.

During the 1960s the country enjoyed some degree of price stability, as the CPI rose from only 1.6 to 2 over nine years. But right after 1970, inflation picked up and began to accelerate following 1973, the year of the first oil price shock. This is remarkable, because Mexico is a major exporter of oil and yet faced the disastrous effects of a sharp rise in energy prices. In the late 1970s, inflation climbed at astounding rates. Between 1975 and 1980, prices nearly tripled and then jumped another 1,000 percent in the next five years. This was followed by another climb of 800 percent between 1985 and 1988. In 1990 also, prices soared, this time by 265 percent in one year.

In 1991, the inflation tiger was rapidly tamed, and by early 1992, inflation had declined substantially, running at a 20 percent annual rate. This is still high by international standards, but it is remarkably low by the Mexican norm.

With inflation out of control during the 1970s and the 1980s, all other variables—wages, exports, imports, GNP, investment— also rose at frantic rates. What is amazing is that in spite of such a frenzied atmosphere, where prices shot up from week to week, the inflation-adjusted, or real, GNP grew at a healthy rate for much of this period. But most of this growth lined the pockets of the wealthy, and inequality soared.

Mexico's economy is a classic example of why figures like real GDP or real per capita GDP are poor measures of a country's standard of living. In order to understand this, take a close look at Table 6.4. Between 1961 and 1980, Mexico's population soared by 89 percent. Yet its real per capita GDP nearly doubled.

The real per capita GDP is also a measure of the nation's overall productivity, suggesting that labor became twice as efficient over the two decades between 1961 and 1980. Yet after 1968 real earnings hardly budged. Real wages went up from 120 to 131, or a meager 9 percent, during the 1970s, while workers became very productive.

During the 1960s, real GDP grew at the rate of 7.3 percent per year, a record that nearly matched the phenomenal growth rate in Japan. Yet the Mexican real wage actually fell slightly between 1968 and 1970. The rapid growth of the sixties was simply a continuation of that of the previous decades, with one major difference. According to economist Rogelio Ramirez, between 1955 and 1970 real minimum wages grew at a healthy 5.5 percent per year.[2] However, all this wage growth occurred before 1968, because, as Table 6.4 shows, industrial wages became stagnant after that year. In this sense, 1968 may be regarded as a landmark year in Mexican annals, for while the economy continued to grow at a healthy pace, wage growth came to a halt.

Apparently the power of the labor unions began to decline in the late 1960s. Until then they had made handsome gains that outpaced the growth in per capita GDP; but following the land-

TABLE 6.4
Trade, Investment, Per Capita GDP Growth, and Real Earnings in
Mexico in Selected Years, 1961–1988

Year	Trade (% of GNP)	Investment (% of GNP)	Per Capita GDP Growth (%)	Index of Real Earnings*
1961	23	15	3.2	NA
1968	19	20	4.1	121
1970	17	18	4.4	120
1973	18	20	4.9	124
1975	17	22	5.1	125
1977	21	20	5.2	140
1980	27	25	6.0	131
1981	26	21	6.4	136
1985	28	21	5.8	100
1986	32	20	5.4	94
1987	34	20	NA	95
1988	NA	NA	NA	94

SOURCES: Table 6.3 and *International Financial Statistics* (Washington, D.C.: International Monetary Fund, 1991).

* 1985 = 100.

mark year of 1968, real wages were more or less constant. Consequently, there was hardly any improvement in the general living standard; only the rich were getting richer. Clearly, GDP is a poor gauge of a country's standard of living.

Mexico was able to expand its GDP through high capital formation and protectionist policies. While Canada and the United States were busy reducing their tariffs, Mexico offered increasing protection to its manufacturing. According to the conventional view, this should have generated low or negative growth in the Mexican GDP. Instead, it produced what some called an economic miracle.

The influence of protectionist policies is revealed by the declining trade/GNP ratio, which fell from 23 percent in 1961 to 17 percent in 1975. In the vernacular of economics, Mexico was then an open economy with restricted trade. Yet the country grew apace with the help of higher capital formation, as the rate of investment climbed from 15 percent to 22 percent in 1975.

Trouble began when Mexico came into increasing contact with the rest of the world, especially the United States, through foreign trade and borrowing from abroad. During the 1970s, the investment/GNP ratio rose from 18 percent to 25 percent, a jump of 39 percent. This enabled the real per capita GDP to grow even faster than in the previous decade—36 percent versus 28 percent. This translates into a 5.1 percent annual rate in the 1970s as compared to 4.8 percent in the 1960s. The impetus to growth came from a government policy aimed at rapidly transforming an agrarian nation into an industrial economy.

Toward this end the state followed inward-looking or protectionist policies. The idea was to protect infant industries in the private sector from foreign competition while reserving some crucial sectors exclusively for the state. Electricity, railroads, and petrochemicals, among others, were barred from private participation.

Protection was granted not just through high tariffs but also through an import license system through which only limited quantities of some goods, mainly raw materials and industrial machinery, could be imported. Foreign investment was permitted, but only in certain sectors such as chemicals, electronics, and transportation.

The government also intended to transform agriculture from a subsistence, low-productivity activity into a mechanized, high-productivity commercialized sector. All in all, the state followed an industrial policy of self-development through protection and import substitution. This was a sharp contrast to the policies followed by Canada and the United States.

At first the results were spectacular. GDP, real wages, per capita incomes, all grew apace as the population increasingly shifted out of agriculture into manufacturing. The fruits of development were also widely distributed, and those who had expected the Mexican venture to fail because of its protectionism were disappointed.

Sometime after 1968, however, the state policy began to betray its contradictions. Secure behind protectionist walls, domestic industries grew increasingly monopolistic; consequently, even though the unions still wielded considerable power in the state monopolies, overall wages became stagnant while business activity continued to soar.

Unable to tame the monopolies and labor unions, the government tried to distribute the fruits of development by sharply expanding its spending as well as state employment. This only increased the power of the bureaucracy, which had already become a monolith in its task of managing foreign trade and the economy. With rising budget deficits came extensive printing of money, which in turn fostered inflation.

Soaring inflation by itself would have forced the state to introduce serious reforms aimed at increasing competition among domestic producers, except that vast offshore reserves of oil were discovered in 1977, a year of exorbitant international petroleum prices. That is when Mexico really opened itself to foreign influence, which until then had been kept under control through limits imposed on imports and foreign investment.

The government then followed a policy not of free trade but of free borrowing from abroad. Multinational banks—Citicorp, Chase Manhattan, Bank of America—flush with petrodollars were only too happy to lend the government all the money it sought. Between 1977 and 1981, Mexico grew like never before. Real GDP jumped by nearly 38 percent during the period, but real wages hardly moved. In fact, the real earnings index fell from 140 to 136.

The billions of dollars borrowed from abroad were squandered on hastily conceived projects that failed badly. The country emerged with its highest-ever per capita GDP but was also saddled with unprecedented debt.

In 1981, the international price of oil began to decline, and the Mexican economy finally collapsed. All the ills of growing inequality and monopolies, hitherto masked by bountiful resources and oil wealth, then erupted.

The first effect, as we have seen, was gargantuan inflation, followed by a deep depression and an unprecedented disaster in real earnings, which from 1981 to 1988 tumbled year after year. Mexico is now plagued by incredible inequality. The poorest 20 percent of the people receive only 3 percent of the national income, whereas the richest 10 percent enjoy a 41 percent share.

Since 1985, Mexico has dramatically altered its policies. It launched a limited experiment with trade liberalization. Consequently, the economy has increasingly become open, as evidenced by its rising trade/GNP ratio. In fact, the trade/GNP ratio is now the highest in Mexico's history. Breaking the power of the domestic monopolies, with or without increased trade, was long overdue. Indeed, inflation is now under better control; however, the depression in real earnings has yet to be arrested.

In recent years Mexico has lured a large number of American companies to its soil through what is called the Maquiladora program. The government offers tax and tariff incentives in return for the companies making goods in Mexico and shipping them back to the United States.

American businesses have responded with great enthusiasm. The Mexican side of the border from California to Texas is littered with the façades of *Fortune* 500 corporations. By moving to Mexico, businesses can not only hire workers for pennies per hour but also elude U.S. regulations regarding child labor, worker safety and health, pollution standards, and, above all, taxes.[3] The likes of Zenith, Xerox, Chrysler, GM, Ford, IBM, Rockwell, Samsonite, and General Electric, among 1,800 other American companies, have established plants south of the Rio Grande.[4]

The Maquiladora factories have gone a long way in stabilizing the Mexican economy, especially in halting the free-fall that began with the fall of the oil price in 1981. But the program has also generated filth, pollution, and stench on both sides of the border.

What trade liberalization has done to the United States since 1973, unrestricted borrowing has done to Mexico since 1977. The lesson of Mexico's development experience is that growth through protectionist industrialization is great—until domestic industries turn increasingly monopolistic behind the tariff walls. For widely different reasons, both Mexico and the United States have been crippled by foreign influences—one by free trade, the other by freely borrowing from abroad.

Germany

Unlike Mexico, Germany's growth experience since the war is straightforward and easy to analyze. Formerly the two states of West Germany and East Germany, the country has turned out to be the biggest beneficiary from trade since the war. The global conflict turned the nation into one vast inferno. The country's industry and infrastructure lay in a shambles. Above all, the nation was divided into two portions, with the eastern portion containing the bulk of the region's productive land and natural resources.

In spite of all these handicaps, West Germany emerged as a dominant economic power soon after the war. With a long tradition of competitive industrialization dating back to the turn of the century, the truncated nation rebounded quickly.

Germany has followed a model of laissez-faire, pure and simple. It has kept its tariffs low and been willing to face foreign competition early on. The country has grown through a program of massive industrialization unaided by the government. Many economic leaps have occurred since the war, and Germany's is one of them. As with all such upswings, a strong and preeminent manufacturing base is the primary factor. Germany defines the standard of quality in many industries. Mercedes-Benz, Volkswagen, BMW, and Siemens are household names around the world. The country is especially strong in chemicals, steel, machine tools, and automobiles.

Key statistics of Germany are presented in Table 6.5 for selected years from 1950 to 1990. Its trade/GNP ratio shows that the economy has become increasingly open over the years. Starting from a low of 24 percent in 1950, the trade/GNP ratio reached an all-time high of 62 percent in 1990. Even though its GNP is about a third of America's, Germany has occasionally been the largest exporter in the world. Germany's is a clear case of how large the gains from trade can be, provided there is a strong manufacturing base.

The increasing openness of the economy has been more than matched by accelerating productivity in manufacturing. Productivity growth was exceptionally high during the 1950s and 1960s, but even after the oil price shock of 1973, the rate remained respectable

TABLE 6.5

Trade, Investment, and Productivity in Germany in Selected Years, 1950–1990

Year	Trade (% of GNP)	Investment (% of GNP)	Manufacturing Productivity*	Productivity Growth (%)
1950	24	19	49	
1960	37	24	100	7.4
1970	43	25	176	5.8
1973	44	24	208	5.7
1980	57	23	269	3.7
1986	60	19	324	3.1
1990	62	20	370	3.4

SOURCES: Bureau of Labor Statistics, U.S. Department of Labor, *Productivity and the Economy: A Chart Book,* 1985 and 1988 (Washington, D.C.: U.S. Government Printing Office, 1986 and 1990); Bureau of Labor Statistics, U.S. Department of Labor, *International Comparisons of Manufacturing Productivity* (Washington, D.C.: U.S. Government Printing Office, 1991); *International Financial Statistics* (Washington, D.C.: International Monetary Fund, 1991).

* 1960 = 100.

by U.S. standards. Capital formation rose steadily between 1950 and 1970 and has slackened somewhat since. This slide is partly responsible for a recent shrinkage in productivity growth. Nevertheless, the German record indicates that high investment and free trade are jointly responsible for the country's extraordinary rise in productivity.

The productivity climb has also been reflected in soaring real earnings. This is displayed in Table 6.6, which shows that the index of real wages jumped from 26 in 1950 to a record high of 112 in 1990. This is a wage growth rate of 3.72 percent per year. Thus in Germany, wages grew in proportion to labor productivity throughout the postwar period. There is no sign so far of any type of agrification at work. The German future seems to be bright.

The lesson of the German economic experience is that manufacturing and foreign trade together are the keys to economic development. This is illustrated in Figure 6.1, which plots the trade/GNP ratio against real wages and productivity. The direction of all

TABLE 6.6
Trade, Productivity, Growth, and Real Earnings in Germany in
Selected Years, 1950–1990

Year	Trade (% of GNP)	Productivity Growth (%)	Index of Real Earnings*	Wage Growth (%)
1950	24		26	
1960	37	7.4	44	5.4
1970	43	5.8	76	5.6
1973	44	5.7	85	3.8
1980	57	3.7	100	2.3
1986	60	3.1	104	0.6
1990	62	3.4	112	1.9

SOURCES: Bureau of Labor Statistics, U.S. Department of Labor, *Productivity and the Economy: A Chart Book,* 1985 and 1988 (Washington, D.C.: U.S. Government Printing Office, 1986 and 1990); Bureau of Labor Statistics, U.S. Department of Labor, *International Comparisons of Manufacturing Productivity* (Washington, D.C.: U.S. Government Printing Office, 1991); *International Financial Statistics* (Washington, D.C.: International Monetary Fund, 1991).

* 1980 = 100.

three lines is upward, indicating that the first is the cause and the other two are the effects. But it may be noted that free trade enriched the country only because it stimulated the high-productivity manufacturing sector.

But Germany's latest experiment with free trade has been a fiasco. On October 3, 1990, West and East Germany were reunited, and Helmut Kohl, now the chancellor of a unified country, rushed to expose the formerly protected industries of the East to full-blooded foreign competition. In addition, the federal government began to pour billions in financial aid into the eastern economy.

However, contrary to the expectations of free traders, the eastern industrial base has all but vanished. The area is now in a full-fledged depression, with unemployment soaring to 40 percent of the labor force.[5]

Mainstream economists blame the economic collapse of the East not on free trade but on its backward technology and factories. To

FIGURE 6.1
Trade, Productivity, and Real Wages in Germany, 1950–1990

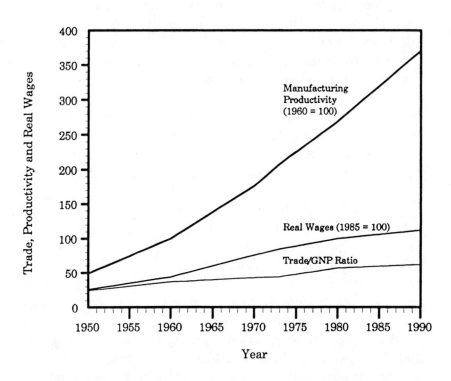

me, this sounds like sour grapes. This latest flirtation with free trade has proved to be a catastrophe, pure and simple.

A proper development strategy for the East would have been a gradual, step-by-step approach. No matter how inadequate its technology, prior to unification the eastern economy did provide secure jobs to virtually all workers. The minimum needs of food, housing, health care, and education were guaranteed to all citizens. The nation did have some industry, including steel, automobiles, armaments, chemicals, and sporting goods. What was the point in decimating this manufacturing base by abruptly exposing it to powerful foreign rivals?

Like mainstream economists, Helmut Kohl had an abiding—in reality a blinding—faith in free trade. It would have been better to break up the former state monopolies of the East and introduce advanced technology into the newly split companies while protecting them from foreign competition. The East should have imported technology but not goods from western Germany and other countries. The helter-skelter introduction of laissez-faire destroyed the eastern stock of capital and forced Germany to borrow billions on the world credit markets, thereby raising interest rates throughout Europe. Such is the carnage of blind faith in dogmas.

Thus, the postwar history of Germany, divided as well as unified, shows that free trade may be either benevolent or predatory depending on what it does to the industrial base. When free trade nourishes manufacturing, the country prospers; when manufacturing suffers because of foreign competition, so does the nation.

Japan

Of all the world's postwar economic leaps, Japan's stands out as the most luminous. A defeated, demoralized nation in 1945, Japan began with an even greater handicap than Germany, which at least has some natural resources. Japan, a cluster of tiny islands, has practically none. It suffers from a paucity of minerals and arable land. Above all, it had little capital left in the aftermath of the war.

Considering these handicaps, the Japanese economic ascendance has been all the more remarkable. Japan overcame its disadvantages through a systematic program of capital accumulation, devotion to education, product quality, hard work, and a national determination to regain the prestige lost by the total defeat in the war.

Unlike Germany, which opened its industries to foreign competition early in the process of development, Japan protected its emerging industries from international rivals. Germany and Japan are case studies in contrast. Both of them have achieved incredible economic growth, but one began with an export-oriented strategy, while the other focused first on the domestic economy. Germany followed a policy of development through foreign competition, while its former ally in the east pursued a policy of development through domestic competition.

Much has been made of the industrial policy of the government of Japan and of Japanese management techniques. However, at the heart of the Japanese upsurge is the force of domestic competition, which is lacking in nearly all other countries. There is no denying that the state played a great role in the process of development. But of all the policies the government pursued, its active stimulus to domestic competition emerges as an indispensable ingredient of Japan's stunning success.

Take a look at the key statistics of Japan, presented in Table 6.7. Unlike in Germany, the trade/GNP ratio in Japan remained constant from 1955 to 1973. While the figure of 22 percent qualifies Japan as an open economy, it does not represent an overly strong degree of openness. Small economies tend to have a higher volume of trade than large economies, and from 1955 to 1970 Japanese economic activity was rather small, relative, at least, to that of the United States and the Soviet Union.

Even though the trade/GNP ratio remained unchanged, the

TABLE 6.7
Trade, Investment, and Productivity in Japan in Selected Years, 1955–1989

Year	Trade (% of GNP)	Investment (% of GNP)	Manufacturing Productivity*	Productivity Growth (%)
1955	22	26	69	
1960	22	30	100	7.7
1970	22	41	279	10.8
1973	21	36	358	8.7
1980	31	32	529	5.7
1986	22	26	725	5.4
1989	27	32	775	6.9

SOURCES: Bureau of Labor Statistics, U.S. Department of Labor, *Productivity and the Economy: A Chart Book,* 1985 and 1988 (Washington, D.C.: U.S. Government Printing Office, 1986 and 1990; Bureau of Labor Statistics, U.S. Department of Labor, *International Comparisons of Manufacturing Productivity* (Washington, D.C.: U.S. Government Printing Office, 1991); *International Financial Statistics* (Washington, D.C.: International Monetary Fund, 1991).

* 1960 = 100.

economy grew apace, fueled mostly by an astounding growth in manufacturing productivity. This in turn was caused by an incredible rate of capital formation, which reached as high as 41 percent of GNP in 1970. Few nations have ever approached such rates of investment, but Japan did it routinely for years. Thus, one reason for Japan's astonishing rate of growth has been its exorbitant level of investment, which went mostly into infrastructure and new technology.

Another reason was the cutthroat competition that existed among firms in various industries. These firms, although protected from foreign rivals, competed intensely with one another. Competition is an engine of innovation, new technology, high-quality products, and low prices. Japan's strategy was to generate a strong demand base at home. It did not pursue an export-oriented plan of development. Consequently, trade was not yet a locomotive for growth. Foreign commerce and GNP grew at the same rate, thus keeping the trade/GNP ratio constant. Japan, like Mexico, followed inward-looking, not outward-looking policies.

As Michael Porter, in a voluminous and scholarly work, puts it: "In a remarkable number of the industries in which Japan achieved strong positions, the nature of domestic demand characteristics provided a unique stimulus to Japanese companies. The domestic market, not foreign markets, led industry development in the vast majority of Japanese industries. Only later did exports become significant."[6]

In order to understand the extent of domestic rivalry among Japanese firms, let us look at the number of companies competing in different industries. Table 6.8 offers this information for various goods that are among the main exports from Japan. There is not a single industry in this group with fewer than nine firms, and in the machine tools sector there are as many as 112 companies. Such is the enormity of domestic competition. Japanese firms have not needed foreign competition to goad them into innovation, new products, and quality control. They have battled one another on their own turf and in the process produced superb goods at low prices. Thus, intense domestic competition and high capital formation were the twin engines of the Japanese upsurge, not trade.

TABLE 6.8
Number of Firms in Selected Industries in Japan

Industry	Number of Firms
Air conditioners	13
Audio equipment	25
Automobiles	9
Cameras	15
Construction equipment	15
Copiers	14
Facsimile machines	10
Machine tools	112
Personal computers	16
Semiconductors	34
Shipbuilding	33
Television sets	15
Videocassette recorders	10

SOURCE: Michael Porter, *The Competitive Advantage of Nations* (New York: Free Press, 1991), p. 412.

In 1973, Japan was hit by the oil price shock, as the country meets all its petroleum needs from imports, whose price quadrupled. This tended to enhance the habitual Japanese anxiety about the lack of natural resources and their sudden shortage abroad. That is when Japan turned its attention to export markets so as to earn enough foreign exchange to pay the rising oil bill. The bloated companies of the United States and Canada, among other nations, were no match for the battle-tested producers from Japan. By now the rest is a familiar story.

Slowly but steadily, Japanese exporters overcame their foreign rivals in markets around the world. Many competitors were wiped out; some others were bought outright. The U.S. industrial base fell prey to the might of Japan.

At first, the Japanese were content to accept U.S. dollars in exchange for their goods. As dollars piled up in their hands, they increasingly turned to purchasing American assets. They bought real estate, stocks, Treasury bonds, complete factory operations, golf courses, office buildings, and more. They did this not only in the United States but also in Canada, Australia, and Great Britain. In effect, these countries paid for Japanese goods with their own exports and assets. They depleted their own capital stock in order to enjoy Japanese delicacies.

After 1973, Japan became more dependent on trade, as its trade/GNP ratio shot up to 31 percent by 1980. This was a huge jump of nearly 50 percent in just seven years. The ratio fell in 1986 as the international oil price collapsed, reducing both imports to and exports from Japan. By 1989, the trade ratio had settled at 27 percent.

The Japanese economy is now more open than its historical norm. The protectionist walls are grudgingly but steadily coming down. Has this helped the country? The answer, though in the affirmative, is not so obvious. Even though capital formation continues to be high, there has been no increase in productivity growth. Trade is now a larger proportion of GNP than before, but productivity growth, though still respectable, is below the historical average.

In fact, there is evidence that Japan is itself suffering from the agrification syndrome, though in a mild way. Because of the huge productivity growth in manufacturing, the industrial relative price in Japan has also dropped. Despite this, as long as export markets were secondary, wages grew at a hefty rate between 1955 and 1973. Take a look at Table 6.9, which shows that real wage growth kept pace with productivity during this period, but after 1973, while productivity growth fell somewhat, wage growth plummeted and nearly came to a halt in 1990. Evidently, wages no longer kept up with productivity as in earlier years. In fact, during the 1980s, wage growth was down to 1.5 percent per year, while productivity was down to 4.3 percent. Thus, with the growth in trade, wages have increasingly lagged behind productivity. And this is exactly what the agrification syndrome does; namely, it increases the divergence between productivity and real earnings. Thus, with growing trade, the growth in Japan's standard of living has declined. Yet only wage growth, not the real wage, has tumbled, unlike the United States.

What is the role of laissez-faire in this regard? Freer trade has

TABLE 6.9
Trade, Productivity, and Real Earnings in Japan in Selected Years,
1955–1990

Year	Trade (% of GNP)	Productivity Growth (%)	Index of Real Earnings*	Wage Growth (%)
1955	22		34	
1960	22	7.7	42	4.3
1970	22	10.8	65	4.5
1973	21	8.7	83	8.4
1980	31	5.7	94	1.7
1986	22	5.4	102	1.4
1989	27	6.9	108	1.9
1990	NA	3.7	109	0.9

SOURCES: Bureau of Labor Statistics, U.S. Department of Labor, *Productivity and the Economy: A Chart Book,* 1985 and 1988 (Washington, D.C.: U.S. Government Printing Office, 1986 and 1990); Bureau of Labor Statistics, U.S. Department of Labor, *International Comparisons of Manufacturing Productivity* (Washington, D.C.: U.S. Government Printing Office, 1991); *International Financial Statistics* (Washington, D.C.: International Monetary Fund, 1991).

*1985 = 100.

helped Japan maintain its lofty living standard. With the country's extreme dependence on imported petrol, the oil price shocks of 1973 and 1979 should have brought Japan to its knees. The Japanese economy should have then collapsed; instead, wages and the living standard continued to rise, though at a mediocre pace. The credit for this goes solely to America's policy of free trade, which enabled Japan to increase its U.S. exports so much that it easily footed its gargantuan oil bill. At the same time, through its surplus dollar earnings, the diminutive island became an international lender, a position the United States had enjoyed ever since 1914. However, wage growth in Japan had to be kept low for its exports to soar. That's why its increasing volume of trade was accompanied by only paltry gains in employee earnings. Nevertheless, America's policy of free trade was instrumental in catapulting Japan into an economic superpower. Though a cluster of small islands, Japan has become a beacon of light and hope to humanity: with courage, hard work, and perseverance, any adversity can be overcome.

South Korea

South Korea, hereafter called Korea, is another success story of the postwar period. Its growth experience is an amalgam of the experience of Germany and Japan. Korea also has few natural resources. It lacks arable land, minerals, energy, and forests. Yet its paucity of resources has not prevented a hardy nation of 43 million people from achieving spectacular growth in productivity and real earnings.

Like Germany, Korea has enjoyed one of the fastest rates of growth in trade, and, like Japan, it has relied heavily on manufacturing and capital formation.

Korea was also devastated during the Second World War, and its subsequent bloody conflict with North Korea, which ended up with the bulk of the region's natural resources, initially diverted its attention toward armament and self-defense. Consequently, Korea's growth, despite substantial aid from the United States, was about average during the 1950s. It was not until the early 1960s that the nation put its heart into a program of rapid economic development.

Table 6.10 portrays a picture of Korea's development since 1961, when the rate of investment was only 12 percent of GNP; but by 1970 gross capital formation had almost doubled. Korea's trade/GNP ratio also followed the same path, nearly doubling from 20 percent to 37 percent over nine years. The country's reaction to the oil price shock of 1973 was similar to Japan's. Following the sharp jump in the price of oil, Korea went after exports and trade with gusto, and by 1980 78 percent of its GNP consisted of foreign commerce. Since then the trade/GNP ratio has declined somewhat. Thus, unlike Japan, which first relied on home demand for speedy development, Korea followed an export-oriented strategy right from the beginning of its commitment to economic development.

However, Korea's strategy of industrialization was similar to

TABLE 6.10
Trade, Investment, Per Capita GDP Growth, and Wage Growth in
South Korea in Selected Years, 1961–1990

Year	Trade (% of GNP)	Investment (% of GNP)	Per Capita GDP Growth (%)	Wage Growth (%)
1961	20	12		
1970	37	23	5.6	3.1
1973	62	23	6.1	6.6
1980	78	32	6.3	9.8
1990	64	37	8.0	8.1

SOURCE: *International Financial Statistics* (Washington D.C.: International Monetary Fund, 1991).

that of Japan. Today the Koreans are highly literate and educated. They have a giant rate of saving and investment, and the internal competition among Korean firms is as intense as any in the world.

In most of the countries with miraculous economic development, domestic rivalry among firms and industries turns out to be a key factor in their competitiveness and affluence. Even though four large groups—Hyundai, Daewoo, Samsung, and Lucky-Goldstar—control vast portions of Korean industry, there is intense competition among firms in most areas. As Michael Porter puts it, an "essential underpinning of Korean competitive advantage is the fierce and even cutthroat rivalry that characterizes every successful Korean industry. . . . A pioneer makes the initial entry, but other competitors soon follow."[7]

Table 6.11 offers a clear picture of the intense domestic rivalry prevailing in many industries. This competition gives an edge to Korean products, which are increasingly found on world markets. That is why the nation's overall productivity, measured by the growth in per capita GDP, has been remarkable since the 1960s. The force of competition has also ensured that the fruits of development are shared by the general population, as since the 1970s the high economic growth has been matched by high growth in wages.

TABLE 6.11
Number of Firms in Selected Industries in Korea

Industry	Number of Firms
Cement	9
Computers	31
Construction	480
Footwear	221
Semiconductors	200
Shipbuilding	250
Steel	13
Television sets	12
Fabrics	2,046
Garments	3,270

SOURCE: Michael Porter, *The Competitive Advantage of Nations* (New York: Free Press, 1990), p. 473.

In Korea's case trade has not yet produced the ugly syndrome of agrification, perhaps because the nation still has a way to go. It is still not in the category of truly advanced nations but is fast approaching that status.

The Korean government has played a special role in the process of development. The role has been both direct and indirect. The state's investment in education and infrastructure is an instance of the government's indirect support. But the government has also been directly involved in export promotion by keeping its currency cheap relative to foreign currencies. In technical language this is called devaluation. A cheap currency translates into cheap domestic goods abroad and expensive foreign goods at home. The first encourages exports, the second discourages imports.

The state also protected infant domestic industries from foreign competition through high tariffs and subsidies during the 1960s and 1970s. Though heavily reliant on foreign commerce, Korea did not adopt free trade, and its economy is still not as unprotected as its competitors'. But protectionism has only helped the country achieve its spectacular economic success.

Taiwan

The success story of Taiwan is similar to that of Korea. Trade, capital formation, domestic rivalry among firms, and the government role are also the main forces behind Taiwan's rise from a pauper in the aftermath of the war to an affluent nation today. There are also two other forces—foreign investment, especially by American and Japanese multinational firms, and U.S. foreign aid.

Unlike Korea, however, Taiwan has paid greater attention to agriculture, has kept its economy freer, and has no foreign debt. In fact, it has a large horde of gold and dollars. Like Japan, it continues to have a huge surplus in its trade with the United States, mainly because U.S. multinationals import a lot from their subsidiaries on the island nation.

Table 6.12 presents a picture resembling that of the Korean experience portrayed by Table 6.10. However, in Taiwan there are few industrial conglomerates controlling the economy. Domestic rivalry among firms is even more intense there than in Korea, which

TABLE 6.12
Trade, Investment, Per Capita GNP Growth, and Wage Growth in Taiwan in Selected Years, 1952–1990

Year	Trade (% of GNP)	Investment (% of GNP)	Per Capita GNP Growth (%)	Wage Growth (%)
1952	23	15		
1960	27	20	4.3	NA
1970	53	27	6.7	NA
1973	77	29	10.8	9.5
1980	97	34	6.2	6.0
1986	88	16	5.5	NA
1990	75	25	7.7	NA

SOURCES: *Taiwan Statistical Data Book,* 1987 (Taipei: Council for Economic Planning and Development, 1989); U.S. Department of Commerce, *Foreign Economic Trends and Their Implications for the United States,* 1989 and 1991 (Washington, D.C.: U.S. Government Printing Office, 1990 and 1992).

has emphasized both heavy and light manufacturing. In Taiwan the focus has been on light industry, and its industrial structure is characterized by a very large number of small firms. For this reason Taiwan's distribution of income is among the most equal in the world.

Italy

Italy was a relative latecomer to the club of high-growth nations. Like Germany and Japan, it was also a defeated country with few natural resources, high unemployment, and little capital available to start the process of reindustrialization. For a while, Italy passed through political instability against a background of multiparty democracy, and initial development was rather mediocre. But after the 1950s, rapid growth and manufacturing productivity helped it join the ranks of leading nations.

Italy imports oil and raw materials and exports compact cars, processed foods, and light manufactures. The country is an enigma in many ways. It has a dual industrial structure. Some of its industries, in which there is intense domestic rivalry, are among the most efficient in the world. Marble, textiles, shoes, jewelry and furniture are notable Italian exports known for their quality, design, and style. On the other hand, Italy is a nation of powerful unions, high welfare spending, and inefficient state monopolies. Most of the large private firms are internationally uncompetitive. They dominate the home market and prosper behind an umbrella of trade barriers and state subsidies.

However, the industries characterized by intense domestic rivalry are very efficient. As Michael Porter points out, "Italian industries composed of many medium sized and small firms are often world leaders."[8]

Table 6.13 highlights the role of trade and capital formation in Italian manufacturing and the standard of living, as measured by the growth in real earnings. The role of investment has been as prominent in Italy's development as trade. Though the trade/GNP ratio has steadily risen since 1961 and is still higher than the historical

TABLE 6.13

Trade, Investment, Productivity Growth, and Wage Growth in
Italy in Selected Years, 1961–1990

Year	Trade (% of GNP)	Investment (% of GNP)	Productivity Growth (%)	Wage Growth (%)
1961	26	23		
1970	30	24	6.1	5.9
1973	34	25	6.5	8.6
1980	44	24	5.7	3.4
1985	44	17	4.8	1.7
1990	39	20	3.5	0.3

SOURCES: *International Financial Statistics* (Washington, D.C.: International Monetary Fund, 1991); Bureau of Labor Statistics, U.S. Department of Labor, *International Comparisons of Manufacturing Productivity,* 1988 and 1990 (Washington, D.C.: U.S. Government Printing Office, 1989 and 1991).

norm, wage growth has tumbled in recent years because of declining capital formation.

Between 1961 and 1980, the trade/GNP ratio rose from a low of 26 percent to a high of 44 percent, while capital formation remained high and steady between 23 percent and 25 percent of GNP. Rising trade generated rising productivity and wage growth between 1961 and 1973. Then came the oil price shock of 1973, which forced an upward jump in the trade/GNP ratio of all energy importers. Trade shot up because of soaring oil prices, which raised imports, which in turn forced a climb in exports. With oil prices plummeting since 1986, Italy's trade/GNP ratio has settled at 39 percent, which is still above its historical average.

In spite of cheaper petrol, wage growth dropped in the 1980s, while productivity growth was still respectable. Manufacturing productivity growth averaged around 4 percent during the 1980s, whereas the overall productivity growth, measured by the rise in real GDP per employee, was 3 percent. With wage growth averaging a mere 0.5 percent, less than half the productivity rise, Italy has now clearly entered the stage of agrification. The worldwide glut in manufacturing is now doing to this country what it has been doing in Canada and Japan. However, Italy has the additional problems of extremely high government debt and a double-digit rate of unemployment; and real earnings in services are actually falling.

France

Even though France was a victor in the Second World War, it suffered nearly the same devastation as the defeated nations. Like its neighbors, France also launched a program of rapid reindustrialization, but unlike Germany, it began by nationalizing a few industries and banks. Since the 1950s, French government intervention in the economy has been extensive. The state has been generous with subsidies to agriculture and official monopolies.

The French have also built a large welfare machine that offers relatively high health and unemployment benefits. Although the economy is based on markets, the government activity participates in business decisions through persuasion and indicative planning.

The state does not impose its plan on private firms, but in their own interest they tend to cooperate with official directives. The government obtains de facto compliance through its ownership of a large number of corporations and financial institutions.

Like its neighbors', the French economy has become increasingly open since 1961 and especially after 1973. The oil price shock elicited the same response from France as from other energy importers. Take a look at Table 6.14, which displays French data on trade, gross investment, and growth in manufacturing productivity and real earnings.

France was a signatory to GATT and other international agreements on tariff reductions. As a result, its trade/GNP ratio has steadily risen. There was also a rise in capital formation after 1961. Thus trade and rising investment have combined to produce high levels of growth in manufacturing productivity, which, however, has been on the decline since 1973. Real wage growth was about half the productivity rate during the 1960s but then picked up substantially under the influence of powerful unions. These gains occurred in spite of stubborn unemployment, which remained high throughout the 1970s and 1980s.

TABLE 6.14

Trade, Investment, Productivity Growth, and Wage Growth in France in Selected Years, 1961–1990

Year	Trade (% of GNP)	Investment (% of GNP)	Productivity Growth (%)	Wage Growth (%)
1961	24	20		
1970	31	24	6.8	3.8
1973	34	25	5.7	5.9
1980	46	23	4.3	4.9
1985	47	19	3.8	2.6
1990	46	21	2.8	0.6

SOURCES: Bureau of Labor Statistics, U.S. Department of Labor, *Productivity and the Economy: A Chart Book,* 1985 and 1988 (Washington, D.C.: U.S. Government Printing Office, 1986 and 1990); Bureau of Labor Statistics, U.S. Department of Labor, *International Comparisons of Manufacturing Productivity* (Washington, D.C.: U.S. Government Printing Office, 1991); *International Financial Statistics* (Washington, D.C.: International Monetary Fund, 1991).

Declining productivity growth eventually convinced the government to ease business regulations. By 1986 almost all price controls on industry had been removed. Since then the government has also been selling its corporations to private groups to mitigate its economic control. However, the policy of privatization has yet to bear fruit, because the productivity rate has continued to slide and real wage growth, especially since 1985, has been paltry.

Between 1985 and 1990 manufacturing productivity grew at an annual rate of 2.8 percent, whereas per capita real GDP grew at a rate of 2.6 percent. Since the wage growth of 0.6 percent was less than a fourth of either productivity measure, we conclude that France has also been in a stage of mild agrification since 1985. Here also real wages in services are declining. Again, the global glut in manufacturing is the culprit.

United Kingdom

The postwar economic experience of the United Kingdom, commonly known as Britain, holds valuable lessons for any country facing a stagnant standard of living. Britain, like France, was a victorious but crippled nation in the worldwide conflict. But the British economic policy was remarkably different from that of other warring parties. The nation went after industrial nationalization and state intervention with gusto in order to create a socialist state.

Regarding commerce, Britain followed an open economy policy, lowering tariffs and, initially at least, other barriers to trade. But before long, with its industry and entrepreneurship stifled under myriad regulations, it resorted to protectionist policies of propping up declining industries through subsidies.

The first wave of nationalization began in 1945 and was not complete until 1951. One after another, electricity, gas, the railways, steel, coal, and airplane manufacture were brought under state control and management. With so many industries nationalized, the labor unions became very powerful, especially during the years of the Labour Party's control of the government.

Compared to its neighbors on the European continent, Britain is well endowed with natural resources of coal and iron and, since the 1970s, of moderate quantities of oil and gas. In the rise of capitalism, the country had a head start in innovations and the development of industry and financial institutions. Even today London is a great financial and communications hub of the world.

However, all these advantages were frittered away after the war by statist economic policies that choked initiative, innovation, entrepreneurship and, above all, competition. From being a technology leader before the war, the country became a technology laggard.

The effect of the monopolistic policies of both management and the unions shows up in the British economic crawl as portrayed in Table 6.15. When a nation once used to great affluence starts from scratch, one would expect a phenomenal improvement in its living standard in the initial phase. That indeed was the experience of most of the participants in the war—but not of Great Britain, which saw mediocre growth in productivity and real earnings during the 1950s. Both manufacturing productivity and real wages grew at an

TABLE 6.15

Trade, Investment, Productivity Growth, and Wage Growth in the United Kingdom in Selected Years, 1950–1990

Year	Trade (% of GNP)	Investment (% of GNP)	Productivity Growth (%)	Wage Growth (%)
1950	45	13		
1960	42	16	2.1	2.1
1970	43	17	3.7	2.6
1973	47	19	5.8	3.8
1980	52	18	0.9	0.5
1985	56	17	5.8	2.8
1990	52	19	4.1	1.5

SOURCES: Bureau of Labor Statistics, U.S. Department of Labor, *Productivity and the Economy: A Chart Book,* 1985 and 1988 (Washington, D.C.: U.S. Government Printing Office, 1986 and 1990; Bureau of Labor Statistics, U.S. Department of Labor, *International Comparisons of Manufacturing Productivity* (Washington, D.C.: U.S. Government Printing Office, 1991); *International Financial Statistics* (Washington, D.C.: International Monetary Fund, 1991).

anemic 2.1 annual percentage rate. Things improved during the 1960s, but not by much.

The best British performance in the growth of productivity and earnings occurred during a short span of three years between 1970 and 1973; but that was not to persist, because in the next seven years wages and productivity were virtually stagnant.

The socialist model that Britain followed after the war had many flaws. With the rise of state and union monopolies, industries faced extreme competitive pressures from Germany and, at least initially, from the United States. The government response was to encourage industrial mergers to strengthen companies. This was a faulty policy, because domestic rivalry, not merger, creates dynamism and competitiveness. For instance, in the auto industry, British Motor Corporation was created out of the marriage of Austin and Morris; but when the new corporation faltered, it was merged with Leyland to create British Leyland. None of this, however, could halt the decay of the automotive and other industries.

During the 1970s, Britain suffered from high unemployment

and inflation combined with a weak currency. The country was called "the sick man of Europe." All this occurred even though large quantities of offshore oil were discovered in the North Sea. Britain's high dependence on trade and a relatively free and open economy were not able to arrest the slide.

Finally, there was a great policy reversal with the election of Margaret Thatcher as prime minister in 1979. The Thatcher government launched a program of privatization and sought to break the power of unions, with some success.

First, the new government lifted exchange controls in 1979, forcing the British industry to compete with foreign rivals on an even keel. This was followed by the sale of shares in state-owned monopolies to private groups. Steel, the telephone service, and airlines were thus privatized. In addition, financial services were deregulated to attract foreign deposits and investment.

The new economic policy initiated a great spurt in productivity, even though capital formation was largely unchanged. From a low of 0.9 percent in the previous period, manufacturing output per hour grew at a respectable 5.8 percent annual rate between 1980 and 1985. Real wage growth also picked up, even though union power declined slightly. But after 1985, the global glut in manufacturing caught up with Britain as well, as, even though productivity continued to rise at a healthy rate of 4.1 percent, wage growth fell to an anemic 1.5 percent. Britain, like other leading industrial nations, has now joined the agrification club.

As in the United States, the British loss of economic power relative to other industrial nations has been associated with a rise in the relative position of services versus manufacturing. While the share of manufacturing as a percentage of GDP has declined in all leading industrial countries, in the United Kingdom this fall has been especially sharp—from a high of 33 percent of GDP in 1960 to a low of 20 percent in 1990.

The lesson to be learned from Britain's experience is that even if the economy becomes highly open through freer trade, absence of domestic rivalry retards the growth of real earnings. Domestic competition is more important than foreign competition in improving the standard of living.

India

In many ways, India's is the same sad story as that of Britain. In other ways, it is worse. India gained freedom from the British yoke in 1947 and almost immediately sought to alleviate the hunger and poverty of its masses. On Independence Day, August 15, 1947, Jawaharlal Nehru, the first prime minister of India, made a solemn promise to the country. "A tryst with destiny" is what he offered to his adoring people. He began with great enthusiasm and intentions. Unfortunately, his misconception of the laws of economics created a yawning chasm between intentions and performance.

India began with many handicaps. Illiteracy, mass poverty, lack of infrastructure, lack of experience with capital formation and industrialization, a huge refugee burden caused by the partition of the country, all made development an almost insurmountable task, to say the least. But India's handicaps were no graver than those of Korea and Japan. In fact, the other two had hardly any natural resources, whereas India was blessed with a vast acreage of arable land and a variety of minerals.

From the start it was correctly felt that the state had a great role to play in the process of development. Railways, bridges, roads, electricity, communications, all had to be constructed from scratch. Schools and colleges had to be opened for the development of education and technology. Agriculture had to be mechanized to feed a growing population. In short, India faced the same daunting task as Korea and Japan. But Korea and Japan succeeded spectacularly, whereas India failed miserably.

What went wrong? At the dawn of independence, India had a great distrust of Britain, its former colonial master. Yet ironically, India followed the British model of development with a mixed economy, choking competition and private initiative in the process. The only difference is that India carried it a step further by blending the British formula with the Soviet program of centralized planning.

Rather than limiting itself to the creation of infrastructure such as educational facilities, roads, railways, and financial institutions, the government entered directly into the process of saving, investment, and production. While state officers were motivated by self-interest, they assumed that the general public had no interest in a better life. The public was thought to be too ignorant or unmotivated to work for its own goals.

Assuming that the people were unwilling to save, the government sharply raised taxes to generate savings for the nation. Most of these taxes were sales or excise duties and tended to fall disproportionately on the poor. Income tax rates were, of course, raised, but they could easily be evaded by the wealthy. The high taxes, of course, discouraged private saving and stifled the initiative to start small businesses, which are normally highly efficient and innovative.

Faced with the same task, Japan had given tax incentives to its people to save and make deposits in post offices or government banks, which in turn channeled these savings as loans to small firms in target sectors such as steel and shipbuilding. But India chose to raise taxes along the Soviet model and then used the revenue to start state monopolies not only in capital-intensive industries but also in the manufacture of light consumer goods.

State-owned companies are especially vulnerable to union pressures. Labor unions initiated restrictive work schedules, inflexible practices, and no-layoff policies. This, combined with the natural inefficiency of monopolies, led to a massive waste of scarce capital and losses in the public sector.

In some sectors such as steel and heavy electrical machinery, one or two private companies were also permitted to exist. The result was that these companies made huge profits because of a lack of any real competition from the inefficient state-owned firms.

Flushed with these profits, private companies soon gained control over government policies and officers, who became corrupt to the core. Numerous state regulations and the need to collect taxes gave rise to a bloated bureaucracy, which stifled innovation and entrepreneurship at every step. High tax rates eventually generated illegal activities and a vast underground economy, which in turn spawned more official corruption.

Distrusting foreign influences, India by and large discouraged foreign private investment. But even where direct investment from abroad was permitted, the planners were so obsessed with monopolies that they effectively reserved the domestic market to one or two foreign producers. Thus multinational firms, prospering behind thick tariff walls, also had a field day, earning vast profits in a country of mass poverty.

Today India is gasping for breath under the choke hold of state monopolies, "black" money, private conglomerates, bureaucratic corruption, and general confusion. Despite the great intentions of its early leaders, the best the country has been able to do is feed its bulging population, while incurring $75 billion of foreign debt in the process. Nehru's "tryst with destiny" has turned into a "tryst with misery."

The absurdity of India's policies comes out starkly from Table 6.16. From 1961 to 1980, the trade/GNP ratio was not more than 15 percent. Even though this compares well with the trade/GNP ratio of the United States prior to 1973, it is astonishingly small in view of the large amount of foreign aid that India has received from the rest of the world. High tariff rates, designed to protect local monopolies, kept the trade/GNP ratio low. In spite of heavy taxation to generate saving and the high level of foreign aid, capital formation also remained low. For all these reasons, real GDP growth during the 1960s and 1970s could not exceed 3.9 percent annually, less than half that of Korea and Japan.

TABLE 6.16
Trade, Investment, and Economic Growth in India in Selected Years, 1961–1989

Year	Trade (% of GNP)	Investment (% of GNP)	GDP Growth (%)	Per Capita GDP Growth (%)
1961	12	15		
1970	9	16	3.9	1.3
1973	15	19	1.8	0.0
1980	14	19	3.9	2.1
1989	17	22	5.7	3.5

SOURCE: *International Financial Statistics* (Washington, D.C.: International Monetary Fund, 1991).

Since 1980 both the trade/GNP ratio and the rate of investment have risen somewhat, and the result showed up in a higher growth rate in the 1980s. Similarly, per capita growth in GDP also improved during the 1980s from its dismal levels in the 1960s and 1970s.

The lesson of India's growth is the same as that of Britain: monopolies, owned privately or by the state, are a great hindrance to economic development.

Australia

Among all the affluent nations, Australia comes closest to the United States in terms of its recent economic ills. America has the highest inequality in income and wealth; Australia is next. The United States also has the highest percentage of poor children, followed by Australia.[9] Both countries have been afflicted with deindustrialization since the early 1970s, and today both are trapped in the vicious circle of agrification.

Australia is tied with the United States for the lowest percentage of labor force (17 percent) employed in manufacturing among the rich nations. In terms of natural resources also, the two have much in common. Both have been blessed by nature with a vast acreage of arable land; both nations, while rich in agriculture, have been built by immigrants.

There are, of course, many differences. Australia is mainly an agrarian economy. Its exports are primarily wheat, wool, dairy products, and minerals. Consumer goods, machine tools, and chemicals are mostly, though not totally, imported. The United States, by contrast, is still a manufacturing power. It has had many setbacks since the early 1970s, yet it still has the largest economy in the world. It continues to be a world leader in aerospace and armaments.

Another difference between the two is not so flattering to America. U.S. workers have suffered far more than their Australian brethren. In the United States real earnings in some sectors have dropped below their 1950 lows; in Australia, only below their 1974 lows.

Although Japan flooded both the U.S. and Australian markets with its manufactures, Australia protected local industries with tariffs, and with some success. That is why even though manufacturing eroded in both English-speaking countries, the erosion was somewhat smaller in Australia. Consequently, Australian workers' earnings did not begin to fall until the mid-1980s.

All this emerges clearly from Table 6.17, which relates Australia's living standard to trade and capital formation. Australia has been an open economy throughout the postwar period, and its high trade/GNP ratio clearly indicates that. However, the ratio has seen only a modest rise since 1962, unlike in Korea, Taiwan, and other Pacific Rim countries. In fact, the trade/GNP ratio jumped in Australia, an energy importer, only in response to the oil price shock of 1973.

Australian capital formation, though not on the scale of that in Japan, Korea, and Germany, has been healthy. Despite an investment rate of at least 25 percent, Australia could not maintain high rates of per capita GDP growth. Unlike its neighbors to the north, the country did not have to start from scratch. In the 1960s its per capita GDP grew annually at a respectable rate of 3.9 percent. But after that its performance went downhill and was not to see such lofty levels again.

TABLE 6.17
Trade, Investment, Per Capita GDP Growth, and Wage Growth in Australia in Selected Years, 1962–1990

Year	Trade (% of GNP)	Investment (% of GNP)	Per Capita GDP Growth (%)	Wage Growth (%)
1962	30	25		
1970	30	26	3.9	3.5
1973	29	31	2.3	2.5
1980	35	25	1.2	1.9
1985	37	25	1.7	0.6
1990	36	27	1.6	−0.6

Source: *International Financial Statistics* (Washington, D.C.: International Monetary Fund, 1991).

Real earnings kept pace with overall productivity until 1973. But then came the inflationary oil price shock and the deluge of imports from Japan. Consequently, wage growth plummeted. In the 1980s, imports also poured in from the NICs, and wage growth dropped even more. Finally, after 1985, it became negative. The gravity of the situation is displayed in Table 6.18.

Table 6.18 reveals the same process of deindustrialization that earlier afflicted the United States. Manufacturing employment in Australia peaked in 1973 and continued to drop until 1985, when it began to pick up some. Still, in 1990 this employment was down 13 percent from its peak.

Despite falling employment in manufacturing, real wages grew until 1985. Since then they have been slowly dropping despite a continuing rise in manufacturing productivity. This is exactly the vicious phenomenon of agrification. The country's protectionism, because of its modest nature, could only delay the inevitable. Wages fell in spite of high trade and strong capital formation. In fact, in

TABLE 6.18
Indexes of Employment, Production, and Real Wages in
Manufacturing in Australia in Selected Years, 1966–1990*

Year	Manufacturing Employment	Manufacturing Productivity†	Real Wages
1966	109	57	67
1970	116	66	79
1973	122	69	85
1980	110	88	97
1985	100	100	100
1990	106	102	97
Annual growth rate, 1966–1990		2.5	1.6

SOURCE: *International Financial Statistics* (Washington, D.C.: International Monetary Fund, 1991).

* 1985 = 100
† Manufacturing production/manufacturing employment.

1985 Australia had the highest trade/GNP ratio (37 percent) in its history, and that is also the year when real earnings began to drop in spite of rising capital formation and productivity. By 1990, wages had tumbled to the 1980 level.

Table 6.18 does not reveal the full gravity of the decline in the living standard because the wage data include all employees. But if we explore the statistics for nonmanagerial employees only, the drop in real earnings is simply stunning. For a better understanding of the Australian predicament, let us look at Table 6.19, which offers a more disaggregated picture of wage trends.

For manufacturing as well as all industries, real earnings in 1990 were the same as those in 1974, whereas for recreational and other services, 1990 wages were down by as much as 9 percent below the 1974 levels. Since nearly 68 percent of the work force is employed in a variety of services, the fall in Australia's living standard is almost as shocking as that of the United States. This is all the more infuriating when you remember that national productivity has risen moderately at the same time.

It is interesting that Australia's living standard began to fall after 1973, the very year in which tariffs were cut by 25 percent across

TABLE 6.19
Real Weekly Earnings of All Nonmanagerial Workers in Australia
in Selected Years, 1974–1990*

Year	All Industries	Manufacturing	Recreational and Other Services
1974	38	37	33
1985	40	39	34
1990	38	37	30
Growth rate, 1974–1990	0	0	−9%

SOURCES: *Average Earnings and Hours of Employees* (Canberra: Australian Bureau of Statistics, Government of Australia, 1991); *International Financial Statistics* (Washington, D.C.: International Monetary Fund, 1991) for CPI data.

* Computed by dividing average weekly earnings in current prices by the CPI.

the board. Economists P. J. Drake and J. P. Nieuwenhuysen describe this event as "the zenith of Australian trade liberalization," which "reduced average effective protection for Australian manufacturing from 36 to 27 percent."[10]

It's a good thing Australia retained a modicum of protection, otherwise its wages would have plummeted as fast as those in the United States, where trade liberalization has been greater and where real earnings in some services have tumbled all the way down to their 1950 lows. It is a great irony of modern life that both the United States and Australia, despite their bounty of natural resources, are the only affluent nations long caught in the sorry trap of agrification. What have they done to deserve this? The answer is clear: for the first time in their history, they have followed the doctrine of free trade.

Conclusion

Among the eleven economies analyzed in the preceding pages, nine—Canada, Mexico, Germany, Japan, Korea, Taiwan, Italy, France, and Britain—are America's major trading partners. Seven of the nine, excluding Mexico and Britain, saw a spectacular rise in their living standard following the war, as their real wages soared. All of them benefited from America's adoption of free trade. Ever since the 1960s, they have shipped a variety of light and heavy manufactures to the United States. Some, such as Canada, Korea and Taiwan, are excessively dependent on the U.S. market, whereas Japan, and to an extent Germany, have become economic superpowers through their exports to the United States.

In Britain, and especially in Mexico, real wages have been stagnant in recent years, but even these nations benefited a great deal from American generosity—Britain through its consistent trade surplus with the United States and Mexico from its Maquiladora program, which lured a number of American companies to its soil.

Unlike in most of its trading partners, real wages in the United States have been tumbling since 1973, the first year of the country's switch to laissez-faire. The conclusion is unmistakable: *every major trading partner except America has benefited from America's adoption of free trade.* No wonder, as Ross Perot lamented during the 1992 presidential election, many U.S. trading partners have hired well-connected Americans to lobby for their interests and perpetuate laissez-faire.[11]

7

America's Experience with Tariffs

Economists frequently claim that historically free trade has been an essential ingredient of U.S. economic success. To the unwary, this claim seems so natural that it is not even worthy of further investigation. Free trade, after all, must be a natural extension of free competition, which is supposed to be the foundation of the American economy. There is an automatic presumption that the United States must have kept its tariffs low all through history, just as they are today and have been since the 1970s. You have heard about the beneficence of free trade all your life; not surprisingly, some of you may believe that laissez-faire must have been the basis of economic policy through much of the American chronicle.

Nothing could be further from the truth. International commerce, whether free or restricted, contributed little to the critical transformations that built and enriched the country. Indeed, America manufactured its success almost entirely at home through the dynamism of its young, immigrant society, which harnessed its immense economic potential.

Let's take a close look at the evolution of U.S. trade policy over the past two centuries. In the dispassionate mirror of history, you will discover an image of the United States that is far different from the portrait offered by free traders. A journey into the past is always informative and eye opening. In our case, the venture not only throws light on the principles that govern the success and failure of an economy but also reveals a way out of the current morass to capture the heights America once commanded.

It is unfortunate that few trade specialists study history, because if they did they wouldn't be such ardent supporters of free trade. To mainstream economists, U.S. history presents special problems, as they have to concoct artificial theories to explain how America became an economic giant in spite of its exorbitant tariffs over more than a century.

The Agrarian Republic: 1783–1808

At the Treaty of Paris in 1783 the Revolutionary War finally came to an end, and the United States of America for the first time emerged as a sovereign nation. As a colony of Great Britain, the American states had provided raw materials for British industry and served as an outlet for its exports. Indeed, Britain went to some lengths to discourage the rise of industry in the Americas, asserting it to be "against the advantage of England."[1] As a result, the new republic bore a strongly agrarian character, with more than 90 percent of its work force engaged in farming, hunting, or forestry. A small, vigorous manufacturing sector had indeed sprouted in the northern colonies, and some elementary goods, such as linens, shoes, and furniture, were supplied by local artisans; but for most of their industrial needs, Americans relied on imports from Europe— mostly England—and paid for them by exporting their farm products.

Soon after gaining independence, however, the United States found itself in the thick of international intrigue and commerce. In 1793, England declared war on France, and before long two other continental powers, Spain and Holland, were drawn into the fray. As a result, the merchant ships of all these countries were withdrawn from the seas. A major void thus occurred in the world trading network, and with it came a unique opportunity for American ships to step into the vacuum and take over the neglected trade.

The newfound opportunities in foreign commerce proved lucrative for American shippers, but did little to alter the agrarian nature of the U.S. economy. The warring nations came to rely heavily upon the United States for farm supplies such as wheat, flour, and cotton, which thus became very profitable. At the same time England turned increasingly to the U.S. market for its manufactures, which had previously been targeted at Europe. All these trends merely accentuated the already agrarian bent of the American economy.

At this point the federal government seemed to be protecting local producers through import duties on glass, iron, and other products, but there was no clear public sentiment for promoting domestic industries. Tariffs were primarily an instrument for generating federal revenues, and domestic manufactures—textiles, machine tools, furniture, iron, glass, footwear—remained insignificant in the economy; in fact, in 1799 less than 5 percent of national income was generated in this sector.

The Foundation of American Industry: 1808–1815

Foreign trade in the early years after independence only intensified the primitive mold of the economy. In fact, the country was able to move out of this mold only after British and French actions led to an abrupt halt in foreign commerce. It was a fortuitous development that virtually forced America to industrialize and become a rich nation.

Neither England nor France took kindly to the growing U.S. role in trade that occurred after independence. They passed a series of decrees and seized a large number of U.S. ships. In order to protect Americans from such seizures, Congress passed the Embargo Act of 1807, which prohibited exports. Trade came virtually to a halt, and although the act was moderated in 1809, another war with England in 1812 pushed America back into economic isolation. Until the end of hostilities in 1815, the United States would remain a solitary island, cut off from other economies.

Commercial isolation had a profound impact on American economic development. U.S. consumers, now denied access to European goods, turned their demand toward domestic manufactures. The local supply fell so short of demand that profits soared. In textiles alone, for example, the profit margin jumped more than 40 percent between 1807 and 1809.

High returns lured vast amounts of capital into manufacturing. All estimates we have for this period reveal an astonishing growth in industry. In cotton textiles the number of spindles climbed from 31,000 in 1809 to almost 500,000 in 1815. A similar bounty was enjoyed by woolen manufactures, where output jumped from $4 million to almost $20 million in 1815.

Virtually all new industry emerged in New York, New Jersey, and the four New England states of Connecticut, Massachusetts, Vermont, and New Hampshire. While only four new factories were established in these states in 1807, 128 were started in 1815. The southern states, however, failed to join in the spree because their landowners considered their work force, which consisted mostly of slaves, to be incapable of operating the factory equipment.[2]

The Development of American Industry: 1815–1900

The rise of manufacturing created a new lobby that had not existed prior to the War of 1812. For the first time, there was a significant economic interest—Northern manufacturers and their workers—that could be hurt by the resumption of trade. Pitted against them were the traditional beneficiaries of international commerce. Farmers, now predominantly in the south, needed world markets for their products and were also anxious to obtain other countries' manufactured goods at cheap prices, for tariffs would only make foreign products more expensive. In addition, shipping interests, including those in New England, feared the loss of revenue that would accompany any restriction of trade.

The battle among these factions for the control of trade policy began in earnest shortly after 1815 and continued unabated for the rest of the century. The conflict went through two distinct phases. The first, lasting from 1815 to the start of the Civil War in 1861, saw political advantage shifting from one faction to the other, with tariffs rising and ebbing with each shift. By contrast, the second, which endured from 1861 to 1900, saw a decisive victory for pro-tariff forces. The average tariff rate then rose well above 40 percent—more than seven times today's level.

U.S. economic experience during this period belies the simplistic association frequently made by mainstream economists between free trade and prosperity. The first phase delivers a body blow to this creed by revealing that the economic surge over these years had little to do with changes in tariff policy. *The second phase delivers a knockout by showing that the period in which America had its highest tariff rates, and the smallest involvement with international trade, was also the one in which the country had its greatest economic success.*

The First Phase: 1815–1861

Outlines of the great tariff debate of the future became clear shortly after peace was declared with England and foreign trade resumed. U.S. farmers quickly profited from renewed access to European markets, but for America's budding manufacturing industry, it was a different story. British producers, anxious to recover their markets, gave Americans an early and harsh lesson in the practice of dumping, which means temporarily selling goods below cost. In 1815 alone, foreign textile manufacturers dumped 71 million yards of fabric into the United States, more than 75 percent of the entire output of the U.S. industry. Prices tumbled, and before long, many of the weaker mills that had sprouted behind the umbrella of the embargo were driven out of business.

The onslaught of foreign competition brought a call for protection from domestic producers. Initially they received little sympathy from the general public, which was glad to revert to prewar economic conditions, with the United States once again exchanging its agricultural products for British wares. Four years passed before the U.S. industry found a substantial backing.

In 1819, the European markets abruptly collapsed, depriving U.S. agriculture of its profitable outlet. Northern farmers quickly joined the call for protected home markets and, together with the injured manufacturing sector, formed a solid front for higher tariffs. On the other hand, Southern farmers, although just as damaged as those in the North, recognized that their long-term interests still lay in keeping the international markets open. Together with the New England shipping interests, they formed the opposition.

The early rounds went to the opposition, but in 1828 the protectionists won a resounding victory that raised tariffs not only on manufactures of glass, iron, textiles, and machine tools but also on raw materials like wool, tobacco, hemp, and flax. Within months, the average tariff rate soared to 62 percent, a level never seen before or since. See Figure 7.1 for a closer look at U.S. tariff history.

Soon it became apparent that the Tariff Bill of 1828 had gone too far. Dubbed the "Tariff of Abominations," the bill proved unpopular even in the North, and eventually Congress passed the Compromise Tariff Act of 1833. Under the act, tariffs would remain high until 1842, when they would be replaced by a uniform 20 percent duty. However, in 1846, the Walker Tariff Act pushed the average tariff to 30 percent.

To free traders, U.S. economic experience before and after the Civil War must come as a great disappointment. In their analysis, by stifling foreign competition high tariffs choke innovation, fuel inflation, and dampen growth and productivity.[3] U.S. history, however, mocks this view. Despite long spells of high protection, industrial output rose almost tenfold between 1810 and 1860. Consumer prices systematically declined between 1816 and 1860, and the period witnessed a rate of technical innovation matching or exceeding that in Europe.

The development of industry during this period is epitomized by the record of cotton textiles. There the number of spindles climbed from just 191,000 in 1820 to 2,112,000 in 1840 and 5,236,000 in 1860, while productivity ballooned. Output per spindle rose from 142 in 1820 to 185 in 1834, 217 in 1849, and 219

FIGURE 7.1
Average U.S. Tariff Rates, 1821–1991

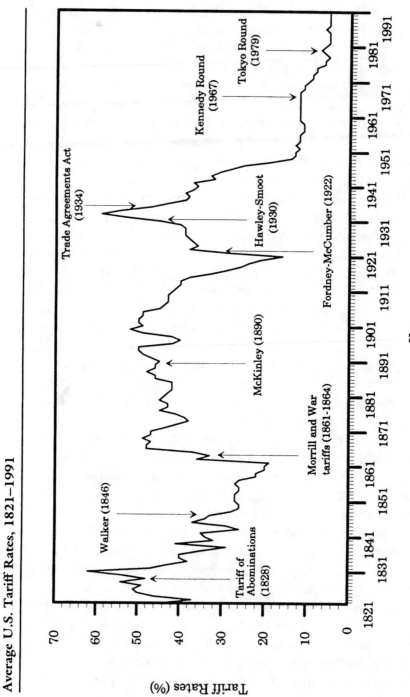

SOURCES: *Historical Statistics of the United States and Statistical Abstract of the United States, 1991.*

in 1859. Indeed, by 1860, spindle productivity had risen so much that real wages in the United States were twice the level of those in Europe.

Despite impressive industrial development, agriculture remained the primary American occupation on the eve of the Civil War. Farming accounted for the largest share of national income (31 percent) as well as the largest share of the active work force (53 percent), although both numbers had diminished since 1820. The growth in industry helped rather than hurt agriculture. The immense expansion of acreage under cultivation could not have occurred without the improvements that took place in farm machinery, such as the steel plow developed by John Deere in 1837 and the mechanical reaper patented by Cyrus McCormick in 1834. These innovations generated tremendous gains in agricultural productivity. Whereas it had taken fifty-six man-hours to grow and harvest an acre of wheat in 1800, it took only thirty-five in 1840. Equally impressive gains were observed in the production of corn and other farm products.

The Second Phase: 1861–1900

The second phase of economic development in the nineteenth century picked up where the first phase left off. The same trends continued, except now at a spectacular speed. Thus, while average tariffs were high in the first phase,. they were higher in the second. Innovation, manufacturing, and agriculture had all made solid progress before; the corresponding achievements now were better, so much so that toward the end of the century, the young republic emerged as the preeminent economic power in the world.[4]

Properly speaking, the second phase of our analysis begins with the year 1865, when Americans returned from the battlefield and once more turned to the task of building themselves and their nation. However, the high tariffs that marked the postwar years first came into effect during the turbulent conflict.

In the early months of 1862, the federal government began to understand the true dimensions of the Civil War and the enormous commitment of resources it would take to win. Toward this end, the federal legislature passed a comprehensive Internal Revenue Act, imposing excise duties on a wide array of commodities and introducing for the first time a general income tax. The legislators felt that the new taxes could give foreign producers an undue edge in local markets. To preempt this possibility, they followed the Revenue Act with the Tariff Act of 1862, which increased tariffs by 15 percent in order to eliminate the cost advantage of imports.

Another round of increases in taxes and tariffs occurred in 1864, and even though internal taxes were gradually dismantled after the end of hostilities in 1865, a powerful lobby of manufacturers persuaded the government to retain the high import duties.

The new rates of protection had a predictable effect on the volume of international trade. Between 1869 and 1899, import growth fell far short of the growth in economic activity. Foreign competition became insignificant to most U.S. manufacturers. Here, then, was the classic profile of an inward-looking economic system—one for which the advocates of free trade reserve their direst predictions. Here was a society which, according to their doctrine, would fritter away its precious resources; a society where the absence of foreign rivalry would lead to choking prices and shoddy products; where producers would have no incentive to innovate and improve; in short, a society that would gradually slide into mediocrity and even poverty.

What actually happened over these years is only too well known. The gross national product of the United States quadrupled between 1869 and 1900 when measured in constant (1929) dollars. In spite of a mushrooming population, real wages jumped 50 percent, retail prices tumbled 37 percent, and annual per capita income rose from $223 in 1869 to almost $500 in 1900.[5]

The advances were most significant in the area where free traders would least expect them: the protected manufacturing sector. Industrial production quadrupled between 1870 and 1900, and at the turn of the century manufacturing had become the premier sector of the economy, accounting for 53 percent of its total product and 22 percent of its labor force. But perhaps the most telling statistic of all is that during this period, the United States, led by manufacturing, became the preeminent economic power in the world. Would free trade have done that? Absolutely not. *If it were up to free traders, America would still be a prominent agrarian economy.*

How could all this happen? Where did the United States find the ingredients and the dynamism required for such success? The answer is not hard to find if sought with a dispassionate mind.

Foreign trade is supposed to benefit a nation by providing two elements indispensable to economic development. The first is the access of producers to a large pool of global consumers, the second is the competitive pressures on domestic industry to become efficient.[6] The U.S. success occurred because the nation was able to generate the ingredients of growth—large consumer markets and vigorous competition—even in the absence of foreign trade. Trade restriction hurts competition only if domestic manufacturers are few in number. The American market was far removed from this scenario.

Despite the growth of the factory system in the 1840s and 1850s, U.S. enterprises were still organized mostly as sole proprietorships or partnerships. Such ventures are limited in scale because they have access to the investible funds of only a few owners. As a result, industries were characterized by a large number of small producers, none commanding any significant market power and all striving to generate the price or quality edge that would distinguish them from their rivals.

There was thus an intense competition among firms, and it was manifested in two directions: technological improvements and innovative strategies for marketing products. A number of new techniques—such as the open-hearth method, among others—revolutionized the steel industry, followed by advancements in electricity, telegraphy, and transportation. The new technology was partly imported from England, partly invented at home.

Direct official aid to industry, however, was marginal. "Of more importance than direct payments," say economists Martin Primack and James Willis, "was government protection of U.S. manufacturing through the use of tariffs."[7] The message of these and other economic historians is thus at odds with that of free traders, who are mostly theorists, unaware of history and much of the reality surrounding them.

Twentieth-Century Developments

As the twentieth century dawned, America found itself in unfamil-
iar territory—that of world economic leadership. The high-tariff
policy had transmuted a meek agrarian nation into a mighty industrial power that was soon to be tested in a global conflagration.

Toward the end of the nineteenth century, U.S. industry had
started to abuse its privileged position behind the tariff walls. There
had been frequent recessions and occasional depressions in the
country, and during each slump, stronger firms would swallow
weaker businesses. The result was the rise of pools, trusts, and
holding companies, all of which are ways of exploiting monopoly
power in any industry. Such abuse of economic power was bound
to generate an antimonopoly sentiment, and it did.

The first manifestation of the antimonopoly mood was antitrust
legislation, which I will examine at length in Chapter 9. The second
was a grudging movement away from protectionism. Thus tariffs
were cut slightly in 1909 and then significantly in 1913 (see Figure
7.1).

By the end of the First World War in 1918, tariffs averaged
below 20 percent, the lowest they had been in more than a century.
Peace, however, was greeted by a steep recession, to which Congress responded with protectionism. The Fordney-McCumber Tariff of 1922 caused the sharpest percentage rise in import duties. In
1920, the average tariff stood at 16 percent; by 1922, it had more
than doubled to 38 percent. On the eve of the Great Depression in
1929, the tariff averaged 40 percent.

Congressional response to the Depression was the same as that
in the postwar recession of 1920–21. Tariffs were raised again
through the Hawley-Smoot Tariff Act of 1930, and by 1932 the
average duty had climbed to 59 percent, which was near the all-time
high of 62 percent reached in 1830.

Soon the new tariff became the scapegoat for the Great Depression, which marked a turning point in America's commercial policy.
All the lessons painstakingly learned over the past 130 years were
quickly forgotten in the early 1930s. Such was the severity of the

economic debacle that President Franklin D. Roosevelt set out to reverse a century-old policy of growth through protectionism.

After 1932, tariffs began to fall. The reversal of Hawley-Smoot and the establishment of a textbook variety of pure free trade now came to be seen as a wonder drug that would revive a comatose economy.

The Roosevelt administration took the initiative in forging a new international order by demanding from Congress the authority to negotiate bilateral tariff reductions with other nations. Although concerned about the health of domestic industries, Congress was unwilling to stand in the way of a popular president and conceded the powers he requested. Between 1934 and 1939, the administration negotiated thirty-one reciprocal trade agreements and extended the resulting tariff reduction to a wider network of nations through a principle called the Most Favored Nation (MFN), under which a concession made in bilateral talks with any trading partner would automatically extend to other partners as well. As a result, average U.S. tariffs plummeted from 54 percent to 37 percent. Although well short of global free trade, the new system was considerably freer.

The outbreak of the Second World War in 1939 disrupted the new policy, and for the next six years Europe, and subsequently the United States and Japan, were absorbed in the hostilities. With the return of peace, the administration once again turned to matters of trade. This time America pursued free trade with greater urgency and vigor.

To the traditional ideological rationale for free trade, several new strategic considerations had been added by the postwar situation. First, the administration was determined to prevent regional animosities from dividing European nations again and felt that the only way to draw them together was through economic integration. Moreover, the democracies of Europe were now seen as menaced by the new and powerful Soviet empire that had arisen in the aftermath of the war. Rapid restoration of European prosperity became a security imperative. Finally, there was self-interest. With the destruction of Europe and Japan, the United States had become the predominant economy in the world, commanding 52 percent of global capital. With little credible competition from other nations, it seemed obvious that American businesses would be the biggest beneficiaries from the opening of world markets.

To Western Europe the United States provided massive aid under the Marshall Plan, and to its Asian allies and Japan it offered advanced technology but modest financial assistance. America also encouraged trade liberalization in the noncommunist world under the auspicies of the General Agreement on Tariffs and Trade (GATT). By opening its own markets, the United States hoped to strengthen the economies of its allies and the Third World, thereby creating a strong bulwark of anti-Soviet states. At the same time, American businesses, especially the multinational corporations, which were already preponderant in international competition, could prosper through greater access to foreign markets.

The world socioeconomic system of a quarter century after the war is often called *Pax Americana*, reminiscent of the *Pax Britannica* that is said to have prevailed during the nineteenth century. In both cases, the international economy was under the hegemony of an overwhelming global power that dominated the earth's economic, political, and military affairs.[8] GATT was the conduit through which the United States hoped to flex its economic muscle around the world.

The most significant feature of GATT was that it provided a framework within which nations could negotiate trade policies. The framework was deliberately structured to hasten the process of liberalization. In order to ensure that all nations had an incentive to participate, it was decided that proposals for trade concessions had to be reciprocal—that is, one nation could not use its greater economic power to extract unilateral concessions from others. Finally, all signatories had to abide by the MFN clause, according to which the concessions granted by a nation to one trading partner would automatically extend to all other trading partners in the relevant industry.

Although the GATT framework was impressive, the range of issues that could be negotiated within it was limited. No nation, except for the United States, was willing to discuss free trade in agricultural products, because there were compelling political pressures within each country to ensure self-sufficiency in food. In the area of manufactured goods, the major focus was on tariffs. The subtler forms of domestic protection, such as subsidies and preferential government procurement, could not be brought to the table. Even with tariffs, member nations insisted on revoking concessions that proved to be disastrous or led to a serious deficit in the balance of payments. But most significantly, member nations could seek access to foreign markets without opening their own, and thus violate the principle of reciprocity, if they could convince others that this was necessary for their economic development.[9]

Despite its shortcomings, GATT was promoted vigorously by various U.S. administrations. Using its considerable leverage over Europe and Japan, America persuaded them to participate in GATT negotiations and lower the high tariff walls they had erected during the war. Such efforts were generally successful. In five rounds of talks, from the First Round in Geneva in 1947 to the Dillon Round, also in Geneva, in 1961–1962, the average tariff rate among member nations was reduced to less than half its 1930 level (47.7 percent, to be exact). Predictably, the volume of world trade increased remarkably, growing at an average rate of 6.8 percent each year between 1948 and 1963.

Not everyone benefited equally from the growth in trade. Indeed, the biggest loser was the United States itself, which often willfully conceded asymmetric benefits to Europe and Japan in order to keep the dialogue alive. The exclusion of agriculture from GATT negotiations hurt America the most, because the country enjoyed a clear comparative advantage in this area. Similarly, in the case of manufactured goods, the United States accepted Japanese protectionism while at the same time giving Japan open access to its own markets.

Even where America extracted reciprocal tariff reductions, U.S. firms benefited little because Europe and Japan did not permit free conversion of their currencies. Thus, while foreign firms could repatriate the profits they earned inside the United States, U.S. firms abroad were not free to do the same. America was well aware of the concessions it had made in order to keep the GATT process alive but believed these costs to be worthwhile because of the benefits it hoped to gain someday, when other economies finally matured and withdrew their protectionist policies. U.S. administrations were under the spell of doctrinaire economists who argued that unilateral free trade was in the best interest of a nation.

Of all the restrictive tendencies that developed in the 1950s, the one that presented the greatest danger to the United States was the gradual process of economic integration within Europe. Starting with the European Coal and Steel Community, which established a free trade zone for coal and steel within Europe, this process broadened into other sectors and ultimately led to the establishment of the European Economic Community (EEC) in 1957. The Community had ambitious objectives. The signatory nations would transform themselves into a single common market, completely harmonize their domestic policies, and allow free migration of labor and capital. The initial steps, however, were more modest and dealt mainly with the first of these objectives, the Common Market. It was agreed that the member countries—France, West Germany, Italy, Belgium, Luxembourg, and the Netherlands—would abolish all tariffs on each other's products and establish a common external tariff against products of other nations.

The Common Market was clearly discriminatory against U.S. producers, and further integration could only increase the disadvantage they faced when competing inside Europe. America now had to respond to this new challenge, and the response it chose was characteristic of its guiding ideology of free trade. Instead of retaliating with protectionist measures of its own, the country decided that the only way to deal with the European challenge without contracting world trade was to bring the new Common Market into the GATT framework and pressure it to liberalize its policies by opening a fresh round of tariff negotiations.

In 1961, the Kennedy administration asked for, and received, broader powers for tariff reduction than had ever been given to a U.S. president by Congress. Armed with these new powers, the administration initiated the sixth round of GATT negotiations, the so-called Kennedy Round, in Geneva. The president had been authorized to cut all tariffs if the European Community and other nations would follow suit. The administration pursued these reductions vigorously, despite the tensions raised within the negotiating body by further advances in European integration.

Finally, in 1967, the Kennedy Round came to a close. The round had been very successful in liberalizing trade in manufactures. On average, tariff rates on manufactured goods fell by 33 percent, and for more than half of the negotiated products, tariffs were reduced by more than 50 percent. Tariffs on nonagricultural products stood at 9.9 percent in the United States, 8.6 percent in the six EEC countries, 10.8 percent in Great Britain, and 10.7 percent in Japan. Never before had tariffs been so low globally.[10]

For U.S. labor, the Trade Expansion Act, which had launched the Kennedy Round, offered an innovative treatment of those whose jobs were threatened by foreign competition. Instead of protecting these jobs, the act established an Adjustment Assistance Program to help workers displaced by increased imports. The idea was to enable laid-off workers to make a smooth transition from import-competing sectors to expanding export industries. Unfortunately, the program did little to assist workers in their most pressing transitional need: new job skills. It merely offered cash payments of up to 65 percent of previous weekly earnings for a period of no more than fifty-two weeks and reasonable relocation expenses.

The main objective of the Kennedy Round was to nudge the European Economic Community in the direction of free trade and to give U.S. businesses a fair chance to compete in the widening European market.[11] However, in 1966, even before the conclusion of the talks, it became apparent that Europe was moving in the opposite direction. That year the EEC formulated the Common Agricultural Policy (CAP). The CAP was designed to maintain farm prices at politically acceptable levels through a series of government price supports. In order to protect overpriced farm products from foreign competition, particularly from the United States, a flexible tariff was imposed on all such imports in a way that equalized the price consumers paid for domestic and foreign commodities. Not surprisingly, the new levy rapidly shrank America's exports of protected items into Europe.

To make matters worse, as the power of the European farm lobby grew, it became increasingly difficult to limit the amounts farmers produced at the inflated prices. In order to divert some of this output from domestic markets, the EEC started giving farmers subsidies to encourage exports. Not only was the United States shut out of its European market, it now began to face stiff competition from subsidized European products in other foreign markets. Needless to say, had America followed such a policy with respect to manufactures, in which it had the comparative disadvantage, the policy would have been a blatant violation of GATT rules.

The problems did not end with agriculture.[12] Increasingly during the 1960s, Europe started expanding its preferential trading agreements with African and Asian countries, many of which had been its former colonies. Such agreements had clearly been barred by the GATT rule of nondiscrimination, but Europe justified them as an indirect form of aid to these countries. From Europe's point of view, these arrangements served a valuable function by reducing the prices European producers had to pay for raw materials and by giving these producers preferred access to the markets of former colonies.

Toward the end of the 1960s, such trade problems were compounded by a new source of trouble: Japan. By 1968, Japan had risen from total devastation to a position where it was surpassed only by America and the Soviet Union in the production of goods and services. U.S. trade policy toward Japan had a lot to do with this resurgence. Despite a complex set of restrictive tariffs and quotas spreading across practically every sector of the Japanese economy, U.S. administrations had actively lobbied for Japan's inclusion into GATT in the early 1950s. The European nations had recognized the potential danger presented by Japan and, despite allowing it entry into GATT in 1955, had withheld from it the Most Favored Nation status that would have given it easy access to their markets. Only America refrained from this discrimination, despite the restrictions that kept U.S. goods out of Japanese markets.[13]

The combination of secure domestic markets and vigorous competition for foreign markets produced a rapid rate of innovation and expansion in Japan, and by the early 1960s Japanese industry seemed to have matured to the point where protection was unnecessary. However, despite significant liberalization of some quotas and foreign exchange rules, Japanese industry remained highly protected. Computers, automobiles, and heavy machinery continued to be regarded as "infant" industries and shielded through barriers to imports. Needless to say, agriculture was also on the list of protected sectors. Since these happened to be precisely the areas in which America was most competitive, it became increasingly difficult for U.S. exports to Japan to grow. At the same time, as a result of successive trade liberalizations, it had become increasingly easy for Japanese goods to penetrate the U.S. market.[14]

All these developments were ominous for America's balance of trade. U.S. exports could not keep pace with the increasing volume of imports. In 1971, the inevitable happened. The U.S. merchandise balance of trade, in surplus since 1893, slid into deficit.[15]

By the mid-1970s, the U.S. economy was no longer as globally dominant as in the late 1940s. As late as 1958, America commanded 58 percent of world capital. By 1975, this figure had shrunk to 32 percent, while Japan's share had risen from 4 percent to 15 percent and that of West Germany from 6 percent to 11 percent. Another important trend was the convergence in the technological structure of these countries. Within twenty-five years after the war, both West Germany and Japan had succeeded in developing sophisticated, capital-intensive industries that were technologically comparable, and in some cases superior, to those in the United States.

Technological convergence meant that U.S. industries could no longer carve out a niche for themselves in their markets. Because of trade liberalization, American goods faced a strong challenge from foreign products that were comparable in design and quality. At the same time, they were also challenged in the low-price segment of their markets by products from Korea, Taiwan, and Brazil, which could use their status as "developing" countries to continue their protectionist policies and aggressive export promotion without stepping outside GATT rules.

Another development since the 1970s has been the growth of services in the industrialized world, a sector in which America still has a technological edge due to its relatively early entry. By the late 1970s, services accounted for more than 65 percent of U.S. GNP and over 50 percent of the GNP in other industrial countries (see Chapter 2). However, international commerce in services is not covered by GATT rules, and as a result other nations overtly used protectionist policies to promote their own service sectors at American expense. Information-oriented products such as semiconductors and telecommunications equipment are still subject to copyright and "national security" restraints, and banking in most parts of the world remains shut to outside agencies. Thus, in services also U.S. goods were and are discriminated against by the world at large.

Under the collective assault of imports and foreign discrimination, the postwar American consensus on free trade policy began to crumble.[16] Shortly after the Kennedy Round was concluded, representatives of local industries such as electronics, textiles, and steel pressured Congress to provide them relief from import competition. They found an unexpected ally in the AFL-CIO, which turned away from its traditional support of free trade in the face of growing dislocation of U.S. manufacturing workers.

By 1968, barely a year after the Kennedy Round concluded, more than a thousand restrictive trade bills were introduced into Congress. When President Lyndon Johnson sought to extend presidential authority to conduct tariff negotiations, opposition was so strong that his bill was never brought to a vote. President Richard Nixon was equally unsuccessful in obtaining an extension of the negotiating authority, and in 1972, it had to deal with the biggest challenge yet to the free trade approach—a bill called the Foreign Trade and Investment Act, which would have imposed significant quotas on imports.

Pressured by rising protectionist sentiment, a stagnant economy, and a steadily mounting trade deficit, President Nixon began to make increasingly belligerent remarks about the need for a "just trading order." His words had little effect on the country's trading partners, but he swiftly got their attention with his New Economic Policy (NEP), launched on August 15, 1971. Not only did NEP propose wage and price controls throughout the economy—measures almost inconceivable from a Republican president—but it imposed an immediate 10 percent surcharge on all dutiable imports and suspended the free convertibility of the U.S. dollar. Both measures were unpleasant to America's trading partners, and the idea was to use them as bargaining chips to extract trade concessions: revision of the CAP and the EEC preference system by the Europeans and removal of import quotas by Japan.[17]

However, this attempt at coercion failed. Europe and Japan did not want to set a precedent for offering unilateral concessions under duress and agreed only to cosmetic measures to open their markets. The main achievement of the effort was a promise by all parties to have another round of multilateral negotiations within the GATT framework. Toward the end of 1972 the details were finalized: talks would begin in Tokyo in September 1973.

The Tokyo Round began under conditions uniquely unfavorable to commercial liberalization. There was a good deal of rancor among affluent nations over recent trade conflicts, and the appeal of protectionism was rising even in the United States, which had been the most ardent champion of free trade. Global issues were particularly contentious, and to make matters worse, the world had just been hit by the first oil price shock, which had raised fears of a worldwide recession.

The biggest achievement of the Tokyo Round came as usual in the traditional area of liberalizing the markets for industrial products. The United States was once again on the losing end. Tariff rates on raw materials were reduced to an average of 0.3 percent, those on finished manufactures to 6.5 percent, and those on semimanufactured goods to 4 percent. Once again, America accepted the lowest tariff rates among all industrial countries, while its major concerns, agriculture and services, went nowhere.[18] There was no significant progress in extending GATT rules to farm products, because the EEC refused to compromise the basic principles of the CAP and Japan had similarly compelling domestic pressures against opening its grain markets. The only concession the Americans could get was an agreement to talk more.

Once again, GATT negotiations proved costly to the United States. As usual, it accepted tariff reductions in its import-competing industries without obtaining similar concessions for its strongest export industries. As a result, the ominous trends that had surfaced in the 1960s intensified. In addition to losing ground to imports at home, America lost further in export markets. Its share of world exports fell from 13.8 percent in 1970 to 11.3 percent in 1980.

Whenever Europe and Japan agree on further talks, they keep their promise. Negotiations come cheap, create delays, and in the end produce generous concessions from the Americans, who despite disastrous losses continue to be under the spell of free trade. In October 1986, a fresh round of multilateral negotiations was declared open at Punta del Este, Uruguay. For the first time, the focus of negotiations is not on tariff reductions but on such issues as trade in services and agricultural products and a further refinement of the GATT rules on nontariff barriers.

Although the new focus is encouraging, there seems little prospect for a breakthrough on these issues, because the same powerful interests that opposed such dialogue during the Tokyo Round are once again at work in the negotiating halls of the Uruguay Round. Developing nations like Brazil and India have already voiced vehement opposition to the idea of expanded trade in critical services like banking, accounting, and financial intermediation. Similarly, the farm lobby in major trading nations is sufficiently powerful to ensure that no significant progress is made toward dismantling agricultural protection. Once again the Americans are expected to get the shaft, while other nations continue to plunder America's manufacturing base.

Pax Americana has now faded into an apparition. The strongest military power in the world faces a nasty budget deficit ranging from $300 billion to $400 billion per year and a still nastier debt in excess of $4 trillion. There is a great irony in the British and U.S. annals: *Pax Britannica* ended because of Britain's ruthless policy of colonial exploitation; *Pax Americana,* by contrast, wilted under American generosity to trading partners. The U.S. economic debacle began in 1973, the first year of America's transition into free trade, and with it also began the demise of U.S. hegemony over the world.[20]

8

The Fallacy of Free Trade

Why are economists and the U. S. administration so obsessed with free trade? In fact, why is the Western world in general so fond of free trade, when all it has brought is nothing but miserable wages to millions of people? Those in Japan and Korea don't care much for commercial liberalization. They have prospered remarkably well under the shelter of protection. Then why is the West so enamored with free trade?

There are two possible answers. One is the enduring memory of the Hawley-Smoot tariff; the other is the lack of a correct theory. It is common experience that contrary facts don't kill an obsolete theory; only a new theory does.

Historians have frequently and rightly denounced the Hawley-Smoot Tariff Act of 1930, which brought the average tariff rate near its peak in U.S. history. But they have denounced the act for wrong reasons. This is one case where emotion has colored logic.

First of all, Hawley-Smoot critics limit their analysis to just three years, 1930 to 1932. They completely ignore the economy's experience immediately before and after these years. Second, they forget that the tariff was enacted against an American background that is totally different from today's.

The Hawley-Smoot Tariff Act

Following the stock market crash in October 1929, the economy plunged into a serious recession. Investment, output, and employment fell swiftly, while interest rates hit the floor. The dramatic drop in the interest rate led to a modest recovery in housing and stock prices in 1930, but unemployment continued to climb. It was against this bleak background that Congress passed the Hawley-Smoot Tariff Act that year. The average tariff soared but for only two years. The slump had deepened even before the passage of the act, as can be seen from Figure 8.1.

This figure plots the trends in the unemployment rate against the tariff rates between 1930 and 1939, a period covering the depression decade that saw major changes in tariff legislation. Two trend lines are shown, the lower one representing the unemployment rate, the upper one the tariff rate. Between 1930 and 1932, the tariff rate shot up from 45 percent to 59 percent, and unemployment climbed from 9 percent to 24 percent of the labor force. From this economists conclude that the Hawley-Smoot tariff deepened the Depression, which had already begun in the middle of 1929.[1] The idea is that raising the tariff in 1930 contributed to the sharp rise in unemployment.

Soon after 1932, however, tariffs tumbled around the world. If the above analysis is correct, unemployment should have vanished by at least 1939, seven years after the tariff reversal. The unemployment rate did fall a bit from 1934 to 1937 but then shot up again, while the tariff rate was essentially constant. Why was this constant tariff associated with rising unemployment?

Now take a look at Figure 8.2, which is very different from Figure 8.1. Between 1921 and 1929, the tariff rate jumped from 29 percent to 40 percent; yet the unemployment rate plummeted from 11 percent to 3 percent. The decade earned the nickname "Roaring Twenties" in spite of—or maybe because of—the huge jump in the

FIGURE 8.1
Tariffs and Unemployment, 1930–1939

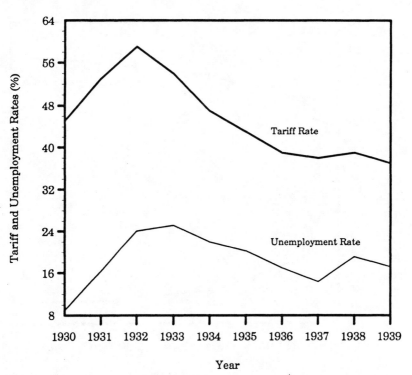

SOURCE: *Historical Statistics of the United States.*

tariff rate. Earnings, productivity, stock prices, profits, GNP and employment, soared, while the average tariffs were as high as those in the middle of the nineteenth century.

During the 1920s, tariffs jumped while unemployment tumbled, whereas during the late 1930s, unemployment rose while tariffs were unchanged. Only between 1930 and 1932 did unemployment and tariffs climb together. From all this evidence, it is ridiculous to conclude that rising tariffs caused unemployment and contributed to the Depression. If anything, the evidence suggests that tariffs generate jobs, not eliminate them.

Even the deleterious effects of the tariff rise in the early 1930s stemmed from bad timing. It was not the tariff increase per se that

FIGURE 8.2
Tariffs and Unemployment, 1921–1929

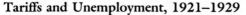

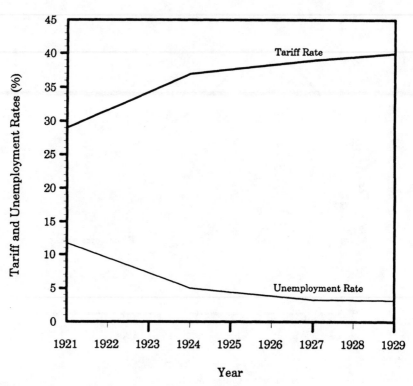

SOURCE: *Historical Statistics of the United States.*

contributed to the Depression in the early thirties but the fact that it was ill timed.

For more than three decades before 1930, the United States had enjoyed a large surplus in its balance of trade. Exports had exceeded imports for thirty-four years straight.[2] American goods had found a welcome mat around the world, much like Japanese goods have since the 1970s. The United States was exporting a wide variety of manufactures—cars, radios, refrigerators, steel, machine tools, the very products the country now imports in such vast quantities. Such was the historical perspective in which the Hawley-Smoot bill was enacted. It amounted to shooting oneself in the foot; it was a self-destructive act, pure and simple. Naturally there was an outcry around the globe. Imagine Japan today, with its trade surplus hovering around $100 billion a year, raising its tariffs. It would be a suicidal act, nothing less. That's what the United States did in 1930.

The fault was not the tariff act but the fact that a nation with a long-lasting and enormous surplus had enacted it. If a deficit country resorts to protectionism, other countries, despite their overt denunciation, may take the action with understanding. But when a surplus nation impedes imports, the action is unpardonable.

If Japan were to raise its tariffs today, the whole world would immediately retaliate. That is how the planet greeted the Hawley-Smoot Tariff, enacting barriers against American products. Since the United States was then a surplus nation, the country was the main loser in the trade war.

Today things are very different. Since 1983, the United States has suffered huge deficits in its foreign commerce. Today a Hawley-Smoot type of tariff should not ignite the world, especially when many other countries, particularly Korea and Japan, continue to follow protectionist economic policies while cheering free trade. And even if the world were to retaliate, America, with its feeble manufacturing base, would not be a loser. Thus, the moral of the whole story is that a trade surplus nation should not resort to protectionism.

The United States is now a deficit nation and has been so ever since 1983. True, the trade deficit has fallen somewhat in the 1990s, partly because of declining real earnings: U.S. wages are much lower than Germany's and slightly below Japan's. (This, however, is no cause for celebration or complacence.) Yet the memory of the 1930s and the faulty lesson drawn from them linger. The 1988 *Economic Report of the President* makes the same mistake as other economists do:

> The lesson of Hawley-Smoot is that passage of protectionist legislation by the United States will increase protectionist activities in the rest of the world, poison the international climate for trade diplomacy in general, and slow the process for trade liberalization for years to

come. Since the United States is a major trading nation, it could suffer major economic losses in the event of increased global protectionism.[3]

Conventional Wisdom on Free Trade

The conventional argument for free trade is naive and simplistic. The acolytes of liberalization make outrageous assumptions and draw incomplete conclusions.

Simplistic theories trap the unwary by equating international trade with the exchange of goods among individuals. Suppose you have ten chairs and need only six; you will be better off by exchanging four chairs for a large table to complete a dining set. Clearly, exchange has enhanced not only your welfare but also that of your trading partner, who valued the chairs enough to make the exchange. From this kind of argument, some conclude that trade is beneficial to all nations as it facilitates exchange of their surplus goods.[4]

More sophisticated versions look at exchange as well as work effort and time. Suppose you and your friend work for a newspaper, putting in eight hours a day, and both of you prepare daily news reports. You are good at typing, but your friend is good at writing. You form a partnership, divide the task, and sell your reports piecemeal. You do the typing while your friend does the writing. In this case the partnership will produce either more reports in the same number of working hours or the same number of reports with some saving in time. Both of you produce more together than the sum of what you would produce working alone. This is the productivity gain of partnership and is based on what is called the principle of absolute advantage.[5]

Each of you has an advantage in doing only one task—you in typing, your friend in writing. You both become more productive when working in unison rather than in isolation.

There is a yet subtler idea called the principle of comparative advantage. Suppose you are better than your friend at typing as well as writing; then you have an absolute advantage in both tasks over your friend. Does a partnership make sense for you now? If you are interested in enhancing your productivity, the answer is most likely yes.

Suppose your advantage in both tasks is greater in typing than in writing. Here again the partnership will be more productive than if each of you were working alone. Even though you are more productive in both jobs than your friend, your productivity edge is greater in typing than writing. For the same sixteen hours a day of work, the partnership will produce more news reports.

Your productivity will be higher because even though you have an absolute advantage in both areas, your comparative advantage is greater in typing. Similarly, your friend may have an absolute disadvantage in both tasks, but his comparative disadvantage is smaller in writing than in typing. If you put all your working hours into typing and your friend into writing, clearly the two of you working together will be more productive. This is the principle of comparative advantage, which suggests that partnership is more efficient even in this case.[6]

Let's now think of nations instead of individuals. Suppose America and Australia both produce wheat and cars. If they formed a partnership and each specialized in the production of the goods in which it had an advantage, whether absolute or comparative, and imported the other product, the partnership would be more productive than before, while both countries could consume both products.

This is essentially the logic behind free trade, which is like a partnership among nations with each concentrating its efforts on sectors in which it has the highest comparative labor productivity. With this in mind, the greater the specialization in goods, the greater the productivity of partnership among nations. But the more you specialize, the more you have to import and pay for it in exports. Thus free trade is the best policy, because trade and hence specialization are then maximized.[7]

Therefore, any policy that restricts trade must reduce world productivity. Hence all forms of protectionism—tariffs, quotas, subsidies, domestic content requirements, and voluntary export restraints, among many others—are bad for international welfare.[8]

The conventional wisdom thus is that trade creates two types of gains: the convenience gain from exchange and the productivity gain from specialization.[9]

What could possibly be wrong with this logic? It is so simple and appealing. In my view, it is deceptively appealing, which may partly explain its popularity among economists. Note that this logic does not even depend on what wage rates prevail in various nations. The world would be more productive with free trade even if wages were very low in some countries and very high in others, because work effort or productivity, not salaries, enters into the principle of comparative advantage. I will shortly have more to say on this point.

Let us go back to the example of partnership between you and your friend. There is absolutely no doubt that you would potentially be more productive working together than alone. But that does not mean you would both earn more. The partnership will definitely make more money, as more news reports will bring it more income. If, before joining your forces, you agree upon a formula for sharing the extra profit, both of you will be better off. Each partner will not only be more productive but will also earn more.

But if you don't have a sharing agreement, one of you could be worse off even with higher potential productivity.

For one thing, suppose the partnership is unable to find a market for all its reports; then one or both partners have to work fewer hours. As long as this is voluntary and appealing, there is no problem. You may have a lower income, but at least you have more leisure time.

But suppose only you, as a typist not so much in demand elsewhere, have to work fewer hours and your share of income falls, while your partner continues to thrive. Then you may be worse off even if you still produce more per hour. You may still be as productive as before, but you will be unhappy because of your reduced income. Your total productivity could also fall, because even with higher hourly output, you could produce less overall if your working hours decline sharply. Thus, if demand for the partnership's output is insufficient, your income could tumble. At this point it would make sense for you to quit and work alone. However, if the partnership has lasted for years, or if your partner is a smart talker and convinces you of the benefits of staying together, you may not leave even if your income drops sharply.

You may stay in the partnership out of a sense of loyalty, out of fear of the unknown, or because you have forgotten how to do both tasks and work alone after many years of specializing in one area. But while you are unhappy inside, you rationalize the status quo with daily pronouncements that the partnership is good for you because at least it raises your hourly output.

Something like this characterizes the U.S. economy today. Free trade may have helped Americans produce more per hour, but because of falling world demand for their products they are earning less than their 1973 salaries, and some even less than their 1950 salaries. America's trading partners, on the other hand, not only produce more per hour but have seen their wages grow significantly since the 1970s. U.S. economists have failed to see the depredations of free trade, because they focus only on productivity and ignore earnings. They are busy rationalizing the status quo. And what would you rather have—higher productivity or higher salaries?

The Outrageous Assumptions of Free Trade

The modern theory of the gains from trade is much more sophisticated than that presented above. But the basic idea is the same. Instead of comparative labor productivity, the modern version emphasizes comparative costs, which are determined by the productivity of various factors—labor, capital, and land—and their earnings. In fact, the modern theory acknowledges that trade may hurt wages in both the short run and the long run.[10] But then other factors benefit so much that their earnings gains outweigh the loss of wages. Hence free trade still makes the nation better off, although it may harm the workers.[11]

This idea can be dismissed easily because it has little practical relevance. In 1991, wages of employees and the self-employed constituted 82 percent of U.S. national income, and capital income the remaining 18 percent. Any theory that ignores wages and focuses only on national aggregates such as social welfare, the real per capita GNP, or national income is really worthy of storage in a dustbin. It is simply preposterous. How can you treat income from labor and from other sources in the same way?

In a high-inequality economy such as America's, only 5 percent of the population derives meaningful income from capital. When economists say that trade benefits a nation while possibly hurting labor, what they are really saying is that at least capital owners thrive, or the rich get richer. Never mind the poor workers who constitute 80 percent of the labor force, at least the affluent prosper from free trade. This means only that free trade definitely promotes the rich man's welfare, not necessarily social welfare, which must apply to the vast majority of the population.

It's not, then, surprising that multinational corporations and their chief executive officers (CEOs), with their industrial fiefs scattered across the globe, adore free trade. You may recall from Chapter 2 that ever since 1973, the first year of America's switch to laissez-faire, the real wages of 80 percent of the population have been shriveling while the rich have grown enormously richer. However, among the beneficiaries of trade liberalization, the CEOs are in a class of their own. Today, the CEOs of General Electric, Du Pont, IBM, Monsanto, Xerox, and Exxon earn millions of dollars per year, even after having fired thousand of hapless employees between 1990 and 1992. Journalists Donald Barlett and James Steele report that Time Warner CEO Steven J. Ross alone made $78.2 million in 1990.[12] As William Greider puts it: "The people at the top are literally leaving everyone else behind. Between 1977 and 1990, the period when average wages were stagnating, compensation for top corporate executives rose by 220 percent."[13]

Even the dubious idea that free trade benefits all nations is based on outrageous assumptions. The theory that laissez-faire, as compared to a closed economy, enriches a country by raising its real per capita GNP assumes that wage rates in different industries are the same. If they are not, then free trade may reduce social welfare.[14] But trade theorists argue that among affluent nations interindustry wages are close to one another. No one, however, has bothered to examine this assumption. In fact, this is an outrageous assumption, because it is a blatant contradiction of facts.

In 1991, U.S. construction workers earned $534 a week, manufacturing workers made $455 a week, but retail trade employees earned only $200 a week (see Table 2.3). These don't look like similar wages. They are far apart and have far-reaching repercussions for gains from trade.

Free traders reply that even such large wage differentials are due only to unequal skills. But in reality people with the same skills working in different industries have sharply unequal salaries. A secretary may earn $40,000 at IBM and only $20,000 per year at a university. The skills are the same, but IBM is a manufacturer, whereas a university provides educational services.

The United States exports mostly services and imports mostly manufactures. Since 1984, America's trade deficit in manufactures has consistently exceeded $100 billion per year; to pay for this deficit, the nation has increasingly relied on the export of services, which in 1990 totaled $131 billion.[15]

How are services traded across countries? Whenever foreigners use facilities or expertise offered by Americans, export of services occurs. When Europeans travel via Delta Airlines, Japanese study at Harvard, Chinese vacation in New York, or Indians buy U.S. technology, movies, and TV shows, paying us royalties, the United States exports services. Such industries include accounting, management, engineering, computer expertise, finance, transportation, communication, education, health care, shipping, insurance, restaurants, advertising, entertainment, and so on. Among the most famous service products are the credit cards offered by American Express, MasterCard, and Visa, as many people travel with them.

Typically, manufacturing firms offer wages much higher than service businesses. As U.S. trade has increased, manufacturing production and employment shares have fallen, whereas services have made corresponding gains. The migration of workers from one sector to the other has not been without cost or discomfort. But suppose that it has been, as is assumed by the free traders. If service and manufacturing salaries were the same, national income would unambiguously rise, because workers who lost jobs in one area could find equally lucrative jobs in another area. With the economy as a whole enjoying higher productivity owing to trade and with wages similar across industries, real per capita GNP would definitely rise.

In reality, as a worker moves from manufacturing to services, GNP falls by the difference between wages in the two sectors. Suppose you work in an auto plant and make $455 per week; because of the surge in car imports, you are laid off and have to go elsewhere for work. Despite your best efforts, you cannot find another auto job or anything related to it, as manufacturing in general is shrinking. As a last resort, after your unemployment compensation runs out, you go to work in a department store for $200 per week. You are now poorer by $255 every week, and so is the nation, for the GNP now declines by the amount of your loss.

If millions of people are in the same predicament as you, the GNP loss will run into billions. In other words, when trade causes a shrinkage in high-wage jobs, the exchange and productivity gains from trade must be offset by income losses due to wage differences. Since these differences are huge, they are eventually bound to overwhelm any gains, generating a net loss from trade.

As stated earlier, trade specialists do recognize this possibility, but they assume that the interindustry wage differentials in affluent countries are rather small. In fact, when wages in some sectors are more than twice those in others, the differentials cannot possibly be small. This assumption is outrageous and makes the entire premise of gains from trade dubious.[16]

The optimality of free trade also assumes that the trading account is balanced within a short period of time. With the U.S. foreign account having been in arrears since the early 1980s, the assumption of balanced trade is specious and invalidates the central message of the theory behind it.[17]

Free Trade and Consumers

Most economists realize that trade may hurt some workers temporarily, but they argue that it definitely benefits consumers, as imports bring prices down and keep a lid on inflation. You see this argument in textbooks and the press so often that before long you tend to accept it on faith. Nothing could be further from the truth. Among misconceptions, this one is superb.

Are consumers different from workers? Aren't they one and the same people? Since the opening of the U.S. economy to free trade in 1973, as much as 80 percent of the labor force has suffered a hefty loss in real income. These people and their families, aren't they consumers as well?

Talk of superstitions, and the consumerism argument really takes the cake. Free trade definitely keeps prices low, but so did the Great Depression.

What matters are not just prices but wages as well. Trade does indeed bring inflation down, but it may also reduce wages, and the wage loss far exceeds the fall in inflation. Hence the abysmal drop in the U.S. living standard.

Pundits suggest that free trade harms only a few workers while benefiting all consumers. They are half right, because experience shows that 80 percent of Americans have seen a dramatic drop in their earnings; of course, the other 20 percent, professionals and employees in high-tech service industries, have benefited from lower inflation.

Stimulus to Competition

Another common argument is that free trade stimulates competition in import-competing domestic industries, which are forced by foreign competition to produce high-quality goods at lower prices. This is a valid point; the U.S. auto industry is a classic case where Japanese competition has led to huge efficiency and quality gains in local firms. Before the arrival of Toyotas, Hondas, Nissans, and Mitsubishis, GM, Ford, and Chrysler made shoddy cars and charged exorbitant prices while pampering their executives. Since the 1980s, however, locally produced cars have improved in design, craftsmanship, and durability.

Trade undoubtedly promotes competition, and protectionism may retard it. However, there are other, less destructive ways to stimulate rivalry among domestic firms. Trade is not the only way, and these other ways may be far superior to free trade. The inherent merit is in the idea of competition, not in commercial liberalization.

The Costs of Free Trade

Many studies in the economic literature deal with the costs of so-called protectionism in the United States. In 1992, the country had the highest trade/GNP ratio in its history, yet some economists complain that America is becoming protectionist.

The costs of protectionism are said to run into billions of dollars per year. These costs take into account consumer losses net of gains to producers in protected industries. Economists David G. Tarr and M. E. Morkre put the annual costs to the United States at $12.7 billion: others, such as Susan Hickok, estimate them to be $14 billion per year.[18]

Of course, all these studies ignore the wage losses resulting from the policy of liberalization. No one has estimated the costs of free trade to the United States, but rough calculations can be easily made.

In 1973, the real weekly earnings of production or nonsupervisory workers averaged $315 in 1982 prices. In 1990, these earnings had dropped to $260, generating a loss of $55 per week per worker. Suppose a person works forty-four weeks a year, with the other eight weeks going into vacations, sick leave, etc. Most people are paid for fifty-two weeks, but let's be conservative in our calculations to estimate the minimum losses from free trade.

The loss of $55 per week when multiplied by forty-four produces an annual loss of $2,420 per person. In 1990, total nonfarm employment was 110 million, of whom 80 percent, or 88 million, were nonsupervisory workers. The aggregate annual loss of these 88 million employees then comes to $212.96 billion in 1982 prices.

This estimate assumes that real earnings have been constant at the 1973 level. But since then national productivity has risen by 18 percent. It is reasonable to assume that average earnings would have risen by at least half of this amount, or some 9 percent, provided trade had been kept at the pre-1973 level. Taking this into account, the earnings loss in 1990 was at least $232 billion in 1982 prices, or $304 billion in current prices, as the 1990 CPI exceeded the 1982 CPI by 31 percent. This is the minimum annual cost of free trade to the United States. Even this minimum is staggering.

Note that this is absolutely the lowest cost of free trade, which has also retarded productivity growth. If real earnings between 1973 and 1990 had risen at the same rate as during the previous seventeen years, the cost would be as high as $350 billion, because 1990 real earnings would have exceeded 1973 levels by 26 percent.

Some may object to this assumption, because the earnings growth might have fallen below the pre-1973 level even if the United States had retained its nearly closed economy status. Still, a minimum annual loss of $304 billion from free trade is no laughing matter.

With the costs of liberalization running so high, it comes as no surprise that the average American remains unconvinced about the benevolence of free trade. Years of official indoctrination have not been able to budge him from the commonsense view that if a policy shifts high-wage manufacturing jobs abroad or workers into low-wage services at home, the country cannot but lose. However, what is straightforward to most is considered naive by economists and the elites. "The elites of media, business, academia and politics," laments Greider, "have already made up their minds on these questions. They are committed to promoting the global economic system—and to defending it from occasional attacks from angry, injured citizens."[19] One would hope that as the truth comes out and the nation learns about the harrowing costs of free trade, the elites will have to change their views.

9

Competitive Protectionism

The chief attraction of free trade is the idea that it brings a vast amount of competition to importable-goods industries. Under capitalism frequent mergers with and acquisitions of other firms enable some businesses to grow fat and feed on the captive domestic market. Corporations become lethargic and their employees insensitive to the needs of consumers. Product quality suffers and prices rise, generating enormous profits for businesses. These profits fill the pockets of executives, who pay themselves large bonuses in both good times and bad, while society bleeds.

Free trade, so it is said, offers a challenge to big business; foreign competition wakes up listless and bloated firms, forcing them to be innovative, energetic, and courteous to their customers. In the absence of this challenge, domestic companies would continue to be inefficient and affluent while preying upon consumers and other companies.

This type of analysis contains a great deal of truth. Since the early 1970s, foreign competition has jolted many U.S. industries, and some of them—auto, steel, computers, machine tools—have indeed become highly efficient and competitive. There is an old saying that money makes the mare go; and it is equally true that competition makes the company go.

Innovation and new products are the results of active rivalry among firms. Competition prods businesses to constantly upgrade their products and offer the best service to their patrons. Similarly, competition among employees compels them to take the initiative and do their best on the job. They become attentive to small steps and minor details, which in turn produce cumulative gains and are often as important as a major breakthrough. In fact, dramatic breakthroughs arise mostly from patience and persistent effort.

In the absence of competition corporations and workers tend to be arrogant and complacent. Patience and perseverance are far from their minds. The inevitable by-products are shoddy goods and service and irritated customers.

Domestic Versus Foreign Competition

Competition is a dynamic process involving perpetual change. There is no such thing as a permanent, exclusive competitive advantage. Knowledge has no limits, and active rivalry among firms compels them to constantly improve and innovate.

However, competition can be domestic as well as foreign in origin, and the two have dramatically different effects on the economy. One is purely beneficial, while the other can be predatory and deadly. In both cases there is a challenge to which businesses must respond to survive; but the origin of this challenge is just as important as its coercive force.

Within limits, foreign competition is a positive factor. It can prod sleeping, bloated monoliths into action and be a locomotive for high productivity and growth; but when carried to extremes, it can be disruptive and destructive.

You have already seen what foreign competition has done to the economies of the United States and Australia. Workers in these countries, in which real wages generally rose with rising productivity, now helplessly watch a steady erosion of their earnings in spite of the still growing productivity. With their economies stagnant for years, the social fabric of these countries is now being torn apart by inequality and poverty. This is double jeopardy: if your work effort and hourly output fall, you can accept a drop in your salary. But when you grow more efficient and still remain underpaid, then you really seethe inside.

That is what excessive foreign competition does. Free trade undoubtedly makes the world more productive, but it does not increase the living standard of every country. Some nations definitely benefit, but some also suffer, and large, resource-rich countries such as Australia and the United States have lately been on the suffering side.

The reason that foreign competition may be predatory is easy to understand. As I have explained in the preceding chapter, as long as wages in different sectors are the same or close to one another, foreign challenge is disruptive but not destructive. Some workers lose jobs in import-competing industries and their lives are temporarily disrupted. This is an inconvenience but no more than that, because soon they will be able to find jobs in expanding export sectors. If they are paid the same, they are no worse off. Before long, as national productivity rises because of the increased specialization induced by trade, everyone's real wages will actually rise, at least over time. In this case, free trade is clearly beneficial to all nations.

In reality, however, salaries from sector to sector are markedly different. Manufacturing workers earn much more than those in retail trade, restaurants, and most other services. If foreign competition forces employment losses in high-wage sectors, there is bound to be an overall wage loss if this competition is carried to the extreme of free trade.

The United States is now a major exporter of services and a monumental importer of manufactures. With rising imports has come a declining level of employment in manufacturing. At first only the employment share dropped, but now the situation is so critical that even the absolute level is falling. An increasing proportion of the labor force has had to find work in the expanding service sector, which pays far less than manufacturing. The export sector has expanded sharply, just as the proponents of free trade had hoped. But since service wages are low, overall there has been a drop in the real wage.

Foreign competition can thus be destructive if it causes a shrinkage of the high-wage sector relative to low-wage industries. However, it can also work the other way. Foreign trade is good to those nations in which it stimulates high-wage industries. The beneficiaries of the growth in international commerce are those countries where manufacturing employment has sharply increased. Japan, Korea, Taiwan, and Germany have reaped enormous gains from trade with the United States, because the high-wage sectors there have expanded at the expense of low-wage industries.

Where does productivity fit into all this? In a global economy, productivity is not the only thing that matters, as far as the real wage is concerned. For instance, during the 1980s U.S. manufacturing productivity growth rose sharply but real wages fell in manufacturing as well as for production workers in all industries. As *The New York Times* reported on October 2, 1992, some GM workers who earned $42,000 per year a decade ago now make only $30,000; this is really shocking, especially when these workers are far more productive than ever before. In general, manufacturing wages have been falling because of the sharper drop in the industrial relative price induced by foreign competition, whereas the overall national wage owes its steady drop to the shrinking employment share in the high-wage sector.

For a high-wage industry to expand relative to overall economic activity, its productivity growth must be tremendous. It has to overcome the cost disadvantage of high salaries, and its productivity must grow even faster than others'. That, of course, is what has fostered the high-wage sectors in Japan, Germany, and South Korea.

But high productivity alone is not enough. For your wages to rise in the presence of cutthroat foreign competition, the high-wage sector has to have a faster productivity growth than the corresponding sector abroad. You had better work with the same intensity as your foreign counterpart; otherwise you may suffer a wage loss. You had better put in the same number of hours as those abroad or else be prepared to accept a shriveling paycheck.

Indeed, this is precisely the advice that free trade buffs offer the American worker. "In a global economy," they say, "you have to be better educated, work harder, and possibly take a pay cut." "We have to save more, invest more, be more productive and competitive in world markets" is their constant refrain. Never mind that in our crime-ridden, divorce-driven, debt-burdened, and tax-averse society, these suggestions are all impractical and hence worthless. What is the point in focusing on exports when this strategy calls for puny wages at home? U.S. exports more than doubled during the 1980s, but real wages continued to tumble.

I will, however, show you that there is a better and infinitely practical alternative available to America, namely, the replacement of foreign competition with domestic competition. Let me reiterate: *The problem is not U.S. productivity, which continues to rise, but free trade.*

Intense foreign competition creates a dog-eat-dog world. As in Lewis Carroll's *Through the Looking Glass,* you have to run as fast as you can just to stay where you are. With domestic competition, on the other hand, you have most of the benefits of foreign competition but none of the perils. Domestic rivalry can be at most disruptive, never destructive. It brings inconvenience and discomfort to losers but does not devastate them: for every loser there is a bigger winner. But with predatory foreign competition, all local import-competing firms and their employees are losers.

Competition in any form forces a firm to constantly improve and seek new technology. In fact, before an industry can take on those abroad, it has to be battle tested at home. Local firms pressure one another to innovate, improve, and cut costs. For instance, if you want to win in the Olympics, you first have to best your domestic rivals; you have to outplay or outrun your local competitors. Without a vigorous local contest, you are unlikely to be an Olympic champion.

In many ways local competition is superior to foreign competition. At home you are all competing on the same turf; no one gets any special treatment. A foreign firm can best yours even with inferior technology if it uses low-cost labor. But in your own country, you all have to pay the same wages, hire from the same pool of workers, secure financing from the same group of banks. There is thus a greater compulsion to innovate and be resourceful. Your success depends on your own intensity of effort, not on any advantage based on natural resources or low wages.[1]

For a developing country with backward technology, domestic rivalry alone is not enough; it will benefit by opening its borders to foreign investment, technology, and competition. India, Pakistan, and Argentina will prosper by expanding their trade contacts with the developed world. But in the case of trade among countries with similar wages and technical knowhow —the United States, Japan, and Europe—domestic competition is superior to foreign competition. It's a greater spur to efficiency.

People don't much care if they lose to a faraway rival, but they strive hard to outperform their neighbors. You want to keep up with the Joneses next door, not those in remote areas.

A domestic rival is a greater spur to competition than a foreign rival. That is why Harvard economist Michael Porter concludes: "Rivalry among a group of domestic competitors is different from and often takes forms far more beneficial to the nation than rivalry with foreign firms."[2]

Moreover, domestic challenge lacks the destructive element of foreign competition. With foreign rivalry, an entire local industry can be wiped out, as has happened to consumer electronics in the United States. But with local competition, some firms within an industry may lose or even go bankrupt, but the industry as a whole benefits. Entire sectors can never be wiped out because of combat among local companies.

Suppose a firm or a small group of firms has discovered a new technique and thus has a cost edge over its rivals, of which some may go bankrupt. Some workers will thus be laid off. But most of them will be able to go to work for the expanding firm, provided it is located in America, not abroad; they will not have to transfer to another line of work or migrate to another geographical area. Interfirm rivalry, then, disrupts their lives but does not devastate them. They don't have to alter their life-style or live in despair. During the 1960s, if Chrysler laid you off, you could easily find a job with General Motors; but not anymore. Nowadays, because of intense foreign competition, a fired autoworker is unlikely to find work with another auto company. He has a better chance of being absorbed into some restaurant or retailing firm at a fraction of his old pay.[3]

All of the major U.S. industries that have so far survived the foreign assault—computers, aviation, autos, chemicals, steel, telecommunications, petroleum refining, primary metals, pharmaceuticals—were founded before the free trade year of 1973. That was the time when U.S. companies faced strong domestic but feeble foreign competition. However, among the new industries that have come up since the 1970s—robotics, video equipment, fax machines—the United States is a minor player. They are all U.S. inventions, yet the Japanese have been dominant in their development and production. The moral is clear: foreign competition may not only hurt old established concerns, it may also stifle the harnessing of new technology.

Domestic competition, by contrast, does not generate such perils. Once upon a time, major U.S. companies of today were the technology leaders in the world. Spurred by local rivalry, they were innovative, vigorous, and dynamic. The introduction of new patents and inventions did not retard their growth, nor did it efface entire industries. However, such times, like ghosts of a distant past, have faded from our memory. Lest we forget, barely two decades ago the United States was the sole economic superpower. Alas, free trade has turned the country into a vast graveyard of rusting plants and factories.

At the extreme, domestic rivalry may hurt an entire industry. Agriculture is an example we have studied before. Here soaring productivity generates declining incomes because of inelastic demand. But the nation as a whole benefits, while farm problems can be tackled through government assistance. Competition among farmers may hurt agriculture, but society is better off, and through adequate subsidies even farm incomes can be restored. By contrast, predatory foreign competition not only destroys entire industries but hurts a vast majority of the nation.

Competitive Protectionism

If domestic rivalry is far superior to the challenge from abroad, then it stands to reason that economic policy should encourage local competition while stifling foreign trade. The government should step in to increase and enforce rivalry at home while protecting domestic firms from global competition. Such an idea may be called competitive protectionism.

For countries well endowed with people and natural resources, competitive protectionism is far superior to free trade. Trade per se has no inherent virtue. It helps because it increases competition, which has an appeal of its own. But trade, as we have seen, can also be destructive, except where domestic substitutes of foreign goods are unavailable. Competitive protectionism retains the merits of competition while avoiding the demerits of free trade.

Competitive protectionism is very different from the traditional concept of trade restriction, which is backed mainly by special interest groups and politicians.[4] The replacement of foreign rivalry with domestic competition is an idea grounded purely in economics. In the case of the United States, it is designed to maximize the living standard—as measured by the real wage of the nonsupervisory workers who constitute 80 percent of the labor force—by harnessing existing technology and resources.

Competitive protectionism calls on the government not only to restrict international commerce but also to abolish all forms of monopolies or oligopolies. The government may use its existing antitrust laws or introduce new legislation. The idea is to increase rivalry among domestic firms sharply while protecting them from the depredations of foreign exporters.

Protection should not be granted on a piecemeal basis, as has been the case in recent years in the United States and Australia, where a few industries such as autos, steel, and textiles have been granted moderate shelter[5] while other trade grew by leaps and bounds. Protection should be extended to the entire high-wage manufacturing sector that has been shedding workers to low-paying service industries. Trade should be reduced to some optimal level, which can be calculated from international trade statistics. For instance, in the United States the standard of living was rising until 1973, the year the country became a free trade economy. Economic policy should first aim at restricting trade to the proportion of GNP prevailing in, say, 1972 or 1970. This means that the trade/GNP ratio, currently at 25 percent, should be cut in half. Later, trade may be restrained further to the level that historically produced the largest increase in the real wage in normal times, excluding wars.

The United States has been a relatively closed economy through much of its history. The new legislation should aim at retrieving that status while spurring domestic competition.

Foreign Investment and Technology

Restrictions applying to trade should not be extended to foreign investment and technology. The international transfer of technology is a great boon to humankind, because it can cure the problems of hunger and deprivation that plague the world. Unlike foreign competition in goods, foreign technology has no predatory effects, except when it harms the environment. But that can be precluded through strict antipollution laws.

There has been a tremendous rise in direct foreign investment across nations since the war. During the 1950s and 1960s, U.S. capital flowed to Europe, Asia, and Australia. American multinational firms opened plants to extract raw materials as well as to produce finished goods abroad.[6]

Throughout the 1940s, the United States enjoyed a large surplus in its balance of trade, a situation that continued during the 1950s and the 1960s. Flush with all that foreign exchange, the U.S. multinationals purchased foreign corporations or built factories in other countries. In the process they transferred advanced technology from which the host countries benefited greatly. The benefits came in the form of greater productivity as well as high-quality products. Of course, the multinationals also profited handsomely, but the flow of benefits was not just a one-way street, as some critics of foreign investment claim.[7]

During the late 1970s and the early 1980s, the U.S. balance of payments ran up increasing deficits. This time foreign producers had a large cache of foreign exchange, or dollars, which they eventually used to acquire American corporations and build new factories in the United States.[8] By 1990 not only the United States but also a host of other countries had large positions in foreign investment.

Figure 9.1 offers a bird's-eye view of direct foreign investment in different countries. The bars represent the percent of such investment in a country's GDP. Since the U.S. GDP is very large, foreign investment percentages in America are small, but with so many countries investing, foreign holdings in the United States now far exceed U.S. holdings abroad.[9]

American investment is large in Germany, Canada, the United Kingdom, and Australia. On the other hand, Britain, Japan, and the Netherlands have large holdings in the United States.

The main benefit of foreign inflow is the state-of-the-art technology that the host country receives without sinking large sums into the process of innovation. The research and development costs have already been incurred by the foreign investors. They bring capital and new technology to the host country, and, unless they restrain competition, their arrival cannot but be beneficial.[10]

It's true that the bulk of foreign inflow springs from the country's own trade deficit, which is especially harmful to an importer of manufactures, and it would be ideal if such inflow could occur without this shortfall. But the deficit would have even deadlier consequences without foreign investment.

In the absence of foreign inflow U.S. interest rates in the 1980s would have been higher, and high interest rates impede all forms of investment. This is one reason the nation was able to maintain its moderate rate of capital formation despite an exceptionally low rate of saving by households. Foreign inflows, then, helped directly as well as indirectly to stabilize investment, despite the huge federal budget deficits.

The United States has had a long tradition of foreign investment in a variety of industries. During the eighteenth and nineteenth centuries such inflows occurred in light manufacturing and

FIGURE 9.1
Foreign Direct Investment, 1990

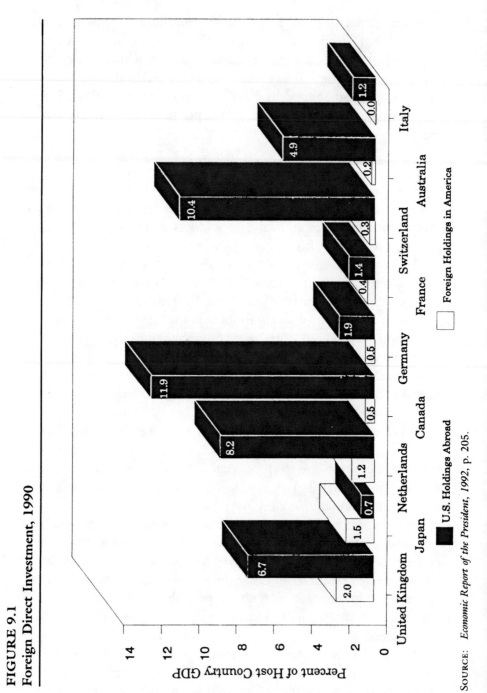

SOURCE: *Economic Report of the President, 1992*, p. 205.

railroads. Not surprisingly, the country had a substantial deficit in its international account. Foreign technology and capital aided in the process of industrialization.[11] It can do the same today.

As far as productivity and real earnings are concerned, the origin of investment makes no difference. It may be of U.S. or foreign source. So long as this investment helps reverse the industrial erosion, the United States will prosper, as will any other nation.

Already the foreign presence in U.S. industry is substantial. Automobiles, consumer electronics, steel, computers, telecommunications, and so on have benefited from significant amounts of foreign-based technology and capital. And nothing should be done to restrain this inflow.[12]

Competitive Versus Monopolistic Protection

The concept of protection is nothing new; it is almost as old as civilization. Even today much of the non-Western world practices it.[13]

Modern protectionism, however, is monopolistic in character; that is to say, governments shield a variety of industries from imports without altering the uncompetitive market structure. In developing countries with high levels of protection, firms have few domestic rivals. This is the case with India, Mexico, Brazil, and Argentina, among others. Monopolistic protectionism thus means shielding domestic monopolistic companies from foreign competition.

U.S. trade is freer today than ever before, but some industries have been able to win a modicum of protection. Notable among them are steel and automobiles, both of which are monopolistic.

Monopolistic protectionism is the worst of all commerical policies because it stifles competition altogether. But exposing monopolistic firms to international competition can also be dangerous if the home firms, despite their best effort, are unable to meet the foreign challenge. This is what has happened in Australia and the United States since the 1970s. With domestic manufacturers unable to compete with foreign companies, millions of high-paying jobs have vanished. But granting protection to such inefficient industries without injecting a strong dose of interfirm rivalry only perpetuates inefficiency.[14]

Free trade can be destructive for nations importing manufactures. Monopolistic protectionism can be, too; but this should not be confused with competitive protectionism. Competitive protectionism retains the best of both worlds, especially for countries well endowed with natural resources. Such nations don't need to import large quantities of raw materials; hence, they don't have to export much to pay for imports. Moreover, these countries don't have to generate a high growth in labor productivity because their other natural resources are so productive. As illustrated by U.S. history, they can enjoy a decent living standard without vast levels of saving and capital formation.

However, monopolistic protectionism is hazardous to the health of any economy, whether rich or poor in resources. This kind of policy has no rational economic basis.

The Historical Perspective

Is there any precedent for competitive protectionism? Yes. In fact, all successful countries have practiced it unintentionally at one time or another. There are even some that have followed it intentionally with astounding success. The modern-day miracles of Japan and Korea were built with overt government policies of competitive protectionism. Both countries limited foreign access to their markets but encouraged intense rivalry among domestic firms.[15]

Take, for instance, the automobile industry. Japan had a very small local market for cars in the 1950s and 1960s, yet it had many auto producers—Toyota, Nissan, Honda, Mitsubishi, Isuzu, Subaru, and Suzuki, among others. The United States, by contrast, had an auto market at least ten times larger. Yet it had only four producers—General Motors, Ford, Chrysler, and American Motors.

In industry after industry, the U.S. market structure was monopolistic, with one or two predominant firms, whereas in Japan, most industries had ten or more major suppliers for a much smaller market. America followed free trade; Japan, competitive protectionism. Today, Japan is the industrial leader of the world, whereas the United States is gasping for breath.

Korea followed the same pattern as Japan, encouraging intense rivalry among local firms while sheltering them from foreign rivals. Australia, on the other hand, essentially followed the United States by broadly reducing tariffs while granting modest subsidies to selected industries. Today, Korea's growth performance is second only to Japan's, whereas Australia suffers from falling wages and mounting foreign debt: another victory for competitive protectionism![16]

How did Korea and Japan get this idea? To my knowledge, no one has ever formalized this concept and analyzed its pros and cons.

Korea and Japan apparently studied the history of early industrialization in affluent nations. They discovered that almost all of them had prospered by developing manufacturing under the umbrella of protectionism. Moreover, in its embryonic stage, manufacturing in most countries was highly competitive.

Table 9.1 displays the average tariff rates in selected years between 1820 and 1913 in the modern-day affluent countries. They are among the wealthiest nations today and are all champions of free trade, with tariffs on their manufactures averaging 5 percent. But look at their history, at how they developed until 1913, when their industries were still fairly competitive. After that year their tariffs did not disappear or even decline, but their markets became uncompetitive. The concept of competitive protection does not apply to them thereafter.

In the early stage of industrialization, gutsy entrepreneurs in every country started new ventures with a small amount of capital or financing. They grew by trial and error. Some failed, some succeeded. Much of the industry was light when compared to today's standards. But in those days, manufacturing, either in factories or at home, was a revolutionary concept because of the relatively sophisticated nature of the new technology.

In the United States, early industry included cotton textiles, lumber, iron, shoes, wagons, leather, and machinery. In Europe, Australia, and Canada, economic development proceeded in much

TABLE 9.1

Manufactured Goods Tariff Rates in Industrial Countries, 1820–1913*

Country	1820	1875	1902	1913
Australia	NA	NA	6	16
Canada	NA	NA	17	26
Denmark	30	15–20	18	14
France	NA	12–15	34	20
Germany	10	4–6	25	13
Italy	NA	8–10	27	18
Sweden	NA	3–5	23	20
United States	40	40–50	73	44

SOURCES: *World Development Report* (Washington, D.C.: The World Bank, 1991), p. 97; Kym Anderson, "Tariffs and the Manufacturing Sector," in *The Australian Economy in the Long Run,* eds. Rodney Maddock and Ian W. McLean (New York: Cambridge University Press, 1987), p. 179.

* Unweighted average percentages.

the same way. But at one time or another all these countries felt it necessary to erect high tariff walls. In fact, the United States, the nation with the fastest rate of industrialization and wage growth, was also the ringleader in protectionism.

Tariffs were introduced partly for their ability to produce revenue and partly to protect industry. Whatever their intended purpose, they helped nations industrialize. Today, these industrial countries are among the wealthiest nations. Such is the proven force of competitive protectionism.

Forms of Protection

Although tariffs on imports have been the principal instrument for regulating trade, protection can be granted in many ways. The idea is to raise the price of imported goods or to reduce the cost of production for domestic import-competing industries.

Tariffs are simply taxes imposed on foreign products at the port of entry. They are mainly of two types. An *ad valorem*, or value, tariff is a certain percentage, normally fixed, by which the product price is raised. A *specific* tariff, by contrast, is on a physical unit, such as a thousand dollars on every car or a hundred dollars on every television set.

Tariffs are easy to administer and can raise substantial revenues for the government. This is one reason why so many countries have used tariffs as the main form of protection today and in the past.[17]

Another form of protection is the *quota*, which is a ceiling on the imported quantity of any product. Quotas can be fixed or variable. An importer is allowed to obtain a fixed quantity of foreign goods or a certain percentage of local production. Even though quotas can also be specific or ad valorem, so far only specific ones have been in vogue. Quotas and tariffs normally have the same effects on domestic prices, except that with quotas the government collects no revenue, which goes to the importing firms.

Quotas, like tariffs, are open restraints on imports. There are many covert restraints as well, used principally by Japan and Korea in recent years. Product standards are the main form of covert protectionism. Here foreign products are simply declared substandard to discourage their access to home markets. Protection can also be conferred through cost savings to producers of import-competing goods. Here the chief instrument is a subsidy related to either an industry's output or its exports. U.S. shipbuilding, for instance, receives financing on favorable terms in addition to direct grants. Agriculture around the world gets payments from national governments. All these are various forms of subsidies.

Economists generally argue that subsidies are better than tariffs and quotas on grounds of social welfare. Free traders dislike all forms of protectionism but contend that subsidies do the least damage.[18] However, in these days of horrendous budget deficits, subsidies, which can cost a lot of money, are not necessarily superior to tariffs, which produce revenue.[19]

Another covert form of protectionism is the use of exchange controls. With these a country simply keeps its own currency cheap relative to foreign currencies. Cheap home currency means cheap home goods and expensive foreign goods. This is, then, yet another way of encouraging exports and discouraging imports.

Tariffs are the best way of granting protection. They are simple and easy to administer and also produce ample revenue for governments strapped by budget deficits. Tariffs definitely raise the prices of import-competing goods when granted to monopolistic industries; but if they are combined with sharply increased competition among local firms, their inflationary effect over time is likely to be minimal.

Competition Policy

Most advanced nations today have some form of antimonopoly or procompetition policy represented by the so-called antitrust laws. However, these laws are either outdated or poorly enforced, especially in the United States.

Antitrust legislation may be broadly defined as a body of rules that businesses must follow in their decisions on production, firm size, and interfirm relations affecting the degree of competition within an industry. Such rules have evolved over a considerable length of time. Laws have been developed to limit the ability of firms to acquire competitors, collude with them to fix prices, or restrain competition in any other form.

Until the eighteenth and early nineteenth centuries, U.S. industries were very competitive even as they flourished behind high tariff walls. Each sector had a large number of firms with little control over market supply and price.

Toward the end of the nineteenth century, however, some business buccaneers got together to fix prices and reduce output in a variety of industries. What businessmen detest most is competition, which increases uncertainty and trims profits. They are also, in general, wary of government intervention and regulations, lest their profits be adversely affected. Regulation is, of course, welcome to them if it cuts competition and ensures a steady and high return.

Toward the end of the nineteenth century, U.S. corporations throve as never before. The economy grew at an unprecedented pace while small businesses were gobbled up by a few giants. The wheeling and dealing that occurred among businessmen at the time earned them the label "robber barons." So outrageous were their practices that the whole country was up in arms. In response, in 1890 Congress passed the Sherman Antitrust Act, which barred any person or corporation from forming monopolies or stifling competition in any way. This, however, turned out to be only a carrot dangled before an aroused public by the business-dominated Congress.

For the next few decades, the Sherman Act was interpreted by the courts in a way that emasculated the labor unions. Their strikes were ruled to be anticompetitive practices, while trusts—the popular form of monopolies in those days—continued to flourish.

Other antimonopoly laws followed the Sherman Act. The Clayton Act was passed in 1914 to bar specific practices such as price discrimination, the use of exclusive or tying contracts, acquisition of stock in competing businesses to crimp competition, and so on. The same year another act established the Federal Trade Commission to investigate and prosecute firms charged with the restraint of competition.

The Clayton Act was amended in 1936, 1938, and 1950 to outlaw deceptive advertising and anticompetitive mergers. None of the antitrust acts, however, overtly prohibits monopoly.

The impact of the antitrust legislation has been extremely limited, in part because Congress has not put teeth into it. Courts have also interpreted the laws to dampen their effectiveness. Controversy has centered on whether bigness itself is outlawed or whether the firm's behavior is what really matters.

The first important cases, both in 1911, involved the American Tobacco Company and Standard Oil. The tobacco giant had already gobbled up 250 rivals, while the oil conglomerate had claimed more than 120 victims. Both these companies were convicted of antitrust violations and were split—Standard Oil into thirty-three subsidiaries and American Tobacco into sixteen. In these cases, the Supreme Court upheld the convictions. But in the case of U.S. Steel in 1920, the company was acquitted of violating the Sherman Act, because even though it controlled nearly 60 percent of the market, its behavior was not considered predatory. Thus was born the rule that mere size unaccompanied by aggressive pricing or conduct was not illegal.

In 1945, however, the Supreme Court reversed itself in a case involving the Aluminum Company of America, or Alcoa, which controlled 90 percent of its market. The Court held the firm to be in violation of antitrust acts because of its huge market share. Here size per se turned out to be a culprit.

Later the United States Shoe Machinery Corporation was also convicted of antitrust violation because of its size. During the 1950s and the 1960s, however, few new precedents were established regarding the competitive practices of businesses, because even though several important actions were initiated by the Justice Department, they were mostly settled through consent decrees. Few required divestiture of companies.

In recent years again, behavior rather than bigness has become the crucial determinant of antitrust violations. Two cases involving International Business Machines (IBM) and American Telephone and Telegraph (AT&T) illustrate the point.

The Justice Department took IBM to court in 1969 for controlling over 70 percent of the mainframe computer market but then dropped the suit in 1982 after long wrangling. In the mind of the new administration, the company's size was no longer the culprit. The IBM case also set a bad precedent in that any company charged with antitrust violations knew it could fight a long war of attrition and ultimately settle out of court on favorable terms.

In the suit involving AT&T in 1982, the company agreed to be split off from local telephone companies and from parts of another subsidiary, Western Electric. Although hailed as a historic breakthrough in the communications industry, the AT&T suit was also over predatory behavior rather than size.

Since the 1970s there have been scattered attempts to apply the antitrust statutes to foreign producers as well. The so-called Matsushita suit of 1974 is a case in point. During the 1950s, several electronic companies in Japan, with the blessings of its Ministry of International Trade and Industry (MITI), formed an export cartel. Television sets were sold at lower prices in the United States than at home. The cartel, through this price discrimination approach—which was barred by the Clayton Act—drove many American firms out of business, and the Japanese gained a large share of the market.

Finally, U.S. firms sued to halt the Japanese practice of export dumping, but the Supreme Court rejected their claim of injury. The Court held that since the export cartel had shown no intent to lower prices, only to raise them later after driving U.S. firms out of business, no harm had been done to U.S. consumers. Hence the cartel was not guilty of predatory pricing.

This is the kind of garbled thinking behind free trade that has crimped the American living standard since 1973. The Court failed to realize that nearly 80 percent of consumers are also the workers and their families who are compelled to live with reduced wages resulting from predatory foreign competition.

During the 1980s, the government adopted an extremely lenient attitude toward antimonopoly violations, even when mergers occurred in an industry with just four firms. The acquisition of American Motors by Chrysler in 1987 is a case in point. This was just one of several hundred large mergers that occurred during the 1980s. Wall Street financiers and investment bankers joined hands to devise new financial instruments to facilitate the merger wave. Corporate giants such as Kraft, Nabisco, Gulf Oil, Getty Oil, RCA, Burlington Industries, TWA, and Federated Stores, among many others, were taken over by other giants. In the process corporate debt skyrocketed. All this occurred with the blessings of the Reagan administration, which presumably believed in competition.

Today, the U.S. market is more monopolistic than ever before. Most industries are either dominated by local giants or are withering under the onslaught of foreign competition.

Many other countries, such as Germany, Japan, and the United Kingdom, also have antimonopoly statutes, mostly enacted after the Second World War. But these countries take a somewhat conciliatory attitude toward cartels, especially when an industry is declining. Although overtly committed to competition, they permit firm mergers and collusion to effect an orderly withdrawal from dying sectors. Despite this conciliation toward cartels, both Germany and Japan have an industrial structure that is much less concentrated than that in the United States. The same goes for Korea, Taiwan, Hong Kong, Singapore, and the much vaunted newly industrialized countries.[20]

10

A Five-Year Plan for Economic Revival

It's now time to recapitulate all we have learned in the preceding pages and to use our knowledge for America's economic revival. Let's first take a look at the facts and the lessons, one at a time.

1. Ever since 1973, when the United States became a free trade economy for the first time in its history, the normally positive link between real wages and productivity has been severed. Real earnings of nonsupervisory workers, who constitute nearly 80 percent of the labor force, have seen a steady shrinkage in spite of rising productivity. Manufacturing wages have sunk to their 1965 level, and in some services such as retailing earnings have tumbled below their 1950 lows. In fact, after-tax retail earnings are now close to the abysmal wages prevailing during the decade of the Great Depression. Such has been the earnings carnage caused by free trade.

2. All this has occurred against a background of modestly rising GNP and per capita national income, so that the earnings debacle has remained hidden from public view; a few econo-mists have recognized it, but the mainstream has seen no cause for alarm.

3. Free trade has led to intense foreign competition in high-wage manufacturing, which first slowed its absorption of new-comers into the labor force, and then in the late 1980s began to shed workers, who in turn had to find jobs in low-paying ser-vices; whence the nationwide slide in real earnings.

4. Real wages fell even in high-productivity manufacturing despite soaring hourly output, because free trade caused a sharp decline in the relative prices of manufactured goods. This is the vicious phenomenon of "agrification," which in the past af-flicted only agriculture, where rising productivity was associated with declining earnings and profits. Hence free trade is respon-sible for the agrification of America.

5. With low-productivity sectors expanding at the cost of high-productivity sectors, free trade has also initiated a slow-down in national productivity growth. This has occurred even though capital formation has been close to the historic norm.

6. Of the twelve countries analyzed in previous chapters—the United States, Britain, Australia, India, Italy, Canada, Mexico, France, Japan, Korea, Germany, and Taiwan—only Germany has pursued free trade through much of its history. All the others, except for India and Mexico, became affluent by adopt-ing competitive protectionism at least over the first two centu-ries of their development. India's economy never got off the ground because it followed the worst possible commerical pol-icy of monopolistic protectionism. When Mexico opened its borders to foreign influences through borrowing abroad, it prospered for a few years during the 1970s but has been in a depression since 1982.

7. All successful countries in the postwar period except Germany owe their prosperity to competitive protectionism. These include Japan, Korea, Taiwan, Hong Kong, and Singapore. Others, such as the United States, Australia, and to some extent Canada, that switched to freer trade have suffered a drop in real earnings in spite of rising productivity. They have been overtaken by the agrification syndrome.

8. Competitive protectionism is thus a proven idea with a lot of success; free trade is historically a relatively new idea with a lot of failure.

9. History shows that countries with a large bounty of natural resources don't need giant growth in labor productivity to become affluent; only those with few resources do. That's why the productivity slowdown in the United States, Canada, and Australia relative to Japan, Korea, and Germany is no cause for alarm. Far more alarming is the laissez-faire policy followed by the laggard nations. In fact, almost every country except America has benefited from the American policy of free trade.

10. The latest victims of free trade are the people of what was formerly called East Germany, which was reunited with West Germany in October 1990. German Chancellor Helmut Kohl rushed to expose the formerly protected economy of the East to intense foreign competition, in the mistaken belief that laissez-faire would quickly bring prosperity to the area. Instead, the opposite occurred. The area's manufacturing, shaky but manageable, has collapsed, real wages have sunk, and unemployment has soared to a depression level of 17 percent.[1] Even after pouring hundreds of billions of dollars into the East, the government has been unable to halt the ill effects of its misguided policy. If those employed in make-work programs are taken into account, the unemployment rate jumps to 40 percent.[2] The great depression of eastern Germany, now in full swing, is a testimony to how fast free trade can decimate manufacturing and thus destroy a protected but viable economy.

Monopolistic Free Trade

U.S. commerical policy since the war has been a classic study in self-contradiction. It is a medley of discordant ideas that have led to unintended consequences. The same goes for mainstream economics, which champions free trade for domestic monopolistic firms.

Nothing illustrates the bankruptcy of U.S. policy better than the fundamental contradiction between free trade and the implementation of antitrust laws. Few firms were ever charged with antimonopoly violations, fewer were convicted, and still fewer were divested of their holdings.

As if that weren't bad enough, monopolistic firms, accustomed to the comforts of a captive domestic market, have increasingly been exposed to competition from hardier foreign businesses, which for years had honed their skills in hand-to-hand combat at home. The result was inevitable: foreign tigers slowly tore off bits of the domestic corporate dinosaurs, and today many U.S. behemoths are on the list of endangered species.

Exposing monopolistic firms to maximum international competition may be called monopolistic free trade. This is the policy the United States has followed since the war. The only thing worse than monopolistic free trade is monopolistic protectionism. There is so much clamor for trade liberalization in America that anytime a distressed sector seeks protection, economists claim the country is growing protectionist. Yet the U.S. volume of trade is now the highest in its history. The American economy has never been more open or free.

But is there any antimonopoly clamor? The country is busy exposing elephantine firms to foreign sharks and still wonders why so many are bleeding and vanishing.

The policy of monopolistic free trade reached a crescendo during the Republican administrations of the 1980s. On the one hand, giant firms swallowed other giants in a frenzy of takeovers, raising monopoly power to unprecedented heights while the Justice Department stood idly by; on the other hand, the administration opened new rounds of global negotiations for still freer trade. The volume of trade as a percentage of GNP had already doubled during the 1970s, only to rise further in the 1980s.

Domestic rivalry is the single most important weapon for fighting international competition;[3] yet the administration did nothing while domestic competition, whatever remained of it, was submerged under the deluge of mergers.[4] In this background, further liberalization of trade was like throwing a bloated amateur into the ring to box with the world champion. One punch, and the weakling hit the floor. During the 1980s, for the first time since the Great Depression, employment in manufacturing fell, and continues to tumble.

Not only has the real wage continued to fall, but the United States has also been saddled with huge trade deficits, which reached a peak of $160 billion in 1987. Since then the deficit has declined somewhat because of the falling dollar and falling U.S. wages but was still running between $75 billion and $100 billion a year in 1992. Even at this level, the deficit costs the nation 2 million jobs a year.

Thus, while the policy of monopolistic free trade began soon after the war, it reached its height in the 1980s only to generate the worst possible effects of deindustrialization, agrification, and deficit trade.

Despite its deadly consequences, the government's misconception of and obsession with free trade continued. Here is an astounding claim from the 1991 *Economic Report of the President*:

> As the world's largest economy, the United States has greatly benefited from the rapid growth of trade.[5]

Where are these benefits? you wonder. There is more:

> Through these international linkages, firms achieve greater productivity . . .[6]

If international linkages have brought greater productivity, why does everyone lament the productivity slide today? The facts reveal a gaping hole between the Bush administration's claims and reality.

North American Free Trade Agreement
(NAFTA)

As if the policy of monopolistic free trade had not done enough damage, the United States compounded its blunders by reaching a free trade agreement with Mexico on August 12, 1992. Commonly known as the North American Free Trade Agreement (NAFTA), the accord also includes Canada, but this does not make much difference because a similar treaty with Canada already exists. The idea is to create a common market of 360 million people along the same lines as the European Common Market or that created by the U.S.-Canada Free Trade Agreement of 1987.

Since 1985 Mexico has reduced its tariff and nontariff barriers to international trade. Even so, its tariffs, quotas, and import license restrictions are far higher than U.S. tariffs on Mexican imports. The fundamental U.S. goal "is the removal of all tariffs and the removal or reduction of nontariff trade barriers."[7] According to the 1991 *Economic Report of the President:*

> . . . a free-trade agreement would boost the international competitiveness of both U.S. and Mexican firms. To reduce costs, companies often allocate phases of a manufacturing process among a number of nations. A free-trade agreement with Mexico would further encourage this natural international division of labor. By lowering the overall costs of U.S. manufacturing firms, a free-trade agreement would make U.S. firms more competitive against imports in the United States and against other countries' exports in the world market. *This gain in manufacturing competitiveness encourages productivity and higher wages.* The proposed free-trade agreement would similarly boost the competitiveness of Mexican firms. Additionally, the two-way reduction in trade barriers would benefit by supporting its market reforms and encouraging economic growth.[8] (My italics.)

NAFTA proposes to eliminate customs duties on nearly ten thousand products over fifteen years. In addition, it aims at an unhindered flow of investment and financial services among North American countries.[9]

In the quote just presented from the Bush administration's report, I have italicized the statement about higher wages. With wages falling since 1973, the government has been reluctant to refer to them in its annual appraisal of the economy. It normally speaks of trade as promoting growth, living standards, real incomes, per capita GNP, or productivity. The 1991 ERP is perhaps the first official statement of a link between free trade and higher wages.

NAFTA will simply compound the ills created by the administration's policy of monopolistic free trade. In the short run, the United States and Canada would feel hardly any effect, while Mexico would face great disruption as a result of opening its borders. This is because the small size of the Mexican economy would barely create a ripple in the economies of its northern neighbors. But unemployment would soar in Mexico because of the large inflow of manufactures from its partners. Indeed, its economy could collapse much like that of the former East Germany, which, following the 1990 unification, was abruptly exposed to intense competition from West Germany and other countries.

Like East Germany, Mexico suffers from backward technology and inefficient, bloated state monopolies. The trauma of exposure to giant northern firms could be fatal to Mexican manufacturing. True, NAFTA proposes to open Mexican markets to its neighbors gradually, and to that extent the foreign onslaught would be contained. Yet the suffering would be massive in the short run, especially since Mexico, which has already been mired in a deep slump since 1982, will not, unlike East Germany, receive huge financial aid. I hope the Mexicans will take a closer look at East Germany's plight before endorsing NAFTA. In fact, the plight of East Germany offers a precious lesson to the United States as well, namely, that free trade can cripple an economy if manufacturing erodes.

Mexico's wage rates are a tiny fraction of those in Canada and the United States. Its productivity is also low and the level of technology relatively primitive. U.S. and Canadian multinationals would relocate their factories to Mexico in search of abysmal wages and train Mexicans to work in low-tech industries. In fact, the process has already begun, as in September 1992, just a month after the signing of NAFTA, Smith Corona decided to relocate its typewriter plant from New York to Mexico. Since these goods would partly come back to Canada and the United States, the result would be a further erosion of the Canadian and American manufacturing base. While manufacturing prices would fall, manufacturing wages would fall even more. Hence real, inflation-adjusted earnings in the two northern countries would plummet.

Since 1965, 1,800 American plants have moved to Mexico, and without any help from NAFTA. With NAFTA thousands more will rush over the border to take advantage of the penurious Mexican wage rates. If U.S. factories are already moving to Mexico in the absence of a free trade accord, it doesn't take a genius to figure out that when the accord actually goes into effect, U.S. businesses will stampede south of the Rio Grande. This would deal another crippling blow to the feeble American economy.

As unemployed manufacturing workers once again move to services, service wages would also decline owing to excess labor supply. U.S. productivity would, of course, rise as the emigrating firms reduce their costs, but real earnings would tumble. The principal beneficiaries would be the multinational firms and their executives, who would continue to be rewarded with multimillion-dollar bonuses.

Mexico would also attract investment from trade surplus countries such as Japan, Korea, and Taiwan, which could reduce their labor costs as well as transportation expenses by shifting some of their low-tech factories to America's southern neighbor, from where they would be able to export their goods to the United States and Canada at zero tariff rates. While U.S. and Canadian multinationals would be able to lower their costs, the foreign multinationals could lower theirs even more. Foreign firms have already been besting monopolistic North American firms in the arena of trade; now they would have an even greater advantage because of reduced transportation costs. Both Canada and the United States would eventually be on the losing end.

For Mexico there would be some benefits in the long run, but it could take at least a decade before they are realized in terms of decent wages. Mexico's industrial structure is also monopolistic, and initially a large number of domestic plants would shut down, thereby further worsening the current depression. Things could get really ugly before they get better. In the long run, however, there might be a payoff, as the country would be sought out by multinationals around the globe.

A Proposal for Competitive Protectionism in America

Monopolistic free trade has already devastated the U.S. economy, and NAFTA would further add to the damage. But something new has to be tried, especially since the current recession, already the longest since the war, could soon turn into a depression.[10]

My proposal is that the United States should reverse its policy of monopolistic free trade and turn to what worked best for it for over two centuries, namely, competitive protectionism. You may recall that U.S. tariffs were associated with rapid industrialization but free trade with rapid deindustrialization. In 1960, U.S. manufacturing imports constituted barely 5 percent of local production; in 1973, they were at 14 percent; and by 1990, they had jumped to over 40 percent. If nothing is done, the country will be nearly stripped of its industrial base. In 1980, 21 million people worked in manufacturing; in 1991, only 18 million remained, while the labor force climbed by 20 million. America's future is bleak if the current trends persist.

Because of poor implementation of ineffective antitrust laws, the U.S. industrial structure is concentrated beyond imagination. The largest corporations belonging to the *Fortune* 500 club produce nearly 70 percent of all output. In industry after industry, just three or four firms control more than half the sales.[11]

When only one firm exists in an industry, we call it a case of pure monopoly; when numerous firms battle in a sector, with none controlling over 10 percent of market share, the industry faces intense competition. Monopoly power is zero in the case of pure competition but 100 percent with pure monopoly. Most industries are neither monopolists nor purely competitive. That's why the concept of market share is so important; it can measure the extent of monopoly power exercised by one firm or a small group of firms.

The development experience of most countries shows that keen domestic rivalry is the single most important determinant of their affluence.[12] But keen rivalry calls for the creation of many small to medium-sized firms, and this is exactly what should be done now. *We should break up large firms controlling more than 10 percent of market share in any industry and at the same time actively guard them from foreign competition.*

In order to assess the degree of monopoly power in an industry, economists have devised the concept of the four-firm concentration ratio. This ratio measures the market share of the four largest firms in any sector. Since large corporations exercise undue control over market prices, the higher the concentration ratio, the greater the industry's monopoly power.

The Bureau of the Census used to compute four-firm concentration ratios roughly every five years. However, the last such computation was made in 1982. The government has failed to update the figures since then, lest the ugly effects of the merger mania of the 1980s on industrial concentration be discovered.

Few doubt that the concentration ratios among domestic producers, excluding foreign firms now operating on U.S. soil, have risen since 1982. But even if they have not, the 1982 Census data, as they are, present a sorry portrait of competition in America. Some of the most crucial sectors of the nation have concentration ratios exceeding 80 percent. For instance, the auto industry had a ratio of 97 percent, indicating that only four firms produced 97 percent of domestic cars. It's not surprising then that such inefficient, bloated firms have lost so much of their territory to smaller foreign rivals, which have been battle-tested at home.

Table 10.1 shows how some of the most concentrated industries were bludgeoned by imports between 1972 and 1990. With feeble enforcement of even feebler antitrust laws, industrial concentration in 1972, 1982, and 1990 was extremely high. Consequently, in the absence of high tariffs, imports in overly monopolistic industries soared. The second and third columns of the table show imports as a percentage of domestic production in selected industries in 1972 and 1990. For instance, in the auto industry, which has a concentration ratio of 97 percent, the import/production ratio nearly doubled to 47 percent. If you look back further, in 1967 the ratio was

TABLE 10.1
Import Performance of Highly Concentrated Industries, 1972 and 1990

Industry	Imports (% of Production, 1972)	Imports (% of Production, 1990)	Four-Firm Concentration Ratio (%)
Automobiles	24	47	97
Household appliances	6	16	94
Glass products	0.3	22	85
Turbines and generators	3	26	84
Telephone and telegraph equipment	2	21	76
Photographic equipment	8	23	74
Television sets	45	195	67
Tires	9	23	66
Primary aluminum	6	20	64
Farm machinery	0.1	26	53
Computers	3	40	50 + *
Steel	13	20	42
Semiconductors	12	50	40

SOURCES: U.S. Department of Commerce, *U.S. Industrial Outlook* (Washington, D.C.: U.S. Government Printing Office, various years); U.S. Bureau of the Census, *1982 Census of Manufactures* (Washington, D.C.: U.S. Government Printing Office, 1982).

* Computers are not included in the Census data; but it is well known that IBM alone has more than half the industry's sales. I have therefore placed its four-firm concentration at simply 50 + %.

only 9 percent, barely a fifth of its 1990 figure. But the real carnage occurred in computers, semiconductors and, above all, consumer electronics such as televisions. In computers, for instance, where IBM has long had a corner on nearly three fourths of the industry, imports were only 3 percent of domestic production in 1972; in 1990, they had soared more than thirteen times to 40 percent. Semiconductor imports were half the U.S. production in 1990, but television sets had an import ratio of 195, suggesting that imports were nearly twice as large as domestic output.

When just four firms control 40 percent or more of a market, we call it a monopolistic industry, the extent of monopoly rising with the extent of control. Anything less than 40 percent signals an industry with intense rivalry. The import performance of such industries is displayed in Table 10.2. There are three low-concentration sectors in which imports soared between 1972 and 1990—women's footwear, textile machinery, and women's dresses. But these are also the sectors where you would expect intense competition from abroad, especially Third World countries, because the level of technology involved is relatively light, simple, and labor intensive. Ignoring the low-tech areas, the other low-concentration industries, such as plastics, pharmaceuticals, and petroleum refining, successfully defended their turf from foreign conquest. The import share of these areas did not exceed 10 percent. The moral of the story is that *high market concentration invites high imports.*

Among highly concentrated industries, aircraft manufacturing, with a concentration ratio of 64 percent, is the only area that has

TABLE 10.2
Import Performance of Unconcentrated and Low-Tech Industries, 1972 and 1990

Industry	Imports (% of Production, 1972)	Imports (% of Production, 1990)	Four-Firm Concentration Ratio (%)
Women's footwear	46	217	38
Petroleum refining	8	10	28
Pharmaceutical preparations	2	8	26
Paints and allied products	1	1	24
Textile machinery	64	94	22
Plastics products	2	5	22
Women's dresses	3	62	6

SOURCES: U.S. Department of Commerce, *U.S. Industrial Outlook* (Washington, D.C.: U.S. Government Printing Office, various years); U.S. Bureau of the Census, *1982 Census of Manufactures* (Washington, D.C.: U.S. Government Printing Office, 1982). Also see U.S. Department of Commerce, *Statistical Abstract of the United States* (Washington, D.C.: U.S. Government Printing Office, 1988), pp. 707 and 716.

remained free from heavy imports; there are two reasons for this. One is the active U.S. official support to this industry in the form of defense subsidies. In fact, with the aid of subsidies, even Europe now has a viable aircraft business. The other reason is that the overhead expense of aerospace firms is so large that it discouraged most other countries in the past. However, the future could be different, because Japan is already launching an assault on America's supremacy in this area. The U.S. government may have to match its Japanese counterpart in this regard.

In order to reverse the silent depression in real earnings, we have to protect manufacturing from foreign invasion. There is absolutely no question about that. But simultaneously we should break up the mammoth firms so as to prevent an increased abuse of monopoly power. The idea is to generate not monopolistic protectionism but competitive protectionism. *The idea is to replace today's foreign competition with domestic competition.*

Other economists have also spoken of a possible link between high concentration and imports. Harvard economist F. M. Scherer and his coauthor, David Ross, suggest this:

> Had the United States Steel Corporation been broken up in 1920, it is at least arguable that the industry would not have performed so sluggishly in the 1950s and 1960s, falling behind technologically and setting the stage for *rapidly increasing imports*. Had U.S. automobile production not been concentrated in the hands of four companies, all with headquarters in Detroit, it seems likely that high-quality compact cars would have been available from domestic sources sooner.[13] (My italics.)

The United States has suffered the depredations of monopolistic free trade since 1973, the watershed year; let us try competitive protectionism, and within a few years the nation will be back on its feet. The technology is there; the factories are there, empty and abandoned. What is lacking is a proper understanding of the nature of international trade.

As a practical matter average tariffs should be raised from the current 5 percent rate to 40 percent in order to reduce the import share of GNP to the 1972 level of roughly 6 percent.[14] Today, this share is about 13 percent.

Tariffs should be granted to all import-competing industries where the four-firm concentration ratio is greater than 40 percent. They should be phased in over five years so that foreign producers have time to adjust to the new policy. But in order to stop the U.S. industrial hemorrhage, there should be an immediate increase from 5 percent to 20 percent, and the remaining 20 percent rise can be phased in over the next four years.

The main sectors to be protected are automobiles, consumer electronics, heavy industrial machinery, farm equipment, household appliances, photographic equipment, primary metals, computers, semiconductors, tires, telephone and telegraph apparatus, light machine tools, robotics, and facsimile machines, among others.

The division of large firms into smaller entities should be accomplished at the same time that the average tariff rate is raised to 20 percent. For instance, General Motors could be divided into four or five independent entities, depending on the current market share of each of its divisions. It could be split into Cadillac, Oldsmobile, Buick, and Chevrolet. Its fifth division, Pontiac, could be merged with Cadillac. Another entity could handle GM's foreign and other operations.

Similarly, Ford Motors should be split into Ford and Lincoln-Mercury. Chrysler, however, is small enough to be left intact.

The split among firms can be accomplished along the lines of the AT&T divestiture in 1982. Instead of owning one share of General Motors, for instance, its stockholders will now own shares of five independent firms, each with its own management.

IBM should also be split into five entities—four to handle domestic operations and one to handle foreign ones. Ideally, most *Fortune* 500 firms should be broken up to enhance domestic rivalry. Even those engaged in exports would become more competitive in world markets if they were split into smaller entities.

However, America's sickness in the arena of imports is critical. In the divestiture of firms, the import sector is where we should begin first. The government should appoint a commission to determine the breakup of giant import-competing corporations. Depending on their size, some may be split into five entities, some into four, and so on. It is imperative that in each import-competing industry there be ten to fifteen vigorous competitors, with none cornering more than 10 percent of the domestic market. In the auto industry, for instance, no single firm should have more than $25 billion in sales, which, though still large, is puny relative to GM's current sales, which exceed $120 billion per year.

Goods produced by unconcentrated industries should not be protected. Domestic competition is already strong in these areas, and no gain would come from competitive protectionism. Thus, plastics, footwear, textiles, and petroleum products, among others, need no protection. Raising tariffs in these goods would raise prices without large gains in productivity, which arise by breaking up corporate dinosaurs.

Research and Development Spending

Once monolithic firms have been split into small entities, they will prod each other to be innovative and competitive; but smaller businesses are usually reluctant to spend large sums on research and development (R and D). This is one area where the government will have to take an active role. As in Germany and Japan, the state should subsidize private R and D spending, of which the reward is at best uncertain.

During the 1980s, U.S. defense spending soared, even though as a share of GNP it remained below its historical norm. Now that the cold war is no more, defense spending ought to be reduced drastically, and a part of the saving should be diverted to R and D.

In the past, natural resources, combined with manufacturing, gave a great competitive edge to a nation. Today their role has declined, but they are still crucial to the living standard. It's true that of late the fastest-growing countries—Germany, Japan, Korea, Taiwan—have all been poor in resources. Their success has been in either the development or the purchase of state-of-the-art technology and the translation of that technology into high-quality products through the medium of intensely competitive firms. But that does not mean they no longer need natural resources, which they still import in abundance.

As long as natural resources are needed in production, even at today's truncated levels, the United States has an advantage over many other nations. But that advantage has to be supplemented with the discovery of new technology and high-tech products, which use far less in resources than current products. The state can play a crucial role in the discovery of new techniques just as it does in the creation of infrastructure.

This is also a way to keep the concentration of industry in check. The benefits of improved infrastructure go to all firms; state-supported technical discoveries should also be diffused among all firms. This would keep a lid on the growth of monopoly power.

At this point, a distinction should be made between new-product technologies and new-process technologies. U.S. firms have focused on the former, whereas their foreign counterparts have emphasized the latter. The trouble is that new products can easily be duplicated, but it is harder to copy a new process.[15]

By stressing process technology, Germany and Japan have come to dominate many product lines initially invented by Americans. Video cameras, video recorders, and fax machines are all U.S. inventions in which the important brand names are Japanese. In today's world, those with better processes for making old or new products are also the global economic leaders.

Science has produced such a variety of goods to meet human needs that few new products will succeed in the already saturated markets. Almost everything on earth can be done by machines. The emphasis should now be on perfecting these machines rather than discovering new ones. For instance, the government should pour vast amounts into reducing industrial pollution, so that already invented products can be built without damaging the environment.

Except in the case of the defense industry, the U.S. government has played a minor role in R and D. This role should be vastly expanded, with a special emphasis on new-process technologies. There the United States should be able to meet and even exceed the efforts of Germany and Japan. Such an effort should be an integral part of the policy of competitive protectionism.

Foreign Direct Investment

When splitting large firms in the United States, we have to take into account the heavy presence of foreign direct investment (FDI), especially in the crucial auto sector, where FDI is diverse and massive. Cross-border transactions involving exports, imports and joint ventures are common in this industry. GM has joint ventures with Toyota and Suzuki, Ford with Mazda, Chrysler with Mitsubishi, and so on. In addition, five Japanese firms—Honda, Mazda, Nissan, Toyota, and Subaru—have independent production facilities in the United States, while Toyota has a joint venture with GM in California and Mitsubishi has one with Chrysler in Illinois.

Table 10.3 presents a detailed account of the complex and intertwined automobile market in the United States in 1990. Total sales were about 9.3 million cars, of which nearly 6.1 million were produced on U.S. soil, while 3.2 million came from various other sources including Canada, Mexico, Japan, Europe, and Korea. Including North American imports, the U.S. Big Three had a 60 percent share of total sales. The domestic production share of the Japanese firms added up to 14 percent, and their import share was about 16 percent, for a combined total of 30 percent.

At this point, several questions arise. First, should we break up GM and Ford in spite of intense local competition from Japanese firms? The answer is yes. From our experience with the voluntary export restraint agreement between the United States and Japan in the 1980s, we know that the Big Three U.S. automakers frittered away the advantage they received from protectionism. They simply raised their prices, reaped huge profits, and paid exorbitant bonuses to their executives. The auto protection of the 1980s enhanced their monopoly power, and they abused it without reversing the erosion of the auto-manufacturing base.

For the purpose of restructuring, the North American operations of the Big Three should be separated from their plants in

TABLE 10.3
Auto Sales in the United States in 1990

Firm	Sales (Thousands of Units)	Market Share (%)
Chrysler	726	7.8
Ford	1,377	14.8
General Motors	2,654	28.6
Honda	435	4.7
Mazda	184	2.0
Mitsubishi	148	1.6
Nissan	96	1.0
Subaru	32	0.3
Toyota	415	4.5
Imports from the rest of North America	826	8.9
Other imports	2,396	25.8
Imports from Japan	(1,521)	(16.4)
Total sales	9,289	100.0

SOURCE: U.S. Department of Commerce, *U.S. Industrial Outlook* (Washington, D.C.: U.S. Government Printing Office, 1992), pp. 36–3 and 36–4.

other parts of the world and included in the domestic market. I propose that the Big Three should be converted into seven independent firms with a total of 60 percent market share. There are six Japanese producers that have a combined share of 30 percent. Under this reorganization, there will then be thirteen firms involved in local production controlling 90 percent of the auto market, the other 10 percent belonging to imports from Europe and Korea.

For the purpose of protection, all U.S. auto imports except those from within North America, where we have separate agreements, should be treated alike. It doesn't matter whether these imports come under American or non-American nameplates. Chrysler's imports from Japan should pay the same tariff as Mercedes-Benz imports from Germany. What is more important is that production facilities, not just assembly of the final product, be located on U.S. soil. Thus, all imported components should be taxed at the same rate as finished goods.

FDI is also strong in other American industries such as electronics, computers and petrochemicals. But nowhere is the complexity of FDI as great as in the auto industry. The automobile formula proposed above can be applied to other sectors as well. That is to say, first separate the North American operations of U.S. firms from their subsidiaries in other countries. Second, break up the big U.S. firms into two to four entities depending on their current market share. Third, form a separate entity dealing with operations outside North America. Finally, apply tariffs uniformly to all qualifying imports from countries outside the North American continent. Note that the qualifying import industries are all those where the four-firm concentration ratio is at least 40 percent.

Likely Effects of U.S. Protectionism

The form of protectionism to which most people object—and rightly so—is monopolistic protectionism. They feel that trade restrictions perpetuate inefficiency and exorbitant profits at the expense of the consumer. They do have a valid point, even though most consumers are also workers harmed by international competition. In the long run, everyone except monopolistic producers suffers, because the deadly combination of monopoly power and import restraints chokes innovation, dynamism and productivity.

However, competitive protectionism granted to concentrated industries cannot have any deleterious effects, especially in an economy like that of the United States that is blessed with natural resources and a large domestic market. Tariffs will reduce competition, but the divestiture of large firms will counter this effect. Overall, the degree of competition will stay the same. It may even increase, because many U.S. firms are among the largest in the world and their divestiture is bound to create intense rivalry at home. Tariffs become inflationary only when competition declines. With competitive protectionism, there is no such danger, especially today, when there is so much excess production capacity caused by the persistent recession.

In the first year, there might be a little extra inflation as the average tariff level is raised from the current 5 percent rate to 20 percent. But this will soon dissipate because of an immediate increase in or restoration of competition.

Thus, the combined effects of the current recession and increased competition are likely to keep tariffs from contributing much to inflation. But while prices stay in check, tariffs will divert American demand from foreign goods to those produced on U.S. soil. Factories will start humming again. Millions of new jobs in manufacturing, paying decent wages at the 1973 level, will be created. This will take the labor supply pressure away from services, so that their salaries will also rise.

Manufacturing will expand at the expense of services, thereby raising productivity growth in the economy. Overqualified people, who have been service workers for lack of good jobs, will get their old jobs back; they will take pride in their work again, and the current glum mood will turn into one of optimism. With the divestiture of large companies, the huge executive bonuses will also plummet. This along with rising real earnings will reverse the tidal wave of growing inequality and poverty.

Will Americans be deprived of high-quality foreign brands? Not at all. Faced with the loss of the huge American market, foreign producers will rush to open plants and factories in the United States. In the auto industry, Americans will not feel the absence of Japanese products for even a year. The production capacity of the Japanese auto plants located in the United States is already scheduled to rise from the current level of 1.6 million units to 2.5 million units by 1995.[16] U.S. protectionism will accelerate this process. The cars we now import from Japan will then be produced in the United States by the same producers. We will see a dramatic fall in imports, but there will be no diminution in the quality of goods available for U.S. consumption.

In the absence of a high tariff, the Big Three will be overwhelmed by Japanese transplants. With tariffs large enough to divert much U.S. demand to home-produced goods, all thirteen firms, seven local and six Japanese, will have a chance to prosper. Some German and other European firms will also most likely move facilities to the United States—provided, of course, that NAFTA is rescinded. Otherwise they would go to Mexico.

In consumer electronics, Sony, Magnavox, Goldstar, Panasonic, and Mitsubishi, among others, will move their production facilities to the United States rather than leave the entire American market to the likes of RCA, Zenith, and General Electric. All the U.S. conglomerates will be broken up, of course.

This process is likely to be duplicated in computers, farm machinery, tires, machine tools, and all other concentrated industries receiving protection. Thus, competitive protectionism will raise real earnings while maintaining the quality of goods consumed by Americans.

The U.S. domestic market is already huge. When income inequality declines because of falling executive wages and rising worker salaries, this market will expand even more, because high inequality is the bane of purchasing power. Competitive protectionism will unleash a virtuous cycle of expanding manufacturing, rising earnings, declining inequality, poverty, and homelessness, and a rapidly growing economy.

Other than extreme concentration of wealth, there is no illness of the U.S. economy that cannot be cured by competitive protectionism. So many factories and plants stand abandoned today because a lot of American demand for goods has gone to high-quality products from abroad. My proposal would divert this demand to goods produced on U.S. soil, by U.S. and foreign firms, and factories would once again buzz with production and excitement. The two-decade-long erosion of the American standard of living would then be reversed.

Tariffs will also raise substantial revenue for the government. As foreign goods are considered to be of high quality, it will take a large increase in the tariff rate to reduce demand for them. This suggests that the government could collect plenty of revenue from import duties. Trade data show that in 1990 merchandise imports were at $498 billion, of which about 64 percent, or $320 billion, were dutiable. The average tariff rate of 5 percent thus generated $16 billion in tariff revenue. Under my proposals, dutiable imports would be cut in half to $160 billion through an average tariff rate of 40 percent. This would generate $64 billion in revenue for the government in 1990 dollars.

If a higher tariff rate is needed to cut dutiable imports in half, the revenue generated would be even higher. In view of America's fondness for foreign products, this might very well be the case. Thus, my proposals would also trim the government's budget deficit.

Foreign Retaliation

U.S. protection is likely to stun the world, which is accustomed to America's self-destructive generosity of free trade. Countries with large trade surpluses with the United States will scream the loudest, because the new policy will hurt them slightly. Why only slightly?

Much of the trade surplus in Japan, Taiwan, Hong Kong, and Singapore has been wasted in their speculative markets, which rose to all-time highs by the end of 1989. While their economies expanded at a brisk pace of 6 to 8 percent per year during the 1980s, their stock and land prices at times rose at an annual rate of 50 percent. While foreign trade increasingly forced Americans into flipping hamburgers or into homelessness, speculators in Japan and the NICs were frolicking with their newfound riches. According to *Wall Street Journal* correspondent Yumiko Ono, in the 1980s, "the rapid rise of stock and real estate prices created a whole class of Japanese nouveaux riches and sent them on a free-spending spree. They took their pooches to yoga class, massaged their bodies with cream mixed with pure gold and blew mountains of cash every night at fancy restaurants."[17] It's true that the Japanese bubble has finally burst, beginning in 1990; still, the colossal speculative mania has done its damage to the economy not only of Japan but of the whole world.

The rate of unemployment in Japan and the NICs is very low—far smaller than in the United States. U.S. protectionism will only equalize these unemployment rates, lowering them in America and raising them elsewhere.

Europe will also be hurt somewhat by U.S. protectionism. But at the dawn of 1993, that continent formed a borderless common market, sharply increasing its own market size. What Europe loses from trade with the United States, it will more than make up from domestic market expansion.

In spite of these considerations there will be retaliation from other countries; but the United States, for many reasons, will be a victor in any trade war.

First, there is the huge trade deficit of some $75 billion to $100 billion a year; the deficit peaked in 1987 at $160 billion and has declined steadily since. Even if it falls to zero, that is no cause for celebration, because any country can balance trade through depreciation of its currency and wages. The real challenge is to eliminate the deficit while maintaining your earnings and the value of your currency.

If present trends continue, the trade deficit, also known as the negative balance on the current account, will fluctuate around $80 billion. High tariffs will eliminate this deficit in one year, creating 2 million manufacturing jobs in the process. This would be the minimum benefit of protectionism in spite of foreign retaliation.

Second, the main characteristic of U.S. foreign commerce is the so-called intraindustry trade. For a variety of reasons, the United States exports and imports vast quantities of nearly identical goods. In 1990, the country imported $87 billion of automotive equipment but also exported some $37 billion of the same product. Its exports of machine tools were $154 billion, but its imports of similar tools were $116 billion. The whole process of intraindustry trade appears to be absurd, but that's another matter to be fully discussed in the next chapter.

Nearly 60 percent of America's trade is in nearly identical products. If foreign countries retaliate against U.S. goods, all the American companies have to do is divert their sales to the domestic market. If goods can be sold abroad, they can also be sold at home, and without incurring transportation expenses.

What, then, is the point of disrupting the current system and reshuffling trade? The point is that our minimum gain from the reshuffle would equal our trade deficit, which would be eliminated in the process.

The United States exports a large quantity of services and farm products, especially to Japan. It so happens that at present there is a worldwide shortage of grains along with a glut of manufactures. With the fall of Communism in the Soviet Union, food is in short supply globally. If Japan ceased to buy U.S. agricultural goods, they could be sold elsewhere in the world.

There is no doubt that the United States would lose some export markets because of its protectionism. But on the whole, the policy would be extremely beneficial. Exporting industries would contract and import-competing ones would expand. But much of the contraction would be in services that have lower productivity and wages, and the expansion would be in the high-productivity manufacturing sector, which pays higher wages.

If we were to extend the antimonopoly policy to exporting industries, breaking them up in the process, there would be further gains from competition. Executive salaries would come down, but workers' wages would go up, generating another expansion of the domestic market. Even mainstream economists argue that a fall in a firm's monopoly power raises labor earnings. Thus if tariffs were accompanied by antimonopoly policies in all concentrated industries, any loss from export markets would be offset by efficiency gains in exporting sectors.

Even if farmers were to suffer somewhat from temporary market disruptions, their loss would be just a fraction of the overall gains. Under current laws the government could easily compensate them from the increased tariff revenue.

There is no doubt that as the United States puts its own house in order, trade surplus areas such as Japan and the NICs will suffer. But the suffering, as explained before, will be mainly done by their wealthy speculators. In any case, the world should not expect the United States to accept deficits permanently. The country cannot perpetually borrow from abroad and still stay healthy.

Economies of Scale

Proponents of monopolistic free trade have long argued that the size of a firm and its efficiency are closely connected. The larger the firm, the lower the production cost per unit of output. Not surprisingly, this logic originates from giant monopolistic firms and their supporters.

The argument goes like this. Modern technology requires a huge investment in plant, equipment, and trained personnel. This investment is fixed regardless of the size of the enterprise. Hence, the bigger the enterprise, the smaller the overhead cost per unit of output. In other words, there are economies associated with scale, and they tend to make a giant venture highly efficient.

The economies-of-scale argument, though valid, is incomplete, because large size also creates diseconomies of scale. As a firm grows, it becomes increasingly difficult for management to attend to minor details, individual markets, and quality control. Large companies tend to have a large bureaucracy. Precious time is lost in red tape, internal wrangling, and petty disputes. At a low-output level, economies of scale are significant; at a high-output level, however, they pale before the diseconomies.

Thus, there is an optimum size at which economies of scale are barely offset by diseconomies. Experience shows that giant firms tend to have huge diseconomies and are periodically overwhelmed by much smaller firms. Thus, Apple and Compaq, though much smaller than IBM, are much more efficient; Ford bests GM in productivity any day.[18] Japan today has very large corporations; but because of their youth, they retain the dynamism they acquired when they were still small, and yet defeated U.S. behemoths in the arena of trade.

Among the affluent nations the average size of the top ten or twenty firms is the largest in the United States, followed by Germany, the United Kingdom, France, and then Japan. The average size of the leading Korean firms is even smaller.[19]

Firm size, when carried to the extreme, becomes a burden on efficiency. Some of those that gobbled up other firms in the 1980s are now busy selling them to raise cash for their survival. In September 1992, for instance, Sears, which had a voracious appetite for other businesses during the 1980s, announced a plan to sell some subsidiaries.[20] Monolithic corporations have monolithic problems. This is what prompts Michael Porter to contend that "the idea that domestic firms will be more efficient if they merge into one or two large national competitors fails the test of logic and history."[21]

When U.S. giants are broken up into smaller units, their efficiency will climb. Under my proposal, even after divestiture, each unit will be large enough to be near its optimum size. For instance, the IBM split-up will amount to a creation of five Apple Computers, each much more efficient than its parent. When GM is split into five entities, each will still have $20 billion to $25 billion in sales, large enough to reap the economies of scale without extravagant diseconomies.

America needs smaller companies if it is to revive. It is in this spirit that Harvard Business Professor Rosabeth Kanter writes:

> One of the major questions about the current management revolution is whether it can reach the larger, older elephantlike American corporations that so desperately need revitalization. In recent years, the creation of jobs in the United States has come from small organizations, and a striking proportion of technological innovation has come from start-ups, not from the corporate giants. . . . Some observers argue that older, larger companies must die off, like dinosaurs, to be succeeded by a new breed suited to its environment.[22]

This revitalization of American industry is precisely what my plan is all about. Breaking U.S. dinosaurs apart will infuse dynamism into manufacturing; but they also need protectionism in the best tradition of U.S. history to make sure that the fruits of the new dynamism accrue to American workers rather than those abroad.

Industrial Policy

The postwar U.S. policy of monopolistic free trade has its critics, who have recently grown in number and influence. What they would do to cure America's economic ills is called industrial policy. Let's now see if their proposals are sound and adequate to do the job.

Among those calling for a national industrial policy are economists Barry Bluestone, Bennett Harrison, Paul Krugman, Laura Tyson, and Lester Thurow;[23] among politicians, Michael Dukakis and Paul Tsongas have been in favor of such a strategy.

The centerpiece of the concept of industrial policy is government subsidy of ailing as well as promising industries. The idea is to establish a state development bank that would pick winners and losers and subsidize them accordingly. The losers would get government aid to protect high-paying jobs, while the winners would get funds to compete with foreign firms allegedly subsidized by other nations.

Industrial policy advocates commonly cite Japan's Ministry of Trade and Industry (MITI) as an organization that has a very successful industrial strategy. MITI primarily offers a vision of where the country should be going. It provides the private sector with up-to-date information about developments in technology and management relations. It targets certain industries and brings representatives of labor and business together to generate new and efficient industries—the so-called winners. The groups are also offered investment aid to be used in scientific research.

To some extent the governments of Germany, France, and other European nations also play a role in the development of their frontline industries. A well-known example is Airbus Industrie, which is jointly owned by the British, French, Spanish, and German governments. The venture was established to develop Europe's own aircraft industry in direct challenge to U.S. monopoly in this sector.

Proponents of industrial policy also believe in managed trade, by which they mean bilateral agreements among trading partners to achieve desirable objectives. Such pacts are not permitted under GATT rules, but nations have them anyway. The United States and Japan had two such agreements in the 1980s regarding autos and computers.

If the United States were to raise its tariffs unilaterally, it would be in violation of several GATT agreements. But violations of GATT rules are common around the world. What is more important for the original GATT charter worked out in 1947 is that the United States applies its new tariffs uniformly to all signatories. Of course, the common market agreements are supposed to be exempt even from the uniformity rule.

Managed trade policy would permit bilateral trade negotiations between GATT signatories to sort out their special problems, such as the persistent trade deficit between America and Japan or between America and the NICs. Bluestone and Harrison would even permit temporary protection to key industries and make it a legitimate part of world trading rules.[24]

Industrial policy and managed trade are steps in the right direction. At least they recognize that the United States has a critical problem. Unlike monopolistic free traders, industrial policy advocates have not buried their heads in the sand in order not to see the danger.

But industrial policy is an impotent response to a gargantuan problem. It's like using bows and arrows to fight an enemy armed with tanks and rockets. Its impact on the U.S. economy would be similar to that of Japan opening all its markets—nil to negligible. Free traders believe that America's trade problems would vanish if only Japan were to remove its import barriers. This is nothing but wishful thinking. At most, it would bring $5 billion to $10 billion in new business, nowhere near the estimated cost—exceeding $300 billion annually—that America now pays for free trade.

Today even the Japanese recognize that their government has a very limited role in the vast success of their industries. The government did make a crucial contribution during the 1950s, when Japan was emerging from the ashes of the Second World War. But now the role is mainly informative.

In fact, the governments of Japan, Korea, and Europe have at best had a mixed record in steering their corporations. Airbus Industrie has gobbled up some $26 billion in subsidies and is still not in a position to outcompete Boeing. The government of Korea wasted billions in targeting chemicals, plastics, and machine tools with only modest results.[25]

In Japan, some of the newest industries such as robotics, fax machines, and photocopiers reveal a modest government role, whereas in steel and shipbuilding, where the state direction was active and strong, the investment return has been relatively low.

Ultimately, the competitive battle is among corporations, not governments. The state can and should provide efficient facilities in education, infrastructure, and R and D; but it cannot do the actual combat in the arena of competition.

State subsidies can be very costly, as shown by the experience of agriculture in many nations; so can industrial subsidies. The U.S.

government, with a giant debt and annual deficit, simply cannot afford them.

Both free traders and industrial policy fans believe in the ultimate benevolence of trade. They would both like to reverse the slide in productivity growth and make America competitive in world markets. If the objective is to restore the U.S. living standard, this strategy simply won't work.

First, it would take a long time, if ever, for the bloated American firms to be globally competitive. After all, other countries are not going to stand still. They save more; they invest more; they have a better educational system, a smaller budget deficit, a society relatively free from litigation, maybe even a better work ethic. With all these disadvantages, America is not likely to catch up in the productivity contest, much less win it outright.

But even if we win this war and somehow raise our annual productivity growth from the current 1 percent to the world-class rate of 4 percent, victory would be worse than defeat. The reason lies in the vicious agrification syndrome, wherein productivity rises but real wages fall. Raising productivity is only half the picture; the other half is making sure that the industrial relative price doesn't drop too fast to overwhelm the effect of productivity growth.

Just imagine this: suppose all competing nations manage to have a productivity growth rate of 4 percent in manufacturing. With the world already awash in manufactures, manufacturing relative prices will fall sharply around the world, producing a worldwide fall in manufacturing earnings. Thus, even if the United States did manage to win the productivity war—a very big if—its real wages would still decline just as they now do in agriculture under similar conditions.

America did not build its standard of living through giant rises in labor productivity. It did not need to because it is blessed with abundant natural resources. Never in its history did it invest or save as much as Japan and Korea do today. Other nations have no choice except to develop through enormous capital formation and growth in labor productivity. They also lack huge internal markets. Trade is a necessity for them. But not for the United States.

To fight Japan and the NICs in the war of competitiveness is to fight them with their own best weapons. Actually, I hate to look at it as a war. I think America has more to defend itself than to hurt others. The best U.S. weapon in self-defense is an enduring tariff, not subsidies or temporary, piecemeal protection.

Many Americans tend to blame Japan for America's plight. This is neither fair nor factual. Japan did not impose free trade on the United States, nor did Japanese companies force U.S. businesses to pay millions in executive compensation while laying off thousands of workers. The merger mania of the 1980s was purely an American product, with all components made in the U.S.A. America's economic ills have been self-made. There is not a single Japanese name associated with the simplistic theory of free trade. The theory was pioneered by Adam Smith, David Ricardo, and Nobel Laureates Paul Samuelson and Milton Friedman, among other Western luminaries. In their minds, they did a great service for their people. Of course, the United States completely ignored their creed for nearly two centuries and thus turned into a global industrial giant. But now the country is paying a hefty price for adopting the ill-conceived and illogical dogmas of free traders. Why bash Japan for the miscues of Western pundits?

Industrial policy advocates ignore the most crucial role that the governments of Japan and Korea played in the development process. Both countries had an aggressive policy of domestic competition, which turns out to be the single most important source of national prosperity. It's competition that makes a country affluent, not government regulation of industry and markets. In fact, the U.S. experience with regulation of airlines, natural gas, and trucking was disappointing. Eventually such regulations became so onerous, inflationary, and counterproductive that in 1978 they were all relaxed.

The government does have an active role to play to ensure affluence, and that is to follow a vigorous antimonopoly or antitrust policy. Monopolistic firms should be broken up; mergers among large and solvent firms should be outlawed. Foreign investors should be asked to open new plants and factories rather than buy existing ones. In short, the U.S. government should follow the time-tested formula for success, namely, replacing foreign competition with domestic competition behind high tariff walls. The complete answer to America's ills is competitive protectionism, not an industrial policy nor the continuation of monopolistic free trade.

We need to restore the link between productivity and real wages. Free trade has severed this link since 1973. Only tariffs can bring about the restoration. True, our productivity is not likely to grow at the global rate, but our wages would grow faster. And that is what economic development is all about.

In short, competitive protectionism would increase tax revenues, resurrect the manufacturing base, raise real earnings for 80 percent of the work force, trim inequality, reduce the rate of poverty, enhance the growth of productivity, cripple the abuse of monopoly power by big business, revitalize the economy, and, above all, restore America's economic leadership in the world.

Summary

A vigorous revival of the American economy would spring from the following five-year, five-point plan:

1. The average tariff rate should be raised from the current 5 percent to 40 percent over five years to protect major manufacturing industries from imports.

2. All protected companies should be broken up into smaller independent firms to create intense local rivalry, thereby replacing foreign competition with domestic competition.

3. Mergers among giant firms should be banned.

4. Foreign investment in the United States in new ventures, rather than in old, established concerns, should be encouraged.

5. The government should invest heavily in research and development and finance this venture by using part of the increased tariff revenues.

11

International Trade and the Environment

A new tumor has emerged on the world body since the 1950s, when many newly independent or war-ravaged countries recognized the need for economic development, growth, and industrialization. At first the affliction was local, internal, and invisible. There were aches here and there, but the body's general health was unaffected. By the 1970s, the tumor had surfaced above the skin, but it was still too small to be easily seen. By the 1980s, it was increasingly painful and visible to the naked eye. And now it is spreading without check in all directions.

The tumor is the unprecedented, worldwide environmental degradation and pollution. The side effects of science, technology, and growing population, thus far hidden from view, have abruptly come to the surface, and with a ferocity that cannot be ignored.

No longer can we ignore auto fumes, noxious chemicals in urban air, vehicular congestion, rivers spewing fire or vomiting dead fish, oil slicks ravaging beaches and birds, smog suffocating our lungs and spirits, airplanes shattering our eardrums, nuclear wastes irradiating our landfills, and countless toxins whose dangers are yet unknown. Nor can we ignore the growing health problems ranging from heart ailments to respiratory failures to deformed and brain-damaged babies.

As *Time* puts it: "The blight is global, from the murky red tides that periodically afflict Japan's Inland Sea to the untreated sewage that befouls the fabled Mediterranean. Pollution threatens the rich, teeming life of the ocean and renders the waters off once famed beaches about as safe to bathe in as an unflushed toilet."[1]

Pollution is not partial to any country or ideology. The East, the West, the North, the South, all suffer from it. Affluence is as much to blame as poverty. The smog in Los Angeles, Tokyo, London, New York, and Frankfurt is as venomous as in Calcutta, Karachi, Istanbul, and Cairo. Environmental sickness is not a capitalist disease, but a disease of unbridled materialism.[2]

Types of Pollution

The environment as a concept is easy to understand. It comprises air, water, land, and light. It provides a habitat in which we live and the resources we use in the process of production and consumption.

As producers and consumers, we litter the land, the rivers, the air, and the seas. The environment provides us resources, of which some are exhausted in the production process and some can be reproduced. Pollution occurs when we use our habitat as a dumping ground for our seemingly inexhaustible wastes.

To some extent, nature recycles these wastes. As we exhale carbon dioxide, plants and trees inhale it and emit oxygen, which we need. Wood, iron, and steel disintegrate into dust over time. Dead plants and animals decompose, merging into the same soil from which their living ingredients originated.

Waste products that disintegrate over time are said to be biodegradable. Most of them are, but some are not. Plastics, rubber, and aluminum, for instance, are either not biodegradable or take a very long time to decompose.

Pollution occurs when the environment is unable to absorb our wastes at the rate we create them. Wherever people cluster, toxins are generated. Thus, pollution is as old as civilization itself; but until this century, it was not a major problem, because the earth and its resources were vast enough to sustain the world's population without damaging the environment. Cities produced wastes, which were absorbed by the environment with relative ease. Energy use was low; nonbiodegradable products were nonexistent. Even though the burning of wood and coal generated fumes, they were easily absorbed by the vast forests. Pollution existed, but it was mostly local, not global.[3]

Today, however, our activities produce such great quantities of waste that the environment can no longer deal with them. The wastes are not only solid but also airborne—and toxic air knows no boundaries. It contains many venoms—carbon dioxide and monoxide, nitrogen oxides, sulfur oxides, and particulates. Together or singly, these wastes produce smog and dizziness, nausea, general fatigue, and damage to plants and animals.[4] They also generate heat and changes in climate that may ultimately dissolve the polar ice floes, raising the sea level and submerging tiny islands and possibly small nations across the globe.

This is the so-called global warming, or greenhouse effect, of air toxins. Another impact is the creation of an ozone hole, which springs mostly from the emission of chlorofluorocarbons (CFCs), used in aerosol propellants, refrigeration, and fire extinguishers. These toxins disperse into the air no matter where they are used and in turn cause ozone depletion around the world.

Such depletion increases our exposure to the sun's ultraviolet radiation and makes us more vulnerable to skin cancer and cataracts. A few years ago, scientists discovered an ozone hole in the atmosphere near the North Pole and warned that northern regions like Canada and Europe would feel the effects of the hole by the year 2000.[5] However, in 1991, another ozone hole was detected in the European skies, causing widespread concern among the populace.

While we are busy pouring millions of tons of toxins into the air, we have not spared the land and the oceans. Water is the elixir of life, and it is being polluted at an enormous rate. Industries dump all sorts of chemicals into lakes and rivers, which in turn flow into the seas.

Land pollution occurs mostly from strip mining and runoffs from the junkyards in which we store our solid wastes. Garbage dumps and landfills stand as modern monuments to our "progress" through industrialization.

Sources of Pollution

While there is general agreement about the gravity of our sickly environment, there is less agreement among scholars about its sources, causes, and cures. There is a widespread myth that industry is the main culprit behind pollution, but modern-day mechanized agriculture is no less culpable.

The most obvious source of pollution is the mushrooming world population, which stood at 1.6 billion at the turn of the century but is now 5.5 billion. Everyone has to be fed, clothed, transported, educated, and employed. In other words, economic activity has to grow just for survival, let alone to provide a decent living standard.

Science and technology have done an admirable job in this struggle, but the environment has been gasping in the process. Among the most prolific contaminants are factories, which discharge poisonous chemicals into rivers and lakes and pump millions of tons of pollutants into the air every year. However, without the humming of these factories, life as we know it would come to a halt.

Agriculture provides us grains, fruits, vegetables, and reproducible raw materials; but it also uses tons of fertilizers as well as pesticides and other chemicals. Many of these chemicals seep into the underground water table and eventually into the lakes and wells that form our major sources of drinking water.

Another important source of pollution is transportation for people and freight. Our cars, trucks, railroads, airplanes, and buses use energy, the waste products of which seep into the atmosphere in one form or another.

Electricity, used by almost every business and household around the world, is another high-profile polluter. No matter how it is generated, some environmental ills occur. Hydroelectricity floods valleys; nuclear power generates radiation and radioactive wastes; coal power creates acid rain; solar energy produces arsenic, among other toxins.

At the same time, under the population pressures, forests in many countries are being eliminated. Particularly alarming is the destruction of Brazil's rain forest, which excels in the absorption of carbon dioxide.

Causes of Pollution

By now you know about the main types and sources of pollution. Some people confuse them with the causes of pollution, which they clearly are not. The causes are economic and man-made, which suggests that there is yet hope of inhabiting a nontoxic world.

Mainstream economists have slowly and grudgingly recognized the tumor of environmental degeneration. Economic theory suggests that pollution occurs because the environment comes nearly free to its users.

Take, for instance, a corporation that economizes in the use of resources because it has to pay a price for them. A firm uses labor, capital, and land, for which it has to pay wages, interest, and rent. It uses these factors sparingly and efficiently because it has to pay for them. But the same firm dumps its wastes into the environment, which is available at little or no cost. If chemical dumping were costly, no firm would do it with abandon.

In the same way, a smoker freely contaminates the air because he does not have to pay for its use. Thus economic agents, both producers and households, abuse the environment because to each individual such environmental costs are negligible.

But the actions of each agent, when added together, become a burdensome national cost. Here we have to distinguish between private and social costs. If polluters had to pay for their actions, private costs would rise, giving them an incentive not to pollute. This would then reduce the social costs of a toxic environment.

The social costs of pollution include those that can be calculated and those that are incalculable. You can, for instance, estimate—

though only roughly—the health cost of pollution; you can also measure the expense in terms of lost wages due to illness and low productivity. But you cannot calculate the mental cost incurred from fatigue and irritation.[6]

Calculable or not, the social cost of pollution is much higher than the private cost. Hence the presence of high levels of toxins and contaminants in the environment. Conventional economists recognize this divergence between private and social costs as the main cause of pollution. If businesses had to pay a heavy price for contaminating the environment, pollution and its social costs would automatically decline. Although this logic contains a great deal of validity, few realize that there is another equally important cause of environmental degradation—international trade.

Foreign Trade—A Major Cause of Pollution

I have already introduced you to the heavy cost of free trade incurred by the United States and every other resource-rich country with a shrinking manufacturing base. You will now see that free trade also generates enormous costs for the environment. From these costs, no nation benefits. Trade liberalization enriches some countries, but no one thrives from its pollutive effects.

Since 1950, the world's population has more than doubled, while global economic activity has quadrupled. But world trade has grown faster than even GDP, especially in the 1960s, when trade growth was nearly twice GDP growth. Overall, between 1950 and 1990, trade grew at 1.5 times the pace of increase in economic activity.[7]

More than 60 percent of global GDP is generated in the Group of Seven countries, also known as the G-7 nations. They are the United States, Japan, Canada, Germany, France, Italy, and Britain. These are the leading industrial as well as trading nations. Their exports constitute nearly 65 percent of the world's total. They are also the biggest polluters. According to the 1991 *World Development Report*, per capita energy consumption in the G-7 nations (or OECD countries, in which the G-7 are included) is at least four times that of the rest of the world.[8]

Thus the economic trends set by the G-7 countries apply to the rest of the world as well. It is very difficult to quantify the level of atmospheric pollution, but the World Resources Institute has come up with a rough measure, which estimates the extent of air pollution by comparing it with that estimated to have prevailed in the preindustrialized world. The quantitative measure focuses on carbon dioxide (CO_2), whose buildup is the main source of global warming or the greenhouse effect.

Figure 11.1 plots the concentration of carbon dioxide, as measured by atmospheric levels of CO_2 as a percentage of the estimated preindustrial level of 280 parts per million (ppm). Also plotted are

FIGURE 11.1
Trade/GNP Ratio of G-7 Countries and Atmospheric
Concentration of Carbon Dioxide, 1960–1990

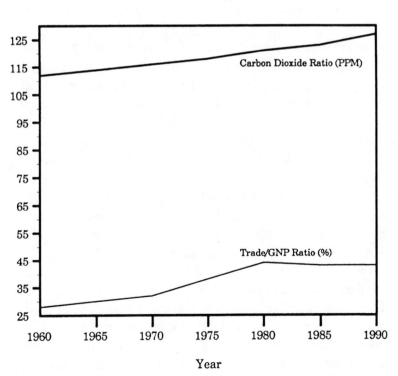

Year

SOURCES: *World Resources, 1990–1991,* and *International Financial Statistics.*

the combined trade/GNP ratio of the G-7 countries from 1960 to 1990.

The two trend lines have moved steadily upward since 1960, although the G-7 volume of trade leveled off during the 1980s. What is worrisome is that the carbon dioxide concentration is moving up in a straight line, with no sign of a letup.

Is there any cause-and-effect relationship between the two? Clearly, rising levels of CO_2 in the atmosphere cannot raise the G-7 volume of trade, but the volume of trade can cause an increase in the toxin. After all, trade occurs through the transportation of goods across vast land areas and the seas. Ships, trucks, wide-bodied jets, and even light vehicles such as cars are involved in the transfer of goods among nations.

Large airplanes such as the Boeing 747 have even made international commerce in perishable goods possible. Fresh fruit, vegetables and seafood can now be transported over huge distances within hours. But airborne trade also pumps millions of tons of jet fuel wastes into the atmosphere, possibly helping to create an ozone hole.

When merchant ships crisscross the globe, carrying raw materials, food, and manufactures across oceans, they also use energy and dump contaminants into the water. When trucks rumble along the roads of Europe, Asia, and Africa carrying goods from one nation to another, they also burn gasoline and pollute. Thus international trade is a major source of environmental degradation.

Since world trade has soared faster than economic activity, trade is a bigger polluter than industrialization. According to *Global Outlook 2000,* the share of transportation in energy consumption rose steadily from 24 percent in 1970 to 31 percent in 1989.[9] In view of the rising trade share of GNP, this is hardly a surprise. It is all the more remarkable because the fuel efficiency of combustion engines has increased by 20 percent since 1971.

Air freight increased from 23 percent of commerical air traffic in 1970 to 25 percent in 1990, whereas the corresponding level of energy consumption rose from 4.2 million metric tons of aviation fuel to 11.2 million tons. Thus, air freight fuel consumption almost tripled in just two decades.[10] In addition, airborne trade emitted

2.1 million tons of nitrogen oxides in 1990; nearly 40 percent of it dispersed into U.S. skies.

A recent assessment of the oceans is downright disheartening. "Chemical contamination and litter can be observed from the poles to the tropics, and from beaches to abysmal depths." Marine pollution arises mostly from sewage, plastics, pesticides, and "oil from routine transport and spills."[11]

Trade also increases the risk of accidental pollution on a vast scale. A third of the industrial waste produced annually is hazardous waste, which is a by-product of the chemical, mineral, and metal processing industries. In 1990, about 18 million tons of this toxin were shipped to other countries for disposal;[12] of this, 20 percent went to developing nations.

In addition, there are many unreported cases of ocean dumping of hazardous substances. International trade in such products is very dangerous, because there are frequent accidents among ships carrying them. Since 1975, there have been 170 documented cases of large accidents involving the shipping of toxic wastes including nuclear materials. Many more collisions have occurred but have not been reported because of their relatively minor damage.

Every year, about 3,000 million tons of crude oil or petroleum products are shipped around the globe. In the process, 2 million tons slip into the marine environment from routine tanker operations like tank cleaning and ballasting and oil spills from tankers and platforms.

This is just routine; it does not include the large oil spills that regularly occur as a result of tanker accidents. The infamous spill of the *Exxon Valdez* in Alaska's Prince William Sound in 1989 was just about the average size. It spilled 38,000 tons of oil into the water and caused a huge loss of aquatic life. Yet it was only one among sixty separate accidents that had occurred over the last two decades and was only one seventh the size of the largest spill on record.

During the 1980s over 3.5 billion tons of goods were shipped annually around the world, the average haul being more than 4,000 nautical miles. Consequently, marine life has been ravaged. If you visit Boston Harbor, you can really see how polluted the seas are. The open seas are, of course, much cleaner than the coastal areas, but the point is that routine shipping leaves a sorry trail of pollution in its wake.

The virulence of limitless shipping is increasingly evident in the sad episodes involving large-scale destruction of marine life. In 1989, nearly 40 percent of the seal population in the North Sea fell prey to a virus and died in a short span of time. This was, of course, the visible carnage that captured headlines. How much more remains unseen, no one knows.

The moral of the story is that international trade is a vast source of pollution, and the environmental costs of global commerce have been totally ignored by orthodox economists. This is a major flaw in the traditional analysis of international economics.

The Energy Intensity of Trade

With our habitat increasingly in a toxic shambles, we need to explore the energy intensity of each economic activity. This is because energy use is a big polluter in every walk of life.

Energy intensity may be defined as the amount of energy used by an activity per dollar of value added by it. For instance, it took 81.2 quadrillion British thermal units (BTUs) of energy to produce a real GNP of $4,118 billion in the United States in 1989. The energy intensity of the U.S. economy was thus 19,700 (or 20,000 when rounded off) BTUs that year.

Activities with a high energy intensity use more energy and hence generate excessive pollution. For purposes of the environment, the smaller the energy intensity, the greater the energy efficiency.

What is the energy intensity of trade? Reliable data at the world level are not available, but you may get an accurate estimate by examining the figures for internal trade in the United States. After all, some American states are larger than some foreign countries, and American domestic trade is typical of global trade. Distances are vast, and interstate commerce occurs by air, river, land, and even sea transport.

Table 11.1 displays the figures for energy intensities in U.S. production and the total transportation sector, of which a part is

TABLE 11.1
Energy Intensity of Production, Transportation, and Domestic
Trade in Selected Years in the United States, 1960–1989*

Year	GNP	Transportation	Domestic Trade
1960	27	32	42
1965	25	31	42
1970	27	34	48
1975	26	40	62
1980	24	31	48
1985	21	30	49
1989	20	31	51

SOURCE: U.S. Department of Commerce, *Statistical Abstract of the United States* (Washington, D.C.: U.S. Government Printing Office, 1991), pp. 569, 602, and 603.

* In thousands of BTUs; figures have been rounded off.

freight. The last column is computed under the assumption that the level of energy consumed by freight transport is 60 percent of the total transportation consumption, because that has generally been the proportion of freight traffic miles to total traffic miles.

Since domestic trade is proportionately linked to freight volume, the energy intensity of the two is nearly identical. Table 11.1 reveals that the energy intensity of GNP in the United States fell between 1960 and 1989, especially after 1973, when energy prices soared due to the oil price shock, but the energy intensity of transportation remained more or less unchanged, whereas that of freight or domestic trade rose slightly.

Both transportation and freight are energy inefficient relative to production. Not only has trade consumed more energy since 1960, it is incredibly wasteful relative to overall economic activity. The energy intensity of domestic trade in 1989 was 51,000 BTUs, more than twice the level of 20,000 BTUs for GNP.

Figure 11.2 displays the significance of this analysis in a vivid way; trade's energy intensity line lies far above that of GNP. What is more alarming is that the gap between the two has increased over time, indicating how wasteful trade today is of environmental resources.

FIGURE 11.2

Energy Intensity of Transportation, GNP, and Trade 1960–1989

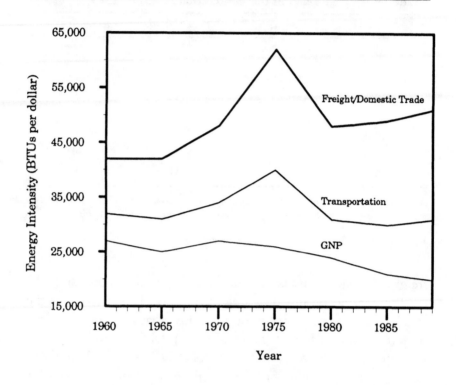

When we apply this lesson globally, international trade comes out as the worst villain in the destruction of the environment. It is the most diabolical polluter in the world and offers a precious lesson in the desirability of economic diversification versus specialization. In other words, in order to meet human wants, local production is preferable to imports so that trade and hence pollution are minimized.

Intraindustry Trade

What is even more disturbing is that so much of the world's trade today occurs in the same or similar products—the intraindustry trade discussed earlier. The United States, for instance, both exports and imports cars; it has reciprocal trade in electronics, machine tools and even farm products.

The United States sends wine to France but also buys some from it; America exports airplanes to Europe but also imports them from there. In 1978, intraindustry trade made up nearly 60 percent of the trade of the G-7 countries and 56 percent of world commerce. That figure is even higher now.[13]

Intraindustry trade should be distinguished from intercommodity trade, which is a one-way exchange of totally different goods. For example, when India exports textiles to the United States in exchange for electric transformers, intercommodity trade occurs. Typically, rich nations have far more intraindustry trade than intercommodity trade.

How do we explain this relatively recent phenomenon? One theory is that consumers demand a wider range of a product than any one country produces. Thus, U.S. consumers want European cars, while Europe demands American cars at the same time.

Another theory is that firms can sell only so much in their own market at a given profit rate. By producing more, they drive their costs down through the economies of scale, and then sell the extra output abroad at a lower but still profitable price. This way they make more money but, importantly, maintain higher prices in local markets. Such a practice is called price discrimination; competitors call it dumping.

The consumer demand theory and the price-dumping hypothesis are mere explanations of the status quo. Few economists question the need for or the costs of intraindustry commerce. The Bush administration proudly announced that in 1990 U.S. consumers had a choice among 567 automobile models.[14] Are there no limits to materialism? Would social welfare fall if auto buyers had only 100 models to choose from?

Intraindustry trade makes a mockery of economists' claims about exchange gains from trade. In Chapter 8, I introduced you to this concept and cited the example of a swap of chairs and tables. If you have ten chairs and another person has two large tables, you certainly gain by exchanging four chairs for one table and completing your kitchen set. So does the other person. In this case, there is a large and mutual exchange gain from trade.

But suppose you have chairs and the other person also has chairs, though of a different variety. How much would you gain by just swapping chairs? Practically nothing. Furthermore, suppose you were in New York and your friend in Los Angeles. Would you consider trading your chairs over such a distance? Most likely not. Even the idea would appear ridiculous to you.

This is exactly what intraindustry trade is—ridiculous. It generates a waste of capital, labor, and the environment on a colossal scale. There is hardly any gain to consumers and not much to producers, either. There is no evidence that intraindustry trade adds much to profits. Then why are all the multinationals engaged in this type of commerce? The answer lies in the "sheep" mentality.

In their quest for money, people often do irrational things just because someone else once did them with some success. This is called the sheep mentality, that is, following others out of peer pressure. During the 1970s, it was fashionable for bankers to chase Third World officials and lend them money. First one New York bank did this, then another, then yet another. Soon this became a worldwide fad among banks, which loaned billions to developing countries. Now these same banks are stuck with huge losses.

History reveals many examples of seemingly rational people lured into irrational behavior just because that is the thing to do at the time. Intraindustry trade is such a case. Compared to its social costs, such commerce is totally irrational. The resources engaged in this activity could be profitably utilized elsewhere; but hardly anyone questions its need. In retrospect, the bankers' actions in the 1970s appear rash and foolish, but at the time they had a lot of defenders. Many economists rationalized their activities as being good for the nation and the world, just as many today justify intraindustry trade in the name of social and global welfare.

Multinational firms are busy opening plants in different countries to make not a finished product but just some components. Thus one plant may make nuts in Asia, another may make bolts in Europe, and a third may put the two together in the United States. Is this a rational way to satisfy human needs and wants? Just imagine how much unnecessary transportation it involves, how much it ravages the environment with no addition to the supply of goods and services.

Trade in Raw Materials

About 60 percent of international trade today is of the intraindustry variety; another 30 percent is in raw materials. Raw materials are mostly imported by Japan, the NICs, Germany, Britain, and Italy; the exporters are mostly the Third World, Canada, Australia, and America. The importers of raw materials pay for them by exporting manufactures.

If we include crude oil, the United States is also a net importer of materials. But since the world oil price is set by the Organization of Petroleum Exporting Countries (OPEC), oil is treated separately by economists.

A part of the oil trade is linked to the trade in other goods. If intraindustry trade were eliminated and countries produced their own manufactures from their own raw materials, global oil demand would plummet. There would be no need to transport so many goods, materials, and oil across the seas. Global energy prices would fall, generating massive growth around the world. Not only would the environment benefit, production costs would also decline because of declining energy prices.

The twins of intraindustry trade and raw materials trade are thus hurting the world economy in many ways. Together they constitute 90 percent of global commerce and have no rational economic basis behind them. In short, they contribute to pollution, high energy prices, and thus a higher global rate of inflation.

Trade and Environmental Policy

You have already seen that producers abuse the environment because it comes to them relatively free of charge. The solution to the pollution problem is, then, obvious. The government should impose heavy taxes on polluters and collect the revenue vigorously. Businesses would then economize on the use of the environment to cut their costs, and pollution would gradually come under control.[15]

However, international trade stands in the way of this simple solution.[16] If a country were to tax its polluters, of whom some compete intensely with foreign rivals, they would be at a disadvantage in world markets.[17] Pollution taxes would bestow a corresponding cost edge on producers abroad. Because of this risk, governments are reluctant to tax their polluters heavily. Thus, international trade is a major barrier to a sound environmental policy.[18]

Nations have to cooperate with one another to cure the ills of pollution. But you cannot even get a global consensus on the issue, let alone international cooperation.

Meanwhile, the world is edging closer to an environmental disaster. Ozone depletion and the greenhouse effect are no laughing matter. They are potentially far deadlier than the thick pall of smog that blackens the sky over many a metropolis. The natural tendency of our planet is to maintain a balanced temperature. As a result, even during the Ice Age the earth's temperature did not drop by more than 5° Celsius (9° Fahrenheit). But in the twentieth century, the greenhouse effect has already caused the earth's average temperature to rise by 2° Celsius, with no end in sight. This amounts to a temperature change of cosmic proportions, with vast but unknown dangers and consequences.

Being the largest energy consumer and polluter in the world, the United States has a special responsibility to clean up the environment. The simple act of raising the average tariff to 40 percent would do just that. It would all but eliminate intraindustry trade—thereby lowering energy imports and prices—and would go a long way in trimming pollution.

There are few economic policies that have vast and varied benefits. Competitive protectionism, in today's milieu, is a rare exception. The pollution reduction would also benefit those nations that might be hurt by higher American tariffs.

12

A Proper Theory of Economic Development and Trade

Change is the essence of life—so proclaim the wise of every generation. With change comes adjustment and with adjustment, struggle and evolution. Old ideas become obsolete, creating the need for new thought, a new paradigm that is more suitable than its precursor.

The ideas that once flowed from the prolific pen of Adam Smith need to be modified in today's world, which is far more polluted than ever. Smith was a relentless champion of competition and international trade. The West has discarded the concept of internal competition and focused on global trade. Today both practices are out of place for a variety of reasons outlined before. Domestic monopolies generate inequality and poverty, while trade imperils the industrial base and the environment.

There is a crying need for a new paradigm, a new understanding of economic development and trade that is consistent with the imperatives of our time. With population around the globe growing rapidly, continuing growth is indispensable; but this growth has to be orderly and constructive. It should not destroy the habitat in which we live and breathe. In this respect, we should borrow from the ideas of my late teacher, P. R. Sarkar, who authored a thesis called "Prout," which is an acronym for progressive (pro) utilization (u) theory (t).

According to Prout, there should be maximum utilization of the "mundane resources" of the world.[1] Otherwise, vast hordes on our planet will remain trapped in a vicious circle of illiteracy, procreation and poverty. We cannot afford to waste a penny of our penurious planet. The maximum utilization of resources is today a matter of survival not just of the weak, but of the fittest as well.

So interdependent has the planet become through communications, trade, and globalization of toxins that the fittest, most affluent nations can ignore the feeble ones only at their own peril. But maximum international trade is not the answer, for, as you have seen before, it ravages the environment without adding much to material development. Free trade is a vast source of global pollution. No theory of development and growth should ignore this dictum.

Net National Income

Economic theory currently recognizes three main factors or primary inputs of production—labor, land, and capital. Businesses combine these inputs with raw materials and technology to generate outputs. But raw materials themselves are produced by the combination of technology with labor, land and capital. Therefore, output growth arises from an increased supply of one or all inputs and/or improved technology. In recent years, growth in Japan and Europe has stemmed mostly from increases in capital stock and new technology, whereas in Canada, America, and Australia labor and land have also been significant contributors.

Inputs can increase in quantity, quality, or both. Education improves the quality of labor, whereas population growth increases its supply. Similarly, saving and investment enhance the supply of capital, which is ultimately turned into office buildings, machinery, and infrastructure. These are goods used over time in the production of other goods.

The quality of capital goods improves only through technology, mainly new-process technology. While repair and maintenance may also make capital more productive, innovation is the chief source of enhanced capital quality.

With land, there is normally a physical limit to quantity, especially today, when most regions of the world are inhabited by people. But land quality can be improved through irrigation, fertilizers, and new mechanization technologies.

Technology may improve the productivity of one or all inputs. So may education. Thus, growth in national output is ultimately the product of growth in inputs, education, and technology. More specifically, economic development springs from growth in population, savings, human intellect, and inventions. This is essentially how current economic theory views growth. It ignores the pollution and environmental degradation that occur in the process of production.

This, however, is a myopic view. According to Sarkar, our environment is an important part of the "mundane resources." It should not be neglected, because it is as essential to the production process as other primary inputs.

A proper theory of development would regard the environment, including water, air, and light, as another factor of production. This is already being done in some disciplines of economics, but in a rather perfunctory way. Theories of economic growth and international trade are two areas that have generally neglected it. Economic theory treats it as a separate branch rather than as an integral part of the discipline's core.

Economists should view the environment in the same way as they do capital goods. Capital depreciates in the production process; so does the environment. Businesses set funds aside for depreciation of capital; they should do the same for environmental depreciation. Capital needs to be periodically renewed through replacement of old machines; renewal of the environment matters just as much.

The trouble is that capital depreciation hurts a business directly, whereas the depreciation of our habitat occurs gradually and hurts a business partially and invisibly. Therefore, businesses ignore environmental costs in their calculation of total costs. Since the environment comes mostly free to them, they abuse it with abandon.

In fact, we all abuse the environment. Energy is the main source of pollution, and most of us overuse it. We all need to change our attitude and regard the environment as a primary factor of production.

Accordingly, the concept of national well-being needs to be redefined. At present, national income is considered to be the best measure of aggregate economic activity, even though it is not as well known as the concept of GNP or GDP. National income equals GNP minus capital depreciation and indirect taxes, such as the sales tax and the excise tax.

However, national income is not a proper gauge of economic activity. It does not take into account environmental depreciation. Even though at the micro level, business consumption of the environment is small and not as visible as the consumption of capital, there is no denying that the nation as a whole suffers from pollution. Hence a proper measure of economic activity would be net national income, defined as national income minus the cost of environmental depreciation.

Currently, economic growth is defined as the rate of increase in national income; a better definition would be the rate of increase in net national income. There are, of course, some practical difficulties with this concept. You can quantify capital depreciation, but how do you estimate environmental depreciation? Since there is no market price for the purity of air or, for the most part, the purity of water, how do we incorporate the cost of the environment into national income?

Fortunately, we don't have to be overly precise in the measurement of environmental costs. In most cases, we are interested in the trends in such costs, not their exact value. A simple way to estimate changes in environmental costs over time is to define an index of such costs, select a base period, and then see how this index performs through the years.

An exploratory but interesting approach to the construction of this index has recently been offered by economist Robert Repetto. He analyzes the case of the electric power industry, which is notorious for pollution. When oil, coal, or nuclear plants are used to produce electricity, the output is not only kilowatt hours but also tons of harmful emissions that seep into the atmosphere. In the dramatic but nerve-wracking words of Repetto:

> A typical 500 megawatt coal-fired power station produces not only 3.5 billion kilowatt hours of electricity per year. All the elements in the 1.5 million tons of coal and 0.15 million tons of limestone it uses as inputs reappear as outputs in some form. Of the 50,000 tons of sulphur in the coal, 5,000 tons are emitted to the atmosphere as sulphur oxides, 5,000 remain in the fly ash, and the remaining 40,000 tons are captured in the scrubber sludge.[2]

This is not all. Several other poisons are also released into the atmosphere. They include 10,000 tons of nitrogen oxides, 225 tons of arsenic and 114 pounds of lead.

Thus, the outputs of an electricity plant are not just billions of kilowatts but also thousands of tons of pollutants that find their way into the air and water. National income estimates include the market value of the kilowatts but exclude the other outputs. A proper estimate, however, would equal the value of the kilowatts minus the value of emissions. The concept of net national income takes these emissions into account.

How do we estimate the value of emissions? Repetto has come up with a measure. The value "of a pollutant equals its incremental cost to those exposed to it."[3]

Suppose you move into an area near a power plant. You were in good health before making your move, but two years later your eyes, nose, and throat burn regularly; you have headaches, your lungs hurt, and so on. You take a vacation from your work and go away for two months, and your painful symptoms disappear. Then you know for sure that your illness was directly caused by the power-plant pollution. The money you spent for medicines and visits to a doctor and the wages you lost because of the forced vacation are the market costs of power pollution.

Today millions of people live and breathe in a toxic atmosphere. Their health costs, low productivity, and lost wages are real, not imaginary.[4] Such costs should be estimated by the government and incorporated into the GDP accounting system.

The Environmental Protection Agency (EPA) has taken a small step in this direction. It is beginning to calculate an index of pollution, which, in the nature of things, is at best a rough measure. But it is a good start. For example, the best EPA estimate for 1987 for sulfur oxide emissions was $637 per ton.

With one coal-fired 500-megawatt power plant emitting 5,000 tons of sulfur oxide, the annual cost of this emission alone is $3.2 million. When other pollutants—particulates, nitrogen oxides, carbon dioxide, lead—along with the thousands of electricity plants are taken into account, the pollution costs of just one industry run into billions of dollars. Add to this the other polluting sectors such as chemicals, steel, automobile, even agriculture, and you get some idea of the enormous cost of pollution to society each year.

With the progress the EPA has made in constructing a pollution index, net national income is not just a theoretical concept anymore. Environmental depreciation can be roughly quantified, and such estimates ought to be included in the national accounting system. The concept of net national income is the only appropriate measure of aggregate economic activity today.

Stages of Economic Growth

From the analysis in the preceding chapters, we can develop an interesting hypothesis regarding the various stages in a country's economic development. The history of most affluent nations reveals an intimacy between the growth of manufacturing and prosperity. There are one or two small nations, such as Singapore and Hong Kong, that became central hubs for trade among other countries and thus became affluent. There are also a few oil-rich nations, such as Saudi Arabia and Kuwait, that prospered from foreign demand for petroleum. With these few exceptions, every other rich country developed through manufacturing and industrialization.

All the advanced countries of today were once pastoral, agrarian economies. They did have some handicrafts and light industry, but more than 75 percent of their population subsisted on farms. Their wealth grew through new inventions, which transformed the agrarian economies into industrial societies. Thus, in the first stage of development in modern affluent nations, workers moved out of agriculture into other occupations, such as transportation, regional trade and other services, and, above all, manufacturing.

Manufacturing, with the highest productivity growth among all sectors, was the locomotive that infused dynamism into other areas. As manufacturing expanded, real wages grew, and so did GNP and net national income. International commerce was relatively insignificant in this process, especially in the case of the United States, where the portion of trade in GNP was rarely above 12 percent.

Since manufacturing was the high-productivity, high-wage sector, most countries granted it protection from foreign competition. This made a lot of sense because the key to higher wages and incomes is a rapid growth of the most productive sector.

Once industrial economies had achieved a certain living standard, the share of manufacturing, in both GNP and the labor force, began a gradual decline. Services began to grow faster than manufacturing. This was not an unwelcome development but a natural evolution of an affluent society.[5]

Services include a variety of industries that perform diverse functions for buyers but have little to do with the production of a tangible product. Businesses offer some services to individuals and households and some to other businesses and institutions.

After reaching a high income threshold, people's need for manufactures is more or less satisfied; they then have extra leisure and consequently demand more entertainment and services. The urbanization associated with industrialization also creates the need for more services, especially for transportation over long distances. Affluence adds to longevity, and retired and older people need more help than younger workers. Thus, for a variety of reasons, services grow faster than manufacturing after a threshold of affluence has been achieved. That defines the second stage of development or industrialization: during the first stage, workers migrate from agriculture mostly to manufacturing; in the second stage, they move increasingly into services.

All this does not mean that agricultural output declines. In fact, the contrary may happen. Because of rapid industrialization, agriculture may be so mechanized that its productivity soars, causing surpluses in farm output in spite of the declining work force. This has been a major problem in some rich nations in the past two centuries.

Note that in the first stage, employment in manufacturing and services grows at the expense of that in agriculture, whereas in the second stage the manufacturing share of the workforce is more or less constant, but the services share rises rapidly. At a relatively late phase in the second stage, the employment share in manufacturing may also decline, but it is a slow, imperceptible fall, insufficient to disrupt the nation's onward march to affluence. In any case, the share of manufacturing in GNP remains more or less constant.

However, when the employment share in manufacturing begins a rapid and visible fall, the third stage of development occurs. This is a backward march toward poverty and high inequality that may spring from a variety of causes, such as the growing monopoly power of giant firms, union militancy, or intense foreign competition. Because of stagnant manufacturing, an ever increasing proportion of the labor force then moves into services. GNP's share of manufacturing also tumbles. Productivity growth slows and may even become negative.

In the first stage, domestic rivalry among companies is strong and, because of high competition, workers and the economy become very efficient; wages then grow at a fast pace. In the second stage, corporate size climbs through mergers and acquisitions, and monopoly power among firms increases. Consequently, wage growth slows. In the third stage, monopoly power has grown so much that wage growth is negligible, while executive compensation soars. This, along with the rising intersectoral wage differentials caused by the decline of manufacturing, creates horrendous inequality in the economy. And an affluent society turns into an inequitable society, where pockets of vast riches mock the misery of the masses.

The polarization of society into the haves and the have nots is the fourth and final stage of development in an industrial economy. At this point, not just the employment share, but the absolute level of employment in manufacturing shrinks, while services forge ahead.

The first two stages are characterized by rapid growth of the middle class and a long-term decline in inequality. The third stage witnesses a shrinking of the middle-income group. In the fourth stage, the middle class all but disappears. Only drastic economic and social reforms can then shake the country out of stagnation.

It is clear that the second stage of industrialization or development is the ideal stage, and through proper economic policy a nation can remain in this phase forever. In the past some countries such as Great Britain were driven out of this stage by the growing monopoly power of corporations and labor unions; others such as the United States moved out of the second stage because of intense foreign competition. Competitive protectionism, therefore, would ensure that the ideal phase of development endures.

Without proper policy, a market economy is likely to go through all four stages. Among the countries examined before, India and Mexico are still in the first stage of development. Though semi-industrialized, they have yet to introduce an element of competition into their markets. As a result, real wages in these countries are still pathetic.

Korea and Taiwan are in the early part of their second stage. Germany, Japan, and France are in the late phase of the second stage. Canada and Italy are in the third stage, whereas Australia, Britain, and the United States entered the early phase of the fourth stage in the 1980s. If the present trends continue, the latter group of nations will be in the thick of the final and vicious stage of development by the year 2000.

Looking at U.S. history, in 1840, nearly 62 percent of the work force was employed in agriculture, about 16 percent in the goods-producing sector (including manufacturing, mining, and construction), and the rest in services such as trade and transportation. By 1910, agriculture's employment share was down to 30 percent, whereas commodities and services divided the rest at roughly 35 percent each. In 1950, agriculture had only 10 percent of the labor force and the goods sector 38 percent, but services' share had jumped to more than 50 percent.

Since the 1950s, the goods sector has seen a slow but steady shrinkage of the employment share, which began to fall rapidly after 1973; since 1979, even the absolute level of employment in manufacturing, mining, and construction has experienced a slow decline.

Until 1910, the United States was in the first stage of industrialization, as labor moved out of farming into goods and services. It remained in the second stage until 1950, during which time workers migrated from agriculture mostly into services. Between 1950 and 1979, the nation was in the third stage of development, as goods' share of employment gradually fell. Since the 1980s, it has been in the fourth stage, with the work force in the goods sector falling by over 2 million by 1991. Only drastic economic reforms can arrest this slide and take the country back into the ideal second stage. Needless to say, competitive protectionism is one such reform.

Since the early 1980s, even Germany, France, and Italy have seen a decline in the employment share of their goods sector. But the decline has been imperceptible.

The Role of International Trade

Where does international trade fit into this process of development? Trade may play a minor or monumental role. It may accelerate or retard development. When trade stimulates manufacturing, it accelerates the rate of growth; when it hurts manufacturing, it retards the development process and may even hurl a country from the second to the third or fourth stage.

Trade may help a nation obtain raw materials from abroad and also provide it with markets for its manufactures. This is how Britain, Germany, France, and Italy, among other colonial powers, developed during the eighteenth and nineteenth centuries. Britain and France especially had many colonies, which were the source of cheap raw materials; the colonies also provided outlets for British and French manufactures.

Thus, colonial powers used trade to their advantage by accelerating their industrialization. A somewhat similar process has helped the economies of Korea, Germany, and Japan since the war. They all import raw materials and ship out manufactured goods. The

Third World, the principal source of raw materials, has plenty of foreign commerce but is poor because of a lack of manufacturing.

During the Second World War, international trade helped Australia and the United States by expanding their manufacturing base. Later, however, ever expanding trade unleashed the reverse process of a shrinking manufacturing sector, and ever since the 1970s, these countries have suffered from a contracting real wage.

Canada has in general benefited from trade, but mainly because U.S. multinationals have poured billions into the country. In this case, the credit for prosperity goes mostly to the foreign direct investment responsible for expanding the industrial base. Trade is again secondary; what is more important is the industrial expansion.

The moral of the story is that there is nothing special about foreign trade. When trade stimulates manufacturing, it enriches a country; when trade retards manufacturing, it hurts a nation. A healthy industrial base with intense domestic competition is far more important to prosperity than international commerce.

International Comparisons

International comparisons among modern affluent societies clearly reveal the significance of manufacturing to prosperity. Take a look at Table 12.1, which analyzes the growth performance of Australia and the Group of Seven (G-7) countries, which include the United States, Great Britain, Canada, France, Germany, Italy, and Japan. All these are leading industrial nations.

The period under study is 1870 to 1990, spanning more than a century. For a hundred years, between 1870 and 1969, the United States was more or less a closed economy, with trade hovering at 10 percent of GNP. In 1970, the U.S. trade/GNP ratio began a steady rise, catapulting America into a free trade economy in 1973 and thereafter. Australia also cut its tariffs sharply at the same time, as did all the G-7 nations. However, Japan retained a series of non-tariff barriers, which largely remain to this day.

Among all nations, the United States was the leader in trade

TABLE 12.1
Growth in Real Per Capita GDP in Selected Affluent Countries,
1870–1990

Country	Per Capita GDP Growth, 1970–1990 (%)	Per Capita GDP Growth, 1870–1969 (%)
Australia	1.6	1.5*
Canada	2.7	1.8
France	2.2	1.7
Germany	2.2	1.9
Great Britain	2.1	1.3
Italy	2.7	1.5
Japan	3.7	NA
United States	1.7	2.0

SOURCES: *International Financial Statistics* (Washington, D.C.: International Monetary Fund, 1991); *Historical Statistics of the United States, Colonial Times to 1970* series F10–16 (Washington, D.C.: Department of Commerce, 1975).

* Author's estimate for 1900–1973, calculated from data in *The Australian Economy in the Long Run*, eds. Rodney Maddock and Ian W. McLean, (New York; Cambridge University Press, 1987), p. 14.

liberalization. Consequently, while others experienced some expansion of commerce, America's trade/GNP ratio more than doubled between 1970 and 1990. The ramifications of U.S. policy are portrayed in Tables 12.1 to 12.4

Table 12.1 shows that for a hundred years, the United States was the world leader in the growth of real per capita GDP. Its 2 percent growth rate exceeded that of every other nation, including Britain and France, the two premier colonial powers until the Second World War, both of which had a variety of advantages accruing from their colonies.

After 1969, however, the per capita growth of every other nation *except* the United States went up. America and Australia were the only nations whose growth fell short of 2 percent. What had not occurred in the century from 1870 to 1969, trade liberalization achieved in the twenty years from 1970 to 1990.

The United States fell from the economic summit because of

trade-induced inertia in manufacturing, as revealed by Table 12.2. In 1990, among the affluent nations, America and Australia had the lowest share of labor force employed in manufacturing. In addition, the United States had the highest employment share in services. Thanks to free trade, America had become a service-preponderant, "fast food" economy relative to other affluent countries.

The United States may now be a laggard in per capita GDP growth, but it is the ringleader in household debt, inequality, and poverty. Table 12.3 shows that except for Japan, the government debt per person is the highest in the United States.

The Japanese debt is somewhat of a surprise but, in a country with an exceptionally high rate of saving, is understandable and may be beneficial. With a mountain of savings, the household debt in Japan is extremely low, but the exact figure is not available. The United States also has a mountain, that of household debt, which is more than twice as high as in the nearest debt-burdened nation for which figures are available—Great Britain.

Table 12.4 reveals the real carnage of free trade. In 1990, the

TABLE 12.2
Manufacturing and Services in Selected Affluent Countries, 1990*

Country	Employment Share in Manufacturing (%)	Employment Share in Services (%)
Australia	18	68
Canada	19	70
France	24	64
Germany	39	57
Great Britain	23	68
Italy	27	58
Japan	27	58
United States	18	71

SOURCE: Michael Wolff et al., *Where We Stand* (New York: Bantam Books, 1992), pp. 148, 149, and 152.

* Numbers have been rounded off.

TABLE 12.3
Domestic Debt in Selected Affluent Countries, 1990*

Country	Government Debt per Person	Household Debt
Australia	3.2	NA
Canada	8.6	NA
France	4.4	27.7
Germany	1.0	27.7
Great Britain	4.6	35.5
Italy	12.1	NA
Japan	14.0	NA
United States	12.4	71.5

SOURCE: Michael Wolff et al., *Where We Stand* (New York: Bantam Books, 1992), pp. 19 and 27.

* In thousands of U.S. dollars.

United States had the worst level of inequality among the affluent nations. In every area dealing with social harmony, justice, and equity, America lagged behind other nations. The United States had the highest level of CEO pay as a percentage of workers' salaries; it also had, after Canada, the largest number of billionaires for every million people, along with the worst index of poverty, as measured by the percentage of families living below 50 percent of the median income line. The nation's income share accruing to the bottom 20 percent of the population was close to the minimum, while its overall index of inequality, on a scale of 1 to 100, was the maximum at 99.

Such has been the carnage of free trade.

International Development and Trade

It must be clear by now that free trade is not always beneficial to a nation. Is it beneficial to the world? The answer is no.

Trade is certainly profitable to countries that must import raw

TABLE 12.4
Inequality Indexes in Selected Affluent Countries, 1990

Country	CEO Pay (Number of Times Average Worker Pay)	Billionaires per Million Population	Poverty Rate (%)	Share of Income of Bottom 20% of Population (%)	Overall Inequality Index
Australia	NA	0.06	12.2	4.4	87
Canada	9.6	0.38	12.6	5.7	83
France	8.9	0.05	NA	6.3	NA
Germany	6.5	0.24	4.9	6.8	66
Great Britain	12.4	0.24	9.7	5.8	78
Italy	7.6	0.16	NA	6.8	NA
Japan	11.6	0.07	NA	8.7	NA
United States	17.5	0.32	17.1	4.6	99

SOURCES: Michael Wolff et al., *Where We Stand* (New York: Bantam Books, 1992), pp. 22, 23, and 151; *World Development Report* (Washington, D.C.: The World Bank, 1991), p. 263.

materials, without which the manufacturing sector cannot exist. It has also been salutary to the oil-exporting countries, which have been able to maintain a relatively high price of petroleum through a cartel. But for others and for the planet as a whole, free trade is harmful. This is because trade is a major source of pollution.

Free trade does indeed maximize the world's national income; but does it maximize the world's net national income, defined earlier as national income minus the cost of environmental depreciation?

The environmental costs of trade are large as well as unnecessary. Trade does not create much value, especially in the presence of unemployment; manufacturing, agriculture, and services do.

The purpose of all economic activity is to satisfy human needs and wants without hurting the environment in which we live and breathe. Since trade pollutes the earth, it is essential that it be kept to the minimum.

Free trade leads to maximum trade, but environmental considerations call for minimum trade. Hence free trade cannot be beneficial to the world. It can maximize only global national income, not net national income.

A New World Economic Order

Maximum utilization of the world's resources requires that waste and pollutants be minimized, subject, of course, to the satisfaction of human needs. After the demise of Soviet Communism, President George Bush proclaimed the need for a new world order, with a planetary economy tied to free trade. This is just the wrong thing to do, for it will add to pollution without generating much new production.

The global trading network today is guided by the GATT rules. These should give way to a new set of rules to create a new world order. Its guiding principle should be the satisfaction of human needs with minimum pollution, which means minimum trade.

There are two types of trade that are wasteful and unnecessary to meet human demands around the world. One is intraindustry trade, which constitutes more than half of global commerce; the other is trade in raw materials, which makes up another third of international commerce. In order to minimize trade-induced pollution, GATT should be replaced by the following set of principles.

1. Monopolistic corporations in all nations should be broken up in order to generate intense domestic competition and preclude the need for foreign competition.

2. Intraindustry trade should be minimized. Multinational corporations should, as much as possible, produce and sell goods in the same nation. Another possibility is for multinational firms to swap their production facilities in different countries. For instance, General Motors exports cars to Europe but also imports them into America from its European facilities. This is clearly unnecessary. It should not export when it can produce the product in Europe itself. Similarly, it should not import when it also

produces cars in the United States. What is the point in generating unnecessary transportation of goods, producing pollution in the process? If GM's plants in Germany are uneconomical without their exports to the United States, the firm should simply sell them to a German manufacturer and use the money for other productive but nonpolluting purposes.

3. International transfer of technology should be augmented. Instead of maximizing global trade, we should maximize the international transfer of capital and technology. For instance, today Japan focuses primarily on exporting goods, creating pollution in the process. If the Japanese companies instead opened plants around the world, local needs would be met by foreign controlled local production and without much trade. Japan would not need to import vast quantities of raw materials in exchange for its exports. Human needs would still be met, but trade in goods and raw materials would be minimum. Japan would import some raw materials for domestic production and would pay for them from its profits earned abroad. Not only would trade be minimized, but the Third World, which mainly exports raw materials, would be industrialized. Germany, another large exporter and polluter, should also maximize technology transfer, not trade.

4. The above principle suggests that countries rich in technology and capital should export them in exchange for raw materials for home production. The Third World should not export primary goods but should either import technology or invite foreign firms to utilize its raw materials in local production. The idea is to locate plants near mineral-rich areas as well as near population centers, so that international trade can be minimized.

5. All resource-rich but industry-poor economies should impose high tariffs on imports of manufactures while vigorously generating competition in domestic markets. This would induce technology-rich countries to locate their plants in tariff-imposing nations. Thus, India, Australia, Canada, Mexico, and the resource-rich nations of Africa and Latin America should follow this policy, combining it with internal competition. Domestic competition would sharply reduce inequality and thus stimulate the demand for goods at home. This in turn would reduce the need for exports and trade.

6. Governments should direct their R and D spending to discoveries that can potentially reduce pollution as well as the optimum size of plants, thereby reducing the need for economies of scale. Some firms enter the arena of exports just to utilize such economies. New technologies should be developed to make this unnecessary. It is worth noting here that the value of economies of scale is often exaggerated. The highly competitive firms of Japan, after all, started small. Similarly, if economies of scale are so important, why do firms have multiple plants in one country to produce the same product?

These are some of the rules that should replace GATT to create a new world economic order.

The migration of factories to mineral-rich areas can trim international trade by as much as 25 percent without reducing the global living standard. The same is true of intraindustry trade. We can eliminate it altogether without much effect on planetary production. In other words, global trade can be cut by at least 75 percent without much harm to overall output. But while the output effect of trimming trade would be small to negligible, the benevolent impact on the environment would be tremendous.

Energy use would plummet, the oil price would tumble, oceans would be safer from oil and chemical spills, the atmosphere would be more secure from toxic gases, the risk of accidents would be smaller, and our ears would be less exposed to deafening noise. Such would be the beneficence of minimum international trade and competitive protectionism.

NOTES

Chapter 1

1. "Why We're So Gloomy," *Time*, January 13, 1992, p. 34; also see Robert Samuelson, "On Being Competitive," *Newsweek*, May 25, 1992, p. 68, and "States of Siege," *U.S. News & World Report*, July 14, 1992, pp. 57–72.

2. *Time*, op. cit.

3. Ibid., p. 36.

4. See, for instance, Barry Bluestone and Bennett Harrison, *The Deindustrialization of America: Plant Closings, Community Abandonment, and the Dismantling of Industry* (New York: Basic Books, 1982); Paul D. Staudohar and H. E. Brown, *Deindustrialization and Plant Closure* (Lexington, Ky.: D.C. Heath and Company, 1987); Katherine S. Newman, *Falling from Grace* (New York: The Free Press, 1988); Gary Burtless, *A Future of Lousy Jobs* (Washington, D.C.: The Brookings Institution, 1990); D. L. Barlett and J. B. Steele, *America: What Went Wrong* (Kansas City: Andrews and McMeel, 1992).

5. Wallace Peterson, "The Silent Depression," *Challenge*, July–August 1991, pp. 29–34.

6. Steven Greenhouse, "Attention America! Snap Out of It," *New York Times,* February 9, 1992, Section 3, p. 1.

7. See, for instance, Martin Neil Baily, "The Productivity Growth Slowdown by Industry," *Brookings Papers* 2 (1982); Congressional Budget Office, *The Productivity Problem: Alternatives for Action* (January 1981); Edward F. Denison, "Explanations of Declining Productivity Growth," Brookings Reprint 354 (1985); Richard R. Nelson, "Technical Advance and Productivity Growth," Yale Working Paper 815 (1986).

8. Barry Bluestone and Bennett Harrison, *The Great U-Turn* (New York: Basic Books, 1988); Barry Bluestone, "Is Deindustrialization a Myth? Capital Mobility versus Absorptive Capacity in the U.S. Economy," *Annals of the American Academy of Political and Social Science* 475 (September 1984): 39–51; Terry Buss and F. Stevens Redburn, *Mass Unemployment: Plant Closings and Community Mental Health* (Beverly Hills, Calif.: Sage Press, 1983); Greg Duncan, *Years of Poverty, Years of Plenty* (Ann Arbor, Mich.: Institute for Social Research, University of Michigan, 1984); Greg Duncan, Martha Hill, and Willard Rogers, "The Changing Fortunes of Young and Old," *American Demographics* 8 (1986): 8:26–33; S. Fineman, *White Collar Unemployment: Impact and Stress* (New York: John Wiley & Sons, 1983); Felician Foltman, *White- and Blue-Collars in a Mill Shutdown: A Case Study in Relative Redundancy* (ILA Paperback No. 6) (Ithaca: New York State School of Labor Relations, Cornell University, 1968); Jeanne Gordus, Paul Jorley, and Louis Ferman, *Plant Closings and Economic Dislocation* (Kalamazoo, Mich.: W. E. Upjohn Institute for Employment Research, 1981); H. G. Kaufman, *Professionals in Search of Work: Coping with the Stress of Job Loss and Underemployment* (New York: John Wiley & Sons, 1982); Ronald Kutscher and Valerie Personick, "Deindustrialization and the Shift to Services," *Monthly Labor Review* 109 (1986), 6:3–13.

9. F. M. Scherer and David Ross, *Industrial Market Structure and Economic Performance* (Boston: Houghton Mifflin, 1990).

10. *Wall Street Journal,* "The Reagan Legacy," August 17, 1992.

Chapter 2

1. Michael Wolff et al., *Where We Stand* (New York: Bantam Books, 1992), 10.

2. U.S. Council of Economic Advisers, *Economic Report of the President* (Washington, D.C.: U.S. Government Printing Office, 1992), 247.

3. Terry Arendell, *Mothers and Divorce: Legal, Economic and Social Dilemmas* (Berkeley: University of California Press, 1986); M. J. Bane and R. Weiss,

"Alone Together: The World of Single-Parent Families," *American Demographics* (1980): 5:323–30; C. Barron, "Down in the Valley," *New York Times Magazine* (September 20, 1987); William D. Beer, *Househusbands: Men and Housework in American Families* (New York: J. F. Bergin/Praeger, 1983); D. Berardo, C. Sheham, and G. Leslie, "A Residue of Tradition: Jobs, Careers, and Spouses' Time in Housework," *Journal of Marriage and the Family* 49 (May 1987): 381–90; W. Berman and D. Turk, "Adaptation to Divorce: Problems and Coping Strategies," *Journal of Marriage and the Family* 43 (1981): 1:179–90.

4. Peterson, "Silent Depression," 32.

5. Sylvia Nassar, "Top 1% Had Greater Net Worth Than Bottom 90% of U.S. Households," *New York Times,* April 21, 1992, p. 1.

6. *New York Times,* September 6, 1992, p. 2F.

7. Barry Bluestone and Bennett Harrison, "The Great American Job Machine: The Proliferation of Low Wage Employment in the U.S. Economy," study prepared for the Joint Economic Committee, U.S. Congress, December 1986.

8. Wolff et al., *Where We Stand,* 4.

Chapter 3

1. Wilfred Ethier, *Modern International Economics* (New York: W. W. Norton, 1991).

2. Ravi Batra, *Studies in the Pure Theory of International Trade* (New York: St. Martin's Press, 1972), chap. 4.

3. Robert Baldwin, *The Political Economy of U.S. Import Policy* (Cambridge, Mass.: MIT Press, 1985).

4. Mordechai E. Kreinin, *International Economics: A Policy Approach* (New York: Harcourt Brace Jovanovich, 1990).

5. Paul R. Krugman and Maurice Obstfeld, *International Economics: Theory and Policy* (Glenview, Ill.: Scott, Foresman and Company, 1988).

6. U.S. Department of Commerce, *Historical Statistics of the United States* (Washington, D.C.: U.S. Government Printing Office, 1975).

7. Gerald M. Meier, *International Economics, The Theory of Policy* (New York: Oxford University Press, 1990).

8. Ravi Batra, *The Great Depression of 1990* (New York: Simon and Schuster, 1987).

9. *Economic Report of the President* (1992), 95.

10. Walter Nicholson, *Microeconomic Theory, Basic Principles and Extensions* (Chicago: Dryden Press, 1989).

11. Ibid.

12. Alan E. Dillingham, Neil Skaggs, and J. Carlson, *Economics* (New York: Allyn and Bacon, 1991), 435.

13. The data are from U.S. Department of Commerce, *Historical Statistics of the United States* (Washington, D.C.: U.S. Government Printing Office, 1975); series D737 is merged with series D726 to obtain one series regarding real annual earnings.

14. All these earnings figures are obtainable by deflating *Historical Statistics of the United States* series D807 by series D727.

15. *Historical Statistics of the United States.*

Chapter 4

1. Bruce Gardner, "Changing Economic Perspectives on the Farm Problem," *Journal of Economic Literature,* March 1992, pp. 62–101.

2. *Economic Report of the President* (1990 and 1991).

3. Edwin Mansfield and N. Behravesh, *Economics* (New York: Norton, 1990), chap. 17.

4. Ibid.

5. Ibid.

6. Ibid.

7. Ibid.

8. Gordon C. Rausser and Eithan Hochman, *Dynamic Agricultural Systems* (New York: North Holland, 1979); Theodore W. Schultz, *Agriculture in an Unstable Economy* (New York: McGraw-Hill, 1945); Theodore W. Schultz, *The Economic Organization of Agriculture* (New York: McGraw-Hill, 1953); Theodore W. Schultz, ed., *Distortions of Agricultural Incentives* (Bloomington: Indiana University Press, 1978).

9. American Agricultural Economic Association, "Measurement of U.S. Agricultural Productivity" (Washington, D.C.: U.S. Department of Agriculture, Technical Bulletin no. 1614, February 1980).

10. Alex F. McCalla and Harold O. Carter, "Alternative Agricultural and Food Policy Directions for the U.S. with Emphasis on a Market-Oriented Approach," in *Agricultural and Food Price and Income Policy,* ed. Robert Spitze (Urbana, Ill.: Agricultural Experiment Station, University of Illinois Special Publication 43, August 1976), 47–70.

11. U.S. Department of Agriculture, *Economic Indicators of the Farm Sector* (Washington, D.C.: U.S. Government Printing Office, 1991).

12. *Historical Statistics of the United States* (1975).

13. Murray R. Benedict, *Farm Policies of the United States, 1790–1950* (New York: Twentieth Century Fund, 1953); Willard W. Cochrane and Mary E. Ryan, *American Farm Policy, 1948–1973* (Minneapolis: University of Minnesota Press, 1976); D. Gale Johnson, "The Food and Agriculture Act of 1977: Implications for Farmers and Taxpayers," in *Contemporary Economic Problems,* ed. William Fellner (Washington, D.C.: American Enterprise Institute, 1978), 167–210; Wayne D. Rasmussen, ed., *Agriculture in the United States,* vol. 4 (New York: Random House, 1975); Vernon W. Ruttan et al., *Agricultural Policy in an Affluent Society* (New York: W. W. Norton, 1969); John T. Schlebecker, *Whereby We Thrive, A History of American Farming, 1607–1972* (Ames: Iowa State University Press, 1975).

14. *Economic Report of the President* (1992).

15. See Chapter 2.

16. Batra, *Great Depression of 1990.*

17. Stevens Redburn and Terry Buss, eds., *Public Policy for Distressed Communities*

(Lexington, Ky.: D. C. Heath, 1981); *New York Times,* "Singer Plant Closing: A Way of Life Ends," February 19, 1982.

18. *New York Times,* "America's Service Economy Begins to Blossom," December 14, 1986.

19. Mansfield and Behravesh, *Economics,* chap. 17.

20. *Economic Report of the President* (1988), 76.

21. Barry Bluestone, "Comment," in *A Future of Lousy Jobs,* ed. Gary Burtless, (Washington, D.C.: The Brookings Institution, 1990), 68–74.

22. See notes 4, 5, and 8 in Chapter 1.

23. William Greider, *Who Will Tell the People* (New York: Simon and Schuster, 1992).

24. Janet Norwood, "The Job Machine Has Not Broken Down," *New York Times,* February 22, 1987, p. D5; Robert Lawrence, "The Myth of Deindustrialization," *Challenge* (November/December 1983), pp. 12–21.

25. *New York Times,* "Global Issues Weigh on Town as Factory Heads to Mexico," September 1, 1992.

26. Bluestone, "Comment."

Chapter 5

1. Bob Davis, "Competitiveness Is a Big Word in D.C.," *Wall Street Journal,* July 1, 1992.

2. Wolff et al., *Where We Stand,* 144.

3. Cf. *Historical Statistics of the United States* (P726 and P736, 1975).

4. Floyd Norris, "Jobs Are in the Government, Not Industry," *New York Times,* September 6, 1992.

Chapter 6

1. Nominal earnings provided by *Canadian Economic Observer*, a monthly from Statistics Canada, are deflated by the Canadian CPI, available from *International Financial Statistics* (Washington, D.C.: International Monetary Fund, 1991).

2. Rogelio Ramirez de la O., "Economic Outlook in the 1980s," in *U.S.-Mexican Industrial Integration*, ed. Sidney Weintraub et al. (Boulder, Colo.: Westview Press, 1991).

3. Donald Barlett and James Steele, *America: What Went Wrong* (Kansas City: Andrews and McMeel, 1992).

4. William Greider, *Who Will Tell the People*.

5. Ferdinand Protzman, "In Thuringia, German Unification Looks Like a Bad Deal," *New York Times*, July 26, 1992.

6. Michael E. Porter, *The Competitive Advantage of Nations* (New York: The Free Press, 1990), 401.

7. Ibid., p. 473

8. Ibid., p. 445.

9. Wolff et al., *Where We Stand*, 23.

10. P. J. Drake and J. P. Neiuwenhuysen, *Economic Growth For Australia* (Melbourne: Oxford University Press, 1988), 14.

11. Ross Perot, *United We Stand* (New York: Hyperion, 1992), 13.

Chapter 7

1. See Stanley Lebergott, *The Americans, an Economic Record* (New York: W. W. Norton, 1984), 131.

2. Jonathan J. Pincus, *Pressure Groups and Politics in Antebellum Tariffs* (New York: Columbia University Press, 1977).

3. J. M. Finger, H. Keith Hall, and Douglas R. Nelson, "The Political Economy of Administered Protection," *American Economic Review,* June 1982, pp. 452–66.

4. David A. Lake, "International Economic Structures and American Economic Policy," in *International Political Economy,* eds. J. A. Frieden and D. A. Lake (New York: St. Martin's Press, 1991), 120–38.

5. *Historical Statistics of the United States,* 1975.

6. John S. Odell and T. D. Willett, *International Trade Policies* (Ann Arbor: University of Michigan Press, 1990), chap. 2.

7. Martin Primack and James Willis, *An Economic History of the United States* (Menlo Park, Calif.: Benjamin Cummins Publishers, 1980), 254.

8. Lake, "The Contemporary Political Economy," 140.

9. Stephen P. Magee and Leslie Young, "Endogenous Protection in the United States, 1900–1984," in *U.S. Trade Policies in a Changing World Economy,* ed. Robert M. Stern (Cambridge, Mass.: MIT Press, 1987), 165–84.

10. Howard P. Marvel and Edward J. Ray, "The Kennedy Round: Evidence on the Regulation of International Trade in the United States," *American Economic Review,* March 1983, pp. 190–7.

11. Baldwin, *Political Economy of U.S. Import Policy.*

12. I. M. Destler, *American Trade Politics: System under Stress* (Washington, D.C.: Institute for International Economics, 1986).

13. Bennett D. Baack and Edward John Ray, "The Political Economy of Tariff Policy: A Case Study of the United States," *Explorations in Economic History* 20 (1983): 73–93.

14. Robert Baldwin and J. David Richardson, *International Trade and Finance,* 3rd ed. (Boston: Little, Brown, 1986).

15. *Economic Report of the President* (1992).

16. Vinod Aggarwal, *Liberal Protectionism: The International Politics of Organized Textile Trade* (Berkeley: University of California Press, 1985).

17. David Lake, *Power, Protection, and Free Trade* (Ithaca, N.Y.: Cornell University Press, 1988).

18. Real Lavergne, *The Political Economy of U.S. Tariffs* (Toronto: Academic Press, 1983).

19. The analysis in this chapter is based on these additional references: Stuart W. Bruchey, *Enterprise: The Dynamic Economy of a Free People* (Cambridge, Mass.: Harvard University Press, 1990); Gilbert C. Fite and Jim Reese, *An Economic History of the United States* (Boston: Houghton Mifflin, 1973); Joan Spero, *The Politics of International Economic Relations* (New York: St. Martin's Press, 1985); Frank W. Taussig, *The Tariff History of the United States* (New York: G. P. Putnam's Sons, 1923); Steven Husted and Michael Melvin, *International Economics* (New York: Harper & Row, 1990); Stephanie Lenway, *The Politics of U.S. International Trade* (Boston: Pitman, 1985); Sidney Ratner, *The Tariff in American History* (New York: Van Nostrand, 1972); W. P. Travis, *The Theory of Trade and Protection* (Cambridge, Mass.: Harvard University Press, 1964).

Chapter 8

1. Richard Caves and Ronald W. Jones, *World Trade and Payments,* 4th ed. (Boston: Little, Brown, 1985).

2. *Historical Statistics of the United States* (1975).

3. *Economic Report of the President* (1988), 149.

4. John Odell and Thomas Willett, eds., "Gains from Exchange," in *International Trade Policies* (Ann Arbor: University of Michigan Press, 1990), chap. 1.

5. Wilfred Ethier, *Modern International Economics* (New York: W. W. Norton, 1983).

6. Mordechai E. Kreinin, *International Economics: A Policy Approach* (New York: Harcourt Brace Jovanovich, 1983).

7. Edward E. Leamer, *Sources of International Comparative Advantage: Theory and Evidence* (Cambridge, Mass.: MIT Press, 1984).

8. J. N. Bhagwati, "The Generalized Theory of Distortions and Welfare," in *Trade Balance of Payments and Growth,* ed. J. Bhagwati, R. Jones, R. Mundell, and R. Vanek, Papers in International Economics in honor of Charles P. Kindleberger (Amsterdam: North Holland Press, 1971), 69–90.

9. W. Max Corden, "The Normative Theory of International Trade," in *Handbook of International Economics,* vol. 1, ed. Ronald W. Jones and Peter Kenen (New York: North Holland Press, 1985), 63–130.

10. Those who are technically inclined may refer to Ravi Batra, "Protection and Real Wages," *Oxford Economic Papers* (November 1968): 353–60.

11. David Greenway, ed., *Current Issues in International Trade Theory and Policy* (New York: St. Martin's Press, 1985).

12. Barlett and Steele, *America: What Went Wrong,* 57.

13. Greider, *Who Will Tell the People,* 397.

14. Ravi Batra, "Factor Market Distortions and the Gains from Trade," *American Economic Review,* September 1973, pp. 706–13; also see E. E. Hagen, "An Economic Justification of Protectionism," *Quarterly Journal of Economics,* November 1958, pp. 496–514; Jagdish Bhagwati and V. K. Ramaswami, "Domestic Distortions, Tariffs and the Theory of Optimum Subsidy," *Journal of Political Economy,* February 1963; pp. 44–50; and Batra, *Studies in the Pure Theory of International Trade,* chap. 10.

15. *Statistical Abstract of the United States, 1991* (Washington, D.C.: U.S. Government Printing Office, 1992).

16. R. J. Barry Jones, "Perspectives on International Political Economy," in *Perspectives on Political Economy,* ed. R. J. Barry Jones (New York: St. Martin's Press, 1983), 1–15.

17. Robert Kuttner, "The Free Trade Fallacy," *New Republic* 28, 1983, pp. 16–21.

18. David G. Tarr and M. E. Morkre, *Aggregate Costs to the United States of Tariffs and Quotas on Imports,* Bureau of Economics Staff Report to the Federal Trade Commission (Washington, D.C.: December 1984); Susan Hickok, "The Consumer Cost of U.S. Trade Restraints," Federal Reserve Bank of New York *Quarterly Review,* Summer 1985, pp. 1–12. Also see Gary Clyde Hufbauer,

Trade Protection in the U.S.: 31 Case Studies (Stockholm: Institute for International Economics, 1986).

19. Greider, *Who Will Tell the People,* 393.

Chapter 9

1. This argument has been advanced by Michael Porter in *Competitive Advantage of Nations.*

2. Ibid., 118.

3. Louis Uchitelle, "America Isn't Creating Enough Jobs," *New York Times,* September 6, 1992.

4. Baldwin, *The Political Economy of U.S. Import Policy.*

5. I. M. Destler, *American Trade Politics: System under Stress* (Washington, D.C.: Institute for International Economics, 1986).

6. Richard E. Caves, *Multinational Enterprise and Economic Analysis* (Cambridge, England: Cambridge University Press, 1982).

7. Alfred Chandler, "The Evolution of Modern Global Competition," in *Competition in Global Industries,* ed. Michael E. Porter (Boston: Harvard Business School Press, 1986), 27–35.

8. Tamir Agmon and Charles P. Kindleberger, *Multinationals from Small Countries* (Cambridge, Mass.: MIT Press, 1977).

9. Ravi Batra, *Surviving the Great Depression of 1990* (New York: Simon and Schuster, 1988).

10. Ravi Batra, "A General Equilibrium Model of Multinational Firms," *Oxford Economic Papers,* July, 1986, pp. 342–53. Ravi Batra and R. Ramachadran, "Multinational Firms," *American Economic Review,* June 1980, pp. 278–90.

11. Roy J. Ruffin, "International Factor Movements," in *Handbook of International Economics,* vol. 1, ed. Ronald W. Jones and Peter Kenen (New York: North Holland Press, 1985), 237–88.

12. *Economic Report of the President* (1992).

13. Helen Milner, *Resisting Protectionism: Global Industries and the Politics of International Trade* (Princeton, N.J.: Princeton University Press, 1988).

14. Lake, *Power, Protection, and Free Trade.*

15. Nigel Campbell, "Sources of Competitive Rivalry in Japan," *Journal of Product Innovation Management,* 4 (1985): 224–31.

16. Porter, *Competitive Advantage of Nations.*

17. W. P. Travis, *The Theory of Trade and Protection* (Cambridge, Mass.: Harvard University Press, 1964).

18. Batra, *Studies in the Pure Theory of International Trade.*

19. See, for instance, Peter Kenen, *The International Economy* (Englewood Cliffs, N. J.: Prentice-Hall, 1989), chap. 9; John S. Odell and T. D. Willett, *International Trade Policies* (Ann Arbor: University of Michigan Press, 1990).

20. The analysis in this section is based on F. M. Scherer and David Ross, *Industrial Market Structure and Economic Performance* (Boston: Houghton Mifflin Company, 1990).

Chapter 10

1. *Dallas Morning News,* September 28, 1992, p. 15a.

2. Ferdinand Pestzman, "German Unification Looks a Bad Deal," *New York Times,* July 26, 1992.

3. Porter, *Competitive Advantage of Nations.*

4. Kevin Phillips, *The Politics of Rich and Poor* (New York: Random House, 1990), chap. 6.

5. *Economic Report of the President* (1991), 233.

6. Ibid., 234.

7. Ibid. (1992), 221.

8. Ibid. (1991), 253.

9. *New York Times,* September 9, 1992.

10. See Batra, *The Great Depression of 1990,* and Ravi Batra, *The Downfall of Capitalism and Communism* (London: Macmillan, 1978, or Dallas, Tex.: Venus Books, 1990).

11. Ansel Sharp, Charles Register, and Richard Leftwich, *Economics of Social Issues* (Homewood, Ill.: Irwin, 1992), chap. 7.

12. Porter, *Competitive Advantage of Nations,* 662–4.

13. F. M. Scherer and David Ross, *Industrial Market Structure and Economic Performance* (Boston: Houghton Mifflin Company, 1990), 482.

14. During the Roaring Twenties, a 40 percent average tariff rate generated the desired import/GNP ratio of approximately 6 percent.

15. On this point, see Lester Thurow, *Head to Head* (New York: William Morrow, 1992), 45–51.

16. U.S. Department of Commerce, *U.S. Industrial Outlook* (Washington, D.C.: U.S. Government Printing Office, 1992).

17. Yumiko Ono, "Behind Calm Exterior, Japanese Feel the Pain of the Nikkei's Plunge," *Wall Street Journal,* April 21, 1992, p. 1.

18. Doron Levin, "General Motors Productivity Trailing Domestic Rivals'," *New York Times,* October 6, 1992.

19. Scherer and Ross, *Industrial Market Structure,* 63.

20. *New York Times,* September 30, 1992.

21. Porter, *Competitive Advantage of Nations,* 662.

22. Rosabeth Kanter, *When Giants Learn to Dance* (New York: Simon and Schuster, 1989), 10.

23. Thurow, *Head to Head;* Paul Krugman, *Strategic Trade Policy and the New International Economics* (Cambridge, Mass.: MIT Press, 1986).

24. Barry Bluestone and Bennett Harrison, *The Great U-Turn.*

25. Porter, *Competitive Advantage of Nations.*

Chapter 11

1. Anastasia Toufexis, "The Dirty Seas," *Time,* August 1, 1988, pp. 44–50; also see "The Rape of the Oceans," *U.S. News and World Report,* June 22, 1992, pp. 64–8.

2. Ezra Mishan, *The Costs of Economic Growth* (Harmondsworth, England: Pelican, 1967).

3. Ansel Sharp, Charles Register, and Richard Leftwich, *Economics of Social Issues,* chap. 6.

4. Albert Gore, *Earth in the Balance* (Boston: Houghton Mifflin, 1992).

5. William K. Reilly, "Statement on Ozone Depletion," Environmental Protection Agency (Washington, D.C., April 4, 1991); "Ozone Loss over U.S. Is Found to be Twice as Bad as Predicted," *New York Times,* April 5, 1991; Douglas G. Cogan, *Stones in a Glass House: CFCs and Ozone Depletion* (Washington, D.C.: Investor Responsibility Research Center, 1988).

6. *World Population Data Sheet* (Washington, D.C.; Population Reference Bureau, 1991); James S. Cannon, *The Health Costs of Air Pollution; A Survey of Studies Published 1984–1989* (New York: American Lung Association, 1990).

7. *Economic Report of the President* (1991 and 1992).

8. *World Development Report* (New York: Oxford University Press, 1991).

9. *Global Outlook 2000* (New York: United Nations Publications, 1990).

10. *Environmental Data Report, 1991–92* (London: United Nations Environmental Program, 1992).

11. *World Resources 1990–91* (Oxford: World Resources Institute, 1991).

12. *Environmental Data Report.*

13. See Peter H. Lindert, *International Economics* (Homewood, Ill.: Irwin), 96; and Nigel Grimwade, *International Trade* (London: Routledge, 1989).

14. See *U.S. Industrial Outlook*, 1991, p. 37–1.

15. Michael Weisskopf, "A Clever Solution for Pollution: Taxes," *Washington Post*, December 12, 1989; Sharp, Register, and Leftwich, *Economics of Social Issues*, chap. 6.

16. *Environmental Challenges to International Trade Policy: A Conference Report* (Washington, D.C.: Overseas Development Council and World Wildlife Fund, 1991).

17. Steven Shrybman, "International Trade and the Environment: An Environmental Assessment of Present GATT Negotiations," *Alternatives* 17 (1990), 2:91–101; Jeffrey J. Schott, "Uruguay Round: What Can Be Achieved," in *Completing the Uruguay Round*, ed. Jeffrey J. Schott (Washington, D.C.: Institute for International Economics, 1990), 1–12.

18. Stewart Hudson, "Trade, Environment, and the Negotiations on the General Agreement on Tariffs and Trade (GATT)" (Washington, D.C.; National Wildlife Federation, September 24, 1990); Clyde H. Farnsworth, "Environment Versus Freer Trade," *New York Times*, February 11, 1991.

Chapter 12

1. P. R. Sarkar, *Prout in a Nutshell: Parts 1–20* (Washington, D.C.: Proutist Universal, 1987); Ravi Batra, *Prout and Economic Reform in India and the Third World* (Bombay: Jaico, 1989).

2. Robert Repetto, "Environmental Productivity and Why It Is So Important," *Challenge*, September–October 1990, p. 34. Also see David Pearce et al., *Blueprint for a Green Economy* (London: Earthscan Publications Ltd., 1989); Frank Bracho, "Towards More Effective Development Indicators," in The Caracas Report on Alternative Development Indicators, *Redefining Wealth and Progress: New Ways to Measure Economic, Social and Environmental Change* (New York: The Bootstrap Press, 1989).

3. Repetto, 35.

4. James S. Cannon, *The Health Costs of Air Pollution: A Survey of Studies Published 1984–1989* (New York: American Lung Association, 1990).

5. Daniel Bell calls it "post-industrial society." See his *The Coming of Post-Industrial Society* (New York: Basic Books, 1973); also see Stephen S. Cohen and John Zysman, *Manufacturing Matters: The Myth of the Post-Industrial Economy* (New York: Basic Books, 1987).

INDEX

Printed in the United States
119655LV00004B/31-66/A